PELICAN BOOKS

A 525

A HISTORY OF MODERN FRANCE
VOLUME TWO

Alfred Cobban was born in 1901. He was educated at Latymer Upper School and Gonville and Caius College, Cambridge.

He has been a lecturer in history at the University of Newcastle upon Tyne, has held a Rockefeller Fellowship for research in France, and has been visiting Professor at Chicago, Harvard, Johns Hopkins, and other American universities.

He is now Professor of French History at the University of London, and editor of *History*.

Among his publications are *Burke and the Revolt against the Eighteenth Century*; *Rousseau and the Modern State*; *Dictatorship, its History and Theory*; and *National Self-determination*. More recently he has written *The Debate on the French Revolution*; *Ambassadors and Secret Agents: the diplomacy of the first Earl of Malmesbury at the Hague*; the history of Vichy France in Toynbee's *Hitler's Europe*; *In Search of Humanity: the Role of the Enlightenment in Modern History*; and articles in the *English Historical Review*, *History*, the *Political Science Quarterly*, *International Affairs*, and many other journals.

A HISTORY
OF MODERN FRANCE

BY ALFRED COBBAN

VOLUME TWO

*From the First Empire to
the Second Empire*

1799–1871

PENGUIN BOOKS
BALTIMORE · MARYLAND

Penguin Books Ltd, Harmondsworth, Middlesex, England
Penguin Books Inc., 3300 Clipper Mill Road, Baltimore 11, Md, U.S.A.
Penguin Books Pty Ltd, Ringwood, Victoria Australia

—

First published 1961
Reprinted 1962, 1963
Second Edition 1965

—

Copyright © Alfred Cobban, 1961, 1965

—

Made and printed in Great Britain
by The Whitefriars Press Ltd
London and Tonbridge
Set in Monotype Baskerville

This book is sold subject to the condition
that it shall not, by way of trade, be lent,
re-sold, hired out, or otherwise disposed
of without the publisher's consent
in any form of binding or cover
other than that in which
it is published

CONTENTS

INTRODUCTION 7

I. THE FIRST EMPIRE
1. *France in 1799*   9
2. *From Consulate to Empire*   12
3. *Napoleonic Foundations of the Nineteenth Century*   18
4. *The Napoleonic Empire: Rise*   38
5. *The Napoleonic Empire: Fall*   55

II. THE CONSTITUTIONAL MONARCHY
1. *The Restoration*   71
2. *Clericalism and Anti-Clericalism*   82
3. *The Foundation of the July Monarchy*   94
4. *Louis-Philippe*   106
5. *An Age of Idealism*   114

III. THE SECOND REPUBLIC AND THE SECOND EMPIRE
1. *1848: from the February Days to the June Days*   133
2. *The Triumph of Louis Napoleon*   146
3. *A Bourgeois Empire*   158
4. *L'Empire c'est la Paix*   171
5. *Towards the Liberal Empire*   184
6. *The Price of Dictatorship*   199
7. *Plus ça Change*   215

CHRONOLOGICAL TABLE   228
FURTHER READING   235
INDEX   240

MAPS

1 The French Empire and its satellite states, 1812	50
2 The eastern frontiers of France, 1814–71	72
3 The conquest of Algeria, 1830–48	111
4 Paris in the nineteenth century	197

INTRODUCTION

THE second volume of this history of modern France originally covered the whole period from 1799 to the Second World War. This meant that the treatment of twentieth-century history in particular had to be much abridged. This fact has been criticized, and in answer to these criticisms I have now divided the former second volume into two parts. To the second volume of the history, which now ends in 1871, I have added a short concluding section. The third volume is largely rewritten and carries the story of France from 1871 to the present day.

I have taken this opportunity to correct a number of slips and must express my gratitude to all who have pointed them out to me.

University College, London   A. COBBAN

I
THE FIRST EMPIRE

1. FRANCE IN 1799

THE pattern of French society, and even its physical setting, received so strong an imprint in the eighteenth century that the mark of that age still remains in many aspects of national life the dominant characteristic of France. In its provincial capitals, the solid eighteenth-century quarters, well-planned enclaves, or graceful urban extensions in a semi-rural setting, still recall the memory of a more elegant age. In Paris, when the older buildings were swept away under the Second Empire and even the street plan modernized out of recognition, the eighteenth century survived in the great town-houses scattered from the Chaussée d'Antin through the faubourg Saint-Honoré to the Seine, and by way of the place de la Concorde across the river to the faubourg Saint-Germain. Under Louis XV, Paris, pushing outwards, had swallowed up the limits traced by Charles V in the fourteenth century and their western extension of 1631 under Louis XIII. The hated wall of the Farmers General, built in 1785 as a customs barrier with imposing monumental gates, took in a vast new area, stretching round the western and northern heights of Passy, Chaillot, Belleville, and Ménilmontant, including – south of the river – the faubourgs Saint-Victor, Saint-Marceau, Saint-Jacques, and Saint-Germain, and curving back round the Champ de Mars. At the end of the eighteenth century much of this new territory was not yet built up; within the barrier, beyond the Bastille and the Temple in the East, were fields and scattered houses with their gardens. In the West the Champs Élysées were woodland crossed by roads and wandering paths, and the Champ de Mars a huge open space. Paris proper still huddled together within the boulevards that marked the site of its former fortifications, a solid agglomeration of high, closely-packed, terraced houses separated by winding, narrow streets and alleys, noisy with street cries, busy with passers-by, crowded and dangerous with carriages and wagons of all kinds, strewn with rubbish and filth lying about in heaps or carried along in the torrents of water pouring after a storm down the wide gutters, across which pedestrians could only pass dry-shod by little plank bridges. After a decade of revolution the house-fronts were dilapidated, their plaster falling, paint-work peeling, and shreds of posters flapping in the wind. At night, when there was no moon, an occasional *lanterne*, jutting out from the wall, shed a feeble and after 1789 a rather sinister light in these dark canyons. For all the fine architecture of the classical age, and the palatial *hôtels* of the wealthy, urban amenities were rare. Voltaire, in 1749, had called for such improvements as fountains to supply pure drinking water, roads adequate for the traffic of a great capital, and worthy public buildings, especially theatres. The narrow and squalid streets of Paris, he declared, should be widened, and fine buildings which were concealed from sight by a huddle of houses freed from their squalid surroundings. It was a century later before his hopes for Paris began to be realized, and then to the artistic taste of the Second Empire instead of that of the age of Louis Quinze.

Paris, at the end of the eighteenth century, was still in some respects an homogeneous city. Though there were faubourgs like Saint-Antoine and Saint-Marceau, inhabited mainly by small masters and their journeymen, and new wealthy quarters like the faubourg Saint-Germain, in much of older Paris the homes of the well-to-do, of the middling people and of the poor existed under the same roof. It might almost be said that class stratification was vertical, the rich and the poor entering by the same door, the former to mount by a short and broad staircase to the impressive apartments of the first floor, the latter to climb high up by ever narrowing stairs till they reached the attics in the mansard roof.

The First Empire

From Paris and the provincial capitals already radiated out the network of great roads that so impressed Arthur Young, as did the lack of traffic on them. The new industrial regions of France have witnessed many changes since the eighteenth century, but the great ports were already considerable cities. They still glory in their eighteenth-century quarters, while to many smaller towns and villages, scattered up and down the length and breadth of the country, alteration has come only slowly and imperceptibly. It was from the provinces that was drawn, then as now, much of the busy, scurrying population of the ant-heap of Paris, and many a Parisian, his fortune made or lost and his active life over, withdrew to pass his declining years in the quiet town or village of his childhood, along with the men who had been boys when he was a boy, who had not stirred from their native soil and who were the millions of France. Perhaps 600,000 lived in Paris at the end of the eighteenth century. The total urban population of France must have been well under two millions. Probably some 95 per cent of France's 26 millions lived in isolated farms, hamlets, villages, and small country towns. Mountain and forest still covered, as they do today, large tracts of country, though under pressure of rural over-population farming had pushed into marginal land on moor and hill-top that has since been abandoned. Agriculture, little influenced by the new methods developed in eighteenth-century England, followed its routine of the Middle Ages. Industry was still largely domestic.

In all these fundamental respects it matters little whether we are writing of 1789 or 1799. The Revolution did not materially add to or subtract from the basic resources of France, though it altered the use that was, or could be, made of them. What France had that still endowed her, at the end of the eighteenth century, with a potentially greater strength than any other country, was the largest population in Europe under a single government, apart from Russia, and even that had only just caught up with France. The application of the steam engine to industry was hardly yet

A History of Modern France

a factor in national strength; and this apart, France had a technical skill and equipment second to none. The Revolution had freed her from the trammels of the *ancien régime*. Paris, which for some five years had tried to rule France, had been disciplined with the aid of the armies drawn from the unpolitical rural millions. All was ready for a great general to concentrate the newly released forces into a centralized despotism and direct them into a bid for world empire.

2. FROM CONSULATE TO EMPIRE

CENTURIES do not usually end so punctually as the French eighteenth century did with the year 1799; though in another sense, as I have suggested, the France of the *ancien régime* still survives. For both its sudden conclusion and its persistence the chief responsibility must be attributed to Bonaparte. With his sense of realism, executive capacity, and ruthless strength of will, he wrote finis to the doubts and feuds of the revolutionaries, and imposed, out of the materials to hand, a new-fashioned framework on France, which was to last in its essentials to the present day. For the very reason that it was an artificial superstructure, which bore the weight of the state without ever being consciously shaped to the society on which it was arbitrarily imposed, it prevented the natural growth of institutions which might otherwise have taken place. This is, of course, wisdom after the event. When Bonaparte was brought to the chief office in the republic, though there was a general feeling that a new period had opened, the politicians who had effected the *coup d'état* did not appreciate what they had done, any more than those who had overthrown Robespierre five years earlier.

On the morrow of *brumaire* Bonaparte himself had only taken the first step, though a long one, on the path to Empire. He had yet to show that he was more than a successful general and to consolidate by the arts of politics what he had staked out a claim to by those of war. The

The First Empire

original proposals for the new constitution came from that self-appointed Solon of the Revolution, Sieyes. Given a third opportunity to demonstrate his genius at making constitutional bricks without straw, he framed a system of legislative bodies ingeniously devised to remove all effective political power from the sovereign people without attributing it to anyone else. In the best revolutionary tradition he was proposing to set up an imposing machine of government without providing any motive power to work it. The central position in the whole complicated system was to be occupied by a Conservative Senate, and if we ask how this was to be created we come to the heart of the matter: it was to be nominated, in effect, by Sieyes. The executive power, on the other hand, was to be entrusted to a Grand Elector with powers so carefully cabined and confined that he could do nothing by himself: this rôle was reserved for Bonaparte. We can hardly be surprised that for the third time Sieyes' plans proved abortive. His proposal for drawing the teeth of democratic sovereignty by attributing the right of voting to electors nominated from above – 'authority must come from above and confidence from below', to quote his new-style formula for democracy – suited Bonaparte well enough, as did the various devices for preventing the legislative chambers from exercising any real power. But Bonaparte was determined that he himself, as First Consul, should have effective and undivided executive authority. Even the other two Consuls were to be little more than rubber stamps. The result of his revision of the constitutional proposals was that whereas the age of divine-right monarchy had ended in 1789, the age of dictatorship began in 1799. Sieyes, who had written the birth-certificate of the Revolution, also signed its death warrant. He accepted, soon after, a large estate from Bonaparte, and confined himself henceforth to drawing-room politics. In a popular vote on the Constitution, which was in effect a plebiscite for or against General Bonaparte, the people performed what was to become its customary role in dictatorships in exemplary fashion: 3,011,007 voted for and 1,562 against.

A History of Modern France

The politicians of Paris did not immediately acknowledge the finality of *brumaire*. No sooner was Bonaparte installed in power than they began to intrigue against him. For his part, the First Consul set about consolidating his position by winning over, through the personal charm which he had at his command, as well as by material favours, men of all parties, revolutionary or royalist, so long as they were willing to forget their principles in his service. All the arts of popularity and propaganda were put to work. The propertied classes, old and new, saw in Bonaparte a saviour of society. A mixture of clemency and force pacified the rebellious departments of the West. The outlines of a new administrative structure for France were drawn up and – more important – put into effective operation. A peace offensive – and peace the French people now ardently longed for, gone the warlike passions of the early nineties – was launched by personal letters from the First Consul to George III and the Emperor; but peace, he was careful to tell the French people, could only come after victory. This was also necessary if he was to be able to put an end to the political intrigues of Paris and consolidate his personal authority.

The military situation was unpromising. When the year 1800 began the remnants of the defeated French army of Italy were still hanging on in Genoa in imminent danger of starvation, and their final collapse would open the door into France. Therefore, leaving Moreau in charge of an offensive on the Rhine, Bonaparte hastily gathered an army at Dijon and descended on Italy by way of the Great St Bernard. The campaign which followed was confused and unplanned. Important documents which might have revealed too much about it were destroyed by Bonaparte subsequently, and his own dispatches are a tissue of lies, so that it is difficult to know exactly what happened. The decisive clash of the French and Austrians at Marengo on 14 June 1800 took Bonaparte by surprise, with his army scattered. He was saved by the return, in the nick of time, of the division he had sent off under Desai. It was a soldiers' battle, won by the staunchness of the Guard and the dash of Desai, who

The First Empire

was killed in the fighting. Bonaparte, in a dispatch from the battle-field, provided for him a romanticized death: a dead man could be no rival. By the battle of Marengo Lombardy was regained and France relieved from the threat of an Austrian invasion. Meanwhile Moreau had advanced through Bavaria, occupied Munich, and in December, after routing the Austrians at Hohenlinden, was within fifty miles of Vienna.

Bonaparte had not waited for the completion of the German campaign to return to Paris, where, he knew, his enemies, Carnot prominent among them, were counting on defeat or at least a stalemate in Italy to enable them to overthrow the Consulate. Instead, hot on the heels of the news of Marengo, Bonaparte came spurring across France to pluck the fruits of victory. The Guards, who had served him so well, were brought back hurriedly to enter Paris with their general on the morning of the Quatorze Juillet, so that their entry could coincide with the celebration of the fête of the Bastille. The faubourg Saint-Antoine, where Robespierre had once been the idol, turned out its *sans-culottes* in their thousands to hail the triumph and welcome the victor.

Peace with victory was now within reach. The Holy Roman Emperor, threatened by French armies advancing from southern Germany on Austria itself and from northern Italy on Venetia, acknowledged defeat. By the treaty of Lunéville, in February 1801, French possessions on the left bank of the Rhine, from Switzerland to the sea, and the French satellite states – the Cisalpine and Ligurian Republics in northern Italy, the Helvetic Republic in Switzerland, and the Batavian Republic of the Dutch – were recognized. The hereditary princes of the Empire who lost territory on the left bank of the Rhine were to be compensated within Germany, and France as a party to the Treaty was to participate in the process of territorial redistribution. This was to open the door to large-scale French intervention in the Holy Roman Empire.

Now only England remained in the way of complete

pacification. To ensure her isolation Bonaparte negotiated an agreement with Russia, and conciliated Spain by the grant of the duchy of Tuscany to the Bourbon Duke of Parma. Under Russian leadership the Armed Neutrality was formed to oppose British attacks on neutral shipping, but the assassination of Paul I of Russia, and the bombardment of Copenhagen, dislocated it. In Egypt the isolated French army had been forced to capitulate by a British expeditionary force. These, however, were peripheral events. Faced with the bankruptcy of their European policy, Pitt and Grenville resigned and a new British government was ready to conclude peace with France. The negotiations were long and difficult, but slowly and reluctantly Great Britain gave up a large part of her conquests: it is true they had mainly been at the expense of former allies and not of France. In March 1802 the Treaty of Amiens was signed; Bonaparte had achieved peace for France and could proceed to collect the fruits of victory.

The change from Consulate to Empire was to be effected with the aid of victories abroad and plots at home. Marengo was followed, on 24 December 1800, by an attempt to blow up Bonaparte on his way to the opera. The attempted assassination was the work of a group of royalists under the Vendean leader, Georges Cadoudal, but the First Consul seized the opportunity to eliminate the unreconciled Jacobins, whom he regarded as his more dangerous opponents. Many of them were sent to rot to death in Guiana or the Seychelles.

The signature of the Treaty of Amiens enabled Bonaparte to secure the passing, by a majority of $3\frac{1}{2}$ millions to eight thousand, of a new plebiscite making him Consul for life. The next step followed fairly soon after. Cadoudal, who had taken refuge in England after the failure of his plot in 1800, organized a new attempt on Bonaparte's life in 1803, possibly with the connivance of Windham among the British ministers. Moreau, whose victory at Hohenlinden had been deliberately played down by Bonaparte to enhance his own glory, and Pichegru, returning secretly from

The First Empire

England where he had taken refuge since his failure to overthrow the Directory, were also implicated. The conspiracy was discovered before it could be put into effect. Cadoudal and his group of desperate men were arrested and executed; Pichegru was imprisoned in the Temple and found strangled one morning. According to the official theory he had committed suicide, as enemies of dictators are apt to do. Moreau, against whom the evidence was weaker, and whose victories were too recent for him to be disposed of so easily, was allowed to go into exile.

Bonaparte now decided that the royalists must be taught a lesson, as the Jacobins had been. The young duc d'Enghien, the last of the Condés, was seized on territory neighbouring France, brought back over the frontier and shot as an *émigré* in foreign service. There was nothing to link him with the plot of Cadoudal: it was an exemplary murder. As a Corsican perhaps Bonaparte regarded it as a legitimate exercise of the right of vendetta, his own life having undoubtedly been threatened by royalist plots. The much-publicized Cadoudal conspiracy also provided an appropriate atmosphere for the final transmutation of the First Consul into the Emperor. The Senate, duly prompted, passed the necessary legislative measures and the subsequent plebiscite, now *de rigueur*, gave popular sanction by 3,572,329 votes against 2,579 to the establishment of an hereditary Empire. This was perhaps less of a shock to republican sentiment than one might think, because, as early as 1789, the term empire had been in use to describe the French state, as a means of avoiding the word monarchy without falling into that of republic. The religious sanction was the one thing lacking, Napoleon felt, to make him a real Emperor. It could be provided. Pius VII was prepared for what to a less holy-minded man might have seemed an humiliation, if it could be regarded as a further step to win France back to the fold, and agreed to perform the ceremony of crowning Napoleon in Notre-Dame. There were many difficulties to be smoothed out but – except that the Pope, or according to the version at the time of the divorcee

A History of Modern France

Josephine herself, insisted that Napoleon should go through a religious ceremony of marriage with her, which he did in strict privacy – in most matters the Emperor had his own way. Anointed by the Pope, Napoleon himself placed the crown on his own head. The day was 2 December 1804.

3. NAPOLEONIC FOUNDATIONS OF THE NINETEENTH CENTURY

WHEN he became First Consul Napoleon Bonaparte was only thirty years old, but already marked as a man of destiny. The impecunious son of what passed for a gentle family in Corsica, after the French conquest he went with government assistance to the school at Brienne and then to the École Militaire, whence he emerged as sub-lieutenant of artillery. The Revolution was the time, the army was the career, for an ambitious young man. Short, but thin and muscular, he had good looks, though little notice should be taken of portraits in which he is already the Byronic hero of the coming romantic movement. He had tremendous energy and a powerful and disciplined memory. He could work continuously for long periods, with only snatches of sleep. In order not to disturb his habits, says his police official, Réal, he had taken care not to form any. He had a thirst for glory, fed partly on the writings of the pre-romantics but more on the history of the great conquerors of the ancient world, Caesar and Alexander, for this was also the period of the classical revival. Although he read Rousseau and was not uninfluenced by the ideals of the Enlightenment, his contribution to the legal code which bears his name showed a natural preference for the more conservative and less enlightened ideas of the *ancien régime*. Politically his bent was towards despotism untrammelled by divine right. His experience of the Revolution had left him with a deep contempt, not unmixed with fear, for the people. For politicians he had the dictator's natural aversion. He was not without humane instincts, and was capable

The First Empire

of kindness in private life, to say nothing of the charm which he could turn on at will; but such qualities vanished when they stood in the way of his success. Even early in his career, before overweening egoism had quite mastered him, when military considerations demanded it he was entirely ruthless. There is no evidence that bloodshed mattered a scrap to him, or that he ever thought, as a Marlborough or a Wellington did, of economizing in the lives of his soldiers. The mass attack on which he relied depended on not counting the cost in dead and wounded. A French Colonel describes him riding, as was his custom, over the field of Borodino after the battle, rubbing his hands and radiant with satisfaction as he counted five dead Russians to every one French corpse. I suppose, the Colonel adds sardonically, he took the bodies of his German allies for Russians. Such nobility as might have been given, even to the career of a military despot, by the service of some end, although a mistaken one, was lacking. Apart from his own personal glory, the only other ambition he had at heart was to found a dynasty. When, in his last campaign, he might have saved much for France by abandoning his dream of Empire, he was incapable of such moderation, or even realism. After all this, to say that he was an adventurer is an anti-climax; but it is not irrelevant or unimportant. Coming from islanders whose social institutions were the *banditti* and the *vendetta*, he carried the same standards into a country where the Revolution had already shown how uncertain were the conquests of the Enlightenment. For fifteen years France and Europe were to be at the mercy of a gambler to whom fate and his own genius gave for a time all the aces. He always cheated at cards and his carriage had diamonds concealed in its lining in case of hurried flight.

The short intermission from continual war that the Treaty of Amiens inaugurated gave Bonaparte the opportunity to establish the bases of a new government. As soon as he became First Consul he began the task of reconstruction. The simulacrum of representative institutions was preserved as a sop to revolutionary tradition, with an advisory Senate, a Legislative Body which could vote but not speak, and a Tribunate which could speak but not vote. Since the last, powerless as it was, did not invariably say just what the Emperor wanted, it was reduced in membership to fifty, divided into sections, and finally, in 1807, abolished. The Legislative Body, chosen by the Senate and composed mostly of obscure former revolutionaries, was then ungagged but remained a passive register of the Emperor's will. The Senate, including many of the great names of the period, at first sight looks a more substantial body, with real legislative powers; but for all their distinction, its members were a mere collection of nominees, serving only to give dignity to their master's decisions.

If we turn from the legislative to the executive, even the façade of limitation on the will of the Emperor disappears. The reorganization of the ministries had mostly been effected during the Revolution. Foreign Affairs, War, and Marine, to which was attached Colonies now that France had lost them all, remained as before 1789. The Keeper of the Seals became the Minister for Justice. The most important changes were the result of amalgamating, and then subdividing on more logical grounds, the Contrôle Général and Maison du Roi, out of which emerged the Ministry of Finances and the Ministry of the Interior. Finally, like all dictators, Bonaparte required a Minister of Police. A State Secretariat was also set up, through which the First Consul controlled and coordinated the policies of his ministers.

Over the Police the ex-terrorist Fouché, later, when titles were handed round, to become the duc d'Otranto, reigned, with the assistance of a choice collection of scoundrels gathered from the police of the *ancien régime* and the underworld of the Revolution. At Foreign Affairs Tallyrand was indispensable. Berthier at the War Office was an invaluable chief of staff. Lucien Bonaparte, the first Minister of the Interior, though efficient showed signs of independence which could not be tolerated, least of all in a brother, and was soon dismissed. Finances were entrusted to Gaudin, formerly a high official of the Contrôle Général. There was,

The First Empire

of course, no first minister, and the ministers never constituted a cabinet. The Emperor consulted them individually, took their advice or gave them their orders as it pleased him, like an *ancien régime* monarch. Louis XIV had at last found a successor and France was again ruled by the *bon plaisir* of an autocrat, but one enfranchised from the bonds of aristocratic and provincial privilege and controlling a new-fashioned and far more efficient administrative machine.

At the centre of the new administrative structure was the Council of State. Napoleon, for all his seizure of arbitrary power, was no mere vulgar dictator imposing unconsidered decisions on a servile nation. An expert himself in the matter of war, he knew the value of experts. He was also, at least when he first came to power, conscious of his own limitations and of his need for a body of specialists who, without possessing political power, could provide him with the advice he needed in all fields of government. The Council of State was intended, in the first place, as the means of his own political education. It was also to draw up laws and administrative regulations and expound them to the legislative bodies: it was in fact the real legislative organ. The Councillors of State took the place of the masters of requests and councillors of the *ancien régime*, from whom the *intendants* and higher officials had been recruited. They formed a permanent corps whence Napoleon could draw *missi dominici* for the varied tasks of imperial government. The sections into which the Council was divided supervised the various fields of government and provided him with a means of checking and controlling the actions of his ministers. The importance he attributed to the Council was well shown in his advice to the former *parlementaire* and constitutional monarchist, Roederer, one of Bonaparte's associates in the *coup d'état* of *brumaire*, not to accept a nomination to the Senate but rather to enter the Council of State. 'In that', the First Consul said, 'there are great things to be done; from that I will draw my ambassadors and ministers.' The advice, as was inevitable with Bonaparte, was not disinterested. He was counting on the Council of State, more than on any other of his administrative bodies, to draw into his service able men from all fields and from all points on the political scale, except the most intransigent republicans and royalists. Former magistrates and high officials of the *ancien régime* sat side by side with men who had made their mark in the struggles of the Revolution, generals of the revolutionary armies with civilian technicians and scientists.

What was to be ultimately the greatest achievement of the Council of State, the creation of a system of administrative law, was as yet a minor activity; but as well as its major rôle in the central government it exercised an unlimited supervision over local administration and all public establishments, and gradually filled in the details of the administrative and financial system sketched out under the Consulate. From its creation in 1800 to 1813, 58,435 separate cases were brought up for examination in the general assembly of the Council; the number dealt with annually rose from 911 in 1800 to 6,285 in 1811. While the Council of State formed the ideal instrument for an absolute régime, its work was far too valuable for any subsequent government to dispense with its services. Though under Napoleon it was no more than an instrument without any independence, the Council of State developed in due course a tradition and an *esprit de corps* of its own and became the unshakeable corner-stone of the French bureaucracy. In the absence of an effective parliamentary system it provided, along with the administrative substructure, the ferroconcrete framework of government, which was to enable French society to survive and emerge comparatively unchanged from so many political upheavals. At the same time, and for this very reason, it also stood in the way of the creation of effective parliamentary institutions. Through the Council of State and his other administrative institutions, the shadow of Napoleon continued to darken the following century. He had given France, when she needed it after the stresses of the Revolution, a steel corset on which

The First Empire

she was to become dependent and from which she was to emancipate herself only slowly and painfully and never completely.

The system of centralized bureaucracy called for the creation of machinery of local administration which could carry the will of the government at Paris into the most remote communes. Administrative centralization, as de Tocqueville pointed out, was not an invention of Napoleon. The modern prefect can trace his ancestry back to the intendants of Louis XIV and Richelieu, and even to the *sénéchaux* and *baillis* of the Middle Ages; but the element of continuity, though important, must not be exaggerated. The *ancien régime* still retained too many medieval relics for the writ of the central government to run unchallenged and unimpeded throughout the provinces. The great achievement of the Revolution, for good or ill, had been to make a *tabula rasa*, administratively speaking, of France. The system of democratic councils with which the Constitutional Assembly endowed, as by a stroke of the pen, its new administrative divisions, could not survive the strains of the Revolution. Already under the Committee of Public Safety a big step had been taken in the direction of the restoration of central control. Under the Directory the local authorities became increasingly weak and corrupt, though the more exaggerated accounts of Directorial decay are perhaps the work of Bonapartist propaganda. However, an official report of 1799 declared, 'The pillage of public funds, attacks directed on public officials, the inertia of a great number of them, the assassination of republicans – such is unfortunately the picture which several departments present.' The picture had at least some truth in it and was perhaps more generally true than was admitted.

Bonaparte and his advisers, in 1800, had no doubt what was wrong: it was the attempt, still surviving in theory, to govern the departments and communes by a system of elected councils. In the basic law on local government of the year VIII the elective principle was eliminated from the appointment of all local officials. Local councils still

23

survived in name, it is true, but their functions were reduced to microscopic proportions. As Chaptal, wealthy proprietor and scientist, ennobled before 1789, and the successor to Lucien Bonaparte at the Ministry of the Interior, put it, 'These popular councils are placed, so to speak, to one side of the line of executive action: they do not hamper in any way the rapid progress of the administration.' In fact adequate precautions were taken to ensure that they should not do so. They were not allowed to meet for a longer period than fifteen days in the year; their chief function was to give their approval to the distribution of taxation between the various *arrondissements*, towns, and villages of the department. All administrative authority in the department was placed in the hands of a prefect, appointed from Paris, with sub-prefects under him. The latter were generally local men and often former revolutionaries, but a job was a job. They had no independent authority. The first list of prefects included many Jacobins who had rallied to Bonaparte, as well as former *ancien régime* officials. The prefects, unlike the sub-prefects, were never local men. There has been much discussion whether they were mere passive agents of the central government. They probably possessed less independence than the former intendants; but since, even now, instructions took eight days to reach Toulouse from Paris, and the newly invented system of telegraphs was only used for important communications, mostly military, detailed control of the prefects' actions was obviously difficult. Lucien Bonaparte in a circular of the year VIII said, 'General ideas must come from the centre. I note with regret that some of you, with praiseworthy intentions doubtless, concern yourselves with the interpretation of the laws. ... It is not this that the government expects of its administration.' That the prefects were the officers of a central government and subject to the same kind of obedience as was expected of officers of the army was made quite clear by putting them into uniform. It was a dignified one – blue coat, white waistcoat and breeches, silver thread on collar, cuffs, and pockets, a *chapeau français*

The First Empire

ornamented with silver, red scarf with silver fringes, and a sword – but one wonders what an intendant would have said if he had been expected to wear a uniform.

The first task of the prefects was that of economic restoration. In a note of 1800 Bonaparte wrote, 'The 36,000 communes in France represent 36,000 orphans, heirs of the old feudal rights, which have been abandoned or pillaged for ten years by the municipal guardians of the Convention and the Directory.' Now the communes were to be taught that they had a master and a more efficient one than the medley of *ancien régime* authorities. This is not to say that the prefects could afford to ride rough-shod over all local feeling. Under the Empire the local notabilities re-emerged as the dominant interest and the prefects and sub-prefects found it wise to remain on friendly terms with them, for their mutual advantage. Of the general ability of the prefects and the valuable work they did in restoring administrative good habits to the departments there can be no question. Taine once expressed the regret of not having had the experience of serving for a year as secretary to one of Napoleon's prefects.

The prefects had other tasks besides that of promoting the economic well-being of their departments. They had to collect favourable votes for the plebiscites: the success with which they performed this duty foretold their future political rôle. Gradually, as the war pressed increasingly heavily on French life, its requirements came to dominate the activities of the prefects. They drew up lists of conscripts, authorized exemptions, sought out deserters, confiscated horses for the army, looked after troops in passage, and guarded prisoners of war. As early as 1801 a prefect is found complaining that the enforcement of conscription occupies one-third of the employees of his prefecture and that these are barely sufficient. Continually increasing military demands bore so heavily on the departments that by 1814 their financial resources had been exhausted.

In the later years of the Empire the personnel of the administration underwent considerable changes. Especially from 1809 onwards, Napoleon, with the weakness of a new man for real gentlemen, tended to appoint former nobles to office. A host of *émigrés* flocked back to take up good jobs, to introduce more easy-going methods into the prefectures, and leave the real work to their secretaries-general. From 1810 all prefects were given the title of count or baron and ordered to assume coats of arms. Many were now secret royalists, ready to accept the Emperor's pay while he was in power, but prepared to desert him with cynical haste in 1814. During the Hundred Days the prefects exhibited what would be a comic, if it were not equally a cowardly and treacherous anxiety to be on the winning side. Official adulation of the Emperor was carried to extreme lengths. A prefect of the Pas-de-Calais, formerly officer of the Royal Normandy regiment, apostrophized his department, when it was about to receive a visit from the Emperor, thus: 'You are about to see him, that Napoleon, proclaimed so justly the greatest of men in the greatest of nations ... *Dieu créa Bonaparte et se reposa.*' As soon as Napoleon lost power the same official addressed his devotions with equal fervour to the duc de Berry, only to renew his loyal protestations to the Emperor when he returned from Elba. Among those with a genius for guessing which way the cat was going to jump and getting there in advance, the prize must be held by M. de Jessaint, prefect of the Marne uninterruptedly from 1800 to 1838. The fact is that the prefectoral system was an immensely powerful instrument in the hands of the central government, but its power was entirely derivative. While the *régime* was strong at the centre the prefects could guarantee to control the rest of the country; but a *coup d'état* in Paris could shatter the whole fabric, for no element capable of standing by itself existed in the provinces. The prefectural system, for all its merits, combined the vices of excessive rigidity and excessive instability. It was to be in no small measure responsible for the alternation of revolution and reaction that marked the history of nineteenth-century France.

Besides creating a unified administrative machinery,

The First Empire

Napoleon laid down the legislative basis on which it was to operate. The idea of reducing the varied laws of France to a uniform, written code was inherited by the Revolution from the *ancien régime*. The work had been begun by the *Ordonnances* drawn up under Colbert and d'Aguesseau. The revolutionary Assemblies set up committees to complete the work of codification, but they were never able to catch up with the mass of their own legislation. In 1800 Bonaparte appointed a committee of distinguished lawyers to draw up a civil code, and gave them five months to do it in. After their draft code had been discussed in the Council of State, the First Consul himself being present at about half of the meetings though of course he had not the legal knowledge to make a serious contribution to them, it was submitted to the legislative bodies, where criticism was so hostile that it did not obtain final acceptance until 1804. The criticism to which the Code was subjected, though it infuriated Napoleon, was largely sound. His rôle was not to frame the Code but to see that the lawyers came to a conclusion, good or bad, without further delay. For some of the worst features he was personally responsible. Such were the deterioration in the legal status of women, who were allowed no control over the family property and could not acquire, sell, or give property without their husband's consent; the reintroduction of confiscation as a legal penalty; and the use of the fiction of civil death. The First Consul's influence was also responsible for the tightening up of the laws of marriage and divorce and the restoration of paternal authority in the family. The great gains of the Revolution, however, were maintained: equality before the law, the principle of religious toleration, the abolition of privileges and seigneurial burdens. Property rights were strictly maintained and there was particular emphasis on the interests of the small owner. Property was to be inherited equally by all legitimate children at death, except for a certain disposable proportion: to this provision has been speculatively attributed the limitation of families in nineteenth-century France. Perhaps the most important feature of the Civil

Code was that all its 2,281 articles could be contained in a single fairly small volume. It was to be the most effective agency for the propagation of the basic principles of the French Revolution that was, or perhaps that could have been, devised. It was carried by the French armies through Europe and thence spread across the world. There followed in France a Code of Civil Procedure, cumbersome and mostly copied from *ancien régime* rules, a Commercial Code, and a severe and arbitrary Criminal Code, which was all the same a model of enlightenment compared with the barbarous laws that still prevailed in Great Britain.

The Revolution had in nothing failed so completely as in its finances. The first step towards their rehabilitation was taken by Gaudin, head of a division in the Contrôle Général before the Revolution and after the 18 *brumaire* Minister of Finances, when he removed the assessment and collection of direct taxation from the control of local authorities and formed a central organization charged with the task. France, however, has never been able to draw the major part of its revenue from the wealthy, and the new rich were no more willing to pay for the privilege of being governed than had been the old privileged orders. All indirect taxes had been abolished by the Constituent Assembly, though the Directory re-introduced them on playing cards and tobacco. Napoleon revived the tax on salt, brought back the hated *droits* on wines and cider, and created a *régie* for their collection. The Directory had also re-established local *octrois*; these were greatly extended under the Empire and the central government took an increasing proportion of them.

In 1800 was founded another of the great and permanent creations of the Consulate, the Bank of France. Though with semi-public functions, this was a private bank, its shareholders represented by a general assembly of the 200 most important, who elected the 15 regents and 3 censors. The Bank, like the other Napoleonic institutions, was to remain a power in France throughout the régimes which followed.

The First Empire

In 1802 the French budget was balanced, but this was only a temporary success. The existence of private and military funds under the direct control of the Emperor prevented the imperial budgets from ever being more than paper exercises, with little relation to the facts. No institutional reforms could put the country on a sound financial basis in time of continual war; and there was never sufficient confidence in the permanence of the régime for the government to draw, as Great Britain did to such a great extent, on loans. Moreover, Napoleon had a profound suspicion of them. He had to fall back, just like the *ancien régime*, on expedients, and live from hand to mouth. And like the Revolution he exploited the conquered countries, to such an extent that it might almost be said that war was a financial necessity for France.

Yet another of the loose ends left by the Revolution for Napoleon to cut and tie up in his own fashion was the problem of a religious settlement, and this also was largely, if not essentially, an administrative question. Whether religious differences still remained, in 1799, a source of danger to France, or whether the increasingly tolerant *modus vivendi* reached by the Directory could have survived, is a much disputed point on which agreement is unlikely to be reached; but it can be agreed that religious persecution during the Revolution had not merely failed to destroy the hold of the Roman Catholic religion on the people, it had strengthened religious feeling and played some part in promoting a religious revival. The more moderate policies of the Directory were perhaps more dangerous to the Church than active dechristianization. The secularization of education – a circular of the year VIII ordered teachers in the central schools to avoid 'everything that pertained to the doctrines and rites of all religions and sects whatever they may be' – may be regarded as initiating a struggle that was to continue to the present day.

The Catholic Church had certainly something to gain in this respect from the renewal of State support. There were also powerful inducements to the State to abandon its policy of religious neutrality and secularization. The complete pacification of the Vendée and Normandy would undoubtedly be greatly facilitated if the support of the clergy could be gained. This would also powerfully aid in the assimilation of the Belgic provinces and other newly acquired territory where the Catholic religion was strong. Bonaparte himself was aware of the sentimental appeal of a vague kind of Rousseauist religiosity, though one can hardly envisage him as a disciple of the Savoyard vicar. Religion, like every other ideal, was to him a means to an end, his own power. Sayings attributed to him represent truly his essential attitude – 'Religion is a kind of inoculation which by satisfying our love of marvels guarantees us against charlatans and sorcerers'; 'Society cannot exist without inequality of wealth, and inequality of wealth cannot exist without religion.' Walking in the park at Malmaison he is alleged to have said, listening to the bells, 'What an impression that must make on the simple and credulous. . . . How can your philosophers and ideologues answer that? The people must have a religion and that religion must be in the hands of the government.'

The Vatican, for its part, despite its denunciations of the Revolution, was prepared to make considerable concessions to regain official recognition in France. The new Pope, Pius VII, elected in 1800, a simple and holy monk with little knowledge of the world, was not violently hostile to the Revolution, and papal agents had been sent secretly to Paris as early as September 1800. The victory over Austria and the Peace of Lunéville in February 1801 made it desirable to come to terms with a France which now controlled all northern Italy. Secretly instituted negotiations were concluded in July 1801. To minimize the inevitable resistance of the strong anti-clerical elements in the legislative bodies, Bonaparte waited until the Peace of Amiens had been concluded before he announced the Concordat, in April 1802. Characteristically, having secured an agreement, he proceeded to distort it in his own interest by means of the issue of Organic Articles. Even so, many of the former

The First Empire

revolutionaries exhibited open hostility to the Concordat and Fouché issued a mocking circular. By the Concordat the Vatican agreed to the institution of a new episcopate which should contain a proportion of bishops from the Constitutional Church, recognized the alienation of Church lands as permanent, and accepted the payment of clerical salaries by the State. Catholicism was described as 'the religion of the great majority of citizens', and its practice was to be free and public so long as it conformed to such police regulations as were required by public order. By the supplementary Organic Articles Bonaparte tried to turn the Concordat into the instrument of a new and stronger Gallicanism. No Papal bull was to be published, nor any Papal representative to function in France, without the permission of the government. The bishops were placed under the close control of the prefects and the lesser clergy lost the considerable independence of episcopal authority they had formerly enjoyed. Subsequent concessions to religious opinion included the suppression of the official ten-day cult, already practically dead, the restoration of Sunday as the day of rest for officials, and of the Gregorian calendar; children were to be given only saints names or those of the great figures of antiquity; the payment of salaries was extended to all clergy and the actual salaries were increased; religious orders reappeared in France, with official sanction for women's orders and for male missionary orders, while others, such as the Jesuits, were tolerated by official connivance; primary, though not higher education, was restored to the control of the clergy.

Despite all these concessions the Vatican was not quite happy about the bargain it had concluded. The Pope protested against the Organic Articles and only consecrated the bishops Bonaparte had chosen from the Constitutional Church after two years' delay. On the face of it the Concordat was a great victory for Bonaparte and a masterstroke of policy. The Emperor was able henceforth to use the clergy as an instrument of government. They celebrated his victories with Te Deums, published his imperial proclamations from their pulpits, delivered patriotic sermons, stimulated conscription, and promoted loyal sentiments. An Imperial Catechism was issued for the purpose of 'binding by religious sanctions the conscience of the people to the august person of the Emperor'. A national fête was created for the day of the Assumption which was also Napoleon's birthday and turned out conveniently to be the Saint's day of a newly discovered St Napoleon. Yet with all this he failed to obtain any permanent religious sanction for his rule. In the last years of the Empire the barely concealed royalist sentiments of most of the clergy undermined the loyalty of the people and prepared the way for his fall.

The religious revival, of which the first great manifesto was Chateaubriand's *Génie du Christianisme* in 1802, would have come about without Napoleon. The Concordat, by pushing Gallican principles farther than ever before, and this in the interests of no divine-right sovereign, did much to discredit Gallicanism and strengthen the ultramontane tendency in the French Church. It also reduced the lower clergy to a position of total dependence on their bishops, and made the bishops themselves much more dependent on the Papacy than formerly. The act by which the Pope, in agreement with Napoleon, deposed the whole episcopate of France, including many lawfully appointed and consecrated bishops, marked a great step forward in the assertion of papal authority. The thirty-seven *ancien régime* bishops who were excluded from their sees by the Concordat kept the allegiance of a small group of the faithful who founded what was called *la petite Église*. The injury to vested interests and nice consciences, and the elevation of a dozen somewhat grisly constitutional bishops, was a cheap price to pay for such a great extension of papal authority. The ultimate result was immensely to strengthen the influence of the Vatican in France. Napoleon had won for himself an unreliable and temporary ally, and he had bequeathed to his successors a Church which would henceforth never willingly be the junior partner of the State. The intermittent struggle between Church and State which be-

The First Empire

devilled French politics for the following century and a half was as much the inheritance of the Napoleonic Concordat as of revolutionary anti-clericalism.

That hierarchical conception of society which made it easy for Napoleon to come to terms with the Roman Church, so long as he imagined that he had safeguarded his own position at the apex of the pyramid, was applied also, though less appropriately, to the organization of the Protestant churches. Their pastors became salaried officials and like the curés took an oath of loyalty. Their synods and consistories were chosen from the wealthier adherents of the faith and controlled by the secular authorities. Louis XIV had failed to extirpate French Protestantism, Napoleon succeeded in domesticating it.

While Napoleon restored official recognition to the Roman Catholic Church, he had no intention of returning the control of education they had possessed under the *ancien régime* to the ecclesiastical authorities. But he needed a system of education to provide administrators and technical experts for the service of the State. The Revolution had destroyed the old system of education but created nothing to put in its place apart from a limited number of Central Schools, which were neither sufficiently traditional in their curriculum, nor sufficiently authoritarian in their discipline, for Bonaparte's taste. They would produce, he thought, liberals and ideologists, for neither of which was there room in the Napoleonic state. Bonaparte himself expounded the basic principles of his theory of education: 'So long as children are not taught that they must be republican or monarchist, catholic or irreligious, etc. ... the State will not be a nation, it will rest on insecure or vague foundations. ... In a properly organized state there is always a body destined to regulate the principles of morality and politics.' Defending the law of 1802 on education, presented to the Legislative Body, ironically enough, by Fourcroy, a leading chemist, another of Bonaparte's necessary experts, Roederer, declared that Latin must be restored to its primacy and quasi-monopoly in the educa-

A History of Modern France

tional system. There followed an almost complete return to the syllabus and methods of the *ancien régime*, which lasted with little change until the reforms of 1865. The Central Schools were replaced by *lycées*, boarding-schools with a semi-military uniform and discipline and military training from the age of twelve.

In these the new *élite* of France was to be formed with the aid of some 6,000 national *bourses*, of which rather more than a third were reserved for the sons of officials and officers. They led on to the specialized schools of law, medicine, and pharmacy, the *école militaire spéciale* and the famous *école normale*, founded in 1808 to prepare for service in schools and universities 300 young men chosen by competitive examination. These were to provide the technical experts needed by the Empire. On a lower level, secondary schools, established by municipalities or individuals, gave the education needed for commercial or minor administrative posts. At the bottom, the primary schools were left to the initiative of the communes and the teaching Orders, and were still too few to bestow even a modicum of literacy upon more than a small fraction of the population. The educational system was placed, by a law of 1808, under the control of a single imperial university. The whole structure formed a rigid hierarchy, under a Grand Master nominated by and responsible to the Emperor. An imposing bureaucratic apparatus centred in Paris was charged with regulating the educational life of France down to the smallest detail. If, today, the Rector of a university cannot appoint his secretary, dismiss a cleaner, or modify an academic course without reference to Paris, it is in obedience to the dead hand of Napoleon.

In the *lycées* religion was kept, by Napoleon's prescription, to the 'necessary minimum'. Primary education, on the other hand, he was content to leave in the hands of the Church. Under the influence of its Grand Master, Fontanes, the University was increasingly subjected to clerical influence. The schools run by priests prospered at the expense of the state *lycées*. Even before his fall the instrument created

The First Empire

by Napoleon to dragoon the mind of France was escaping from his control, and the conflict between secular and clerical education, which was to be one of the dominant themes in the history of the following century, was emerging.

Where the task was simply one of repression, the success of the Napoleonic system was less qualified. The press became a mere instrument of imperial propaganda, and papers which were not sufficiently docile soon disappeared. A censorship controlled the publication of books. Theatres were put under the Ministry of Police and reduced in Paris to eight. Even in the midst of a desperate war, at Moscow in October 1812, Napoleon could concern himself with drawing up the regulations for the Comédie-Française, a gesture illustrating less his interest in the promotion of the drama than his determination to ensure that every medium for the expression of opinion remained under strict control.

The First Empire was hardly the milieu from which literature was likely to emerge, and very little did. The mock-heroics of *Ossian*, translated in 1801, suited the Emperor's literary taste. The romantic melancholy of Chateaubriand's *Atala* and *René*, Mme de Staël's assertion, in *Delphine* and *Corinne*, of woman's right to happiness, but also of the unhappiness that is the fate of superior persons, Joseph de Maistre's theocratic ideals, had no appeal to him. Of these authors only Chateaubriand stayed under Napoleon's rule. Most of the writing of the Empire falls into the category of journalism or propaganda rather than literature.

In painting also the Empire has little to its credit. Fragonard, when he died in 1809, had long been an anachronism. David was capable of magnificent portraits, but he was prepared to serve Napoleon as faithfully as he had served the Jacobins and wasted his talents on huge, neo-classical, historical set pieces. In such a painting as his *Sabine Women interrupting the battle between Romans and Sabines*, every figure, down to the smallest child, is posed in a rhetorical attitude, consciously playing a part on the stage of history, just like David's own contemporaries of the

35

Revolution and Empire. The whole scene is as moving as the waxworks of Mme Tussaud which also date from the same period. A more poetical spirit is infused by Prud'hon into his classical compositions: the Empress Josephine reclines in reverie and classical *déshabillé* on mossy rocks amid a romantic landscape. But most of the painting of the period is frank propaganda. David rearranges the Coronation of Napoleon to order, as he had already done the Tennis-court Oath. Napoleon's charger rears up as his master with an heroic gesture points the way across the Alps to a stage army in the background. The baron Gros paints huge battle scenes to the glorification of the Emperor and his Marshals. He was perhaps the most successful of the official painters of the Empire until he committed suicide.

Napoleon himself was represented *ad nauseam*, the hero leading the charge across the bridge at Lodi, presenting the eagles to his legions, riding his chariot in a Roman triumph or apotheosized as a classical deity, sparing the conquered on the battlefield or subjecting the proud, visiting the victims of plague, rousing by his very presence the spirit of devotion in the wounded and dying. It is quite clear that the French painters of the period and Goya – of course, a painter on a different scale of magnitude – were not illustrating the same war. But it would be a mistake to judge the political success of Napoleon's artists by their artistic merits. Their influence in the formation of the Napoleonic legend and in creating and perpetuating a romantic attitude to war is not to be underestimated. More important for the history of art is the group of young men – Ingres, Vernet, Géricault – which was appearing in the last years of the Empire.

The decorative taste of the Empire was luxurious and heavy, adding Egyptian and Etruscan motives to the influence of the now triumphant classical revival. The provincial cities were not important enough to receive much imperial attention, and there the eighteenth century largely survived, but considerable steps were taken towards

The First Empire

the spoiling of Paris. Napoleon required a grandiose setting for the capital of his Empire, and of course a classical one. Triumphal arches – such as the Étoile and the Carrousel – were *de rigueur*. For public buildings the correct thing was temples; so we have the temple of Finance – the Bourse with its sixty-four Corinthian columns, the temple of religion – the Madeleine, the temple of the laws – the palais Bourbon, all heavy pastiches and all equally unsuited to the purposes for which they were intended. The proportions of the place Vendôme were ruined by sticking in its middle, in place of the destroyed royal statue, a monstrous column, in imitation of that of Trajan. To enable the Napoleonic monuments to be seen, the process of driving long straight roads through Paris, which was to be carried much further under the Second Empire, was begun. Unlike the lath and plaster erections of the Revolution, the buildings of the Empire were made to last – unfortunately, for they embody too well the Emperor's chief aesthetic rule: *'Ce qui est grand est toujours beau.'*

Literature and art could not be expected to flourish in the hard climate of the Empire. Speculation about society was even less likely to be encouraged. In 1803 Napoleon suppressed the Academy of Moral and Political Sciences. On the other hand the natural and mathematical sciences have usually seemed able to accommodate themselves quite happily to absolutism. Apart from the guillotining of Lavoisier as a Farmer General, the Revolution and Empire did nothing to check scientific progress. The older generation of mathematicians and physicists such as Lagrange, Laplace, whose name is identified with the theory of nebulae, Monge, mathematician and accomplice of Bonaparte, and the botanist Lamarck, overlapped with younger men – Cuvier, who brought geology and palaeontology to the aid of zoological studies, Ampère, the founder of electromagnetism, and the astronomer Arago. In psychology, Destutt de Tracy and Cabanis continued the materialist theories of Condillac.

All this – art or science – is incidental or irrelevant to the history of the Empire. Napoleon's peculiar and lasting achievement was the work of the Consulate – that administrative reorganization, which, in perspective, can be seen as bequeathing not only to France but to much of the rest of the world, the most powerful instrument of bureaucratic control that the Western world had known since the Roman Empire. It was not a framework for the kind of society that the idealistic liberals of 1789 had imagined themselves to be inaugurating, nor should we treat the Napoleonic system, as it often has been treated, as the mere logical sequel to the *ancien régime* and the Revolution, and Napoleon simply as the heir of Louis XIV and the Committee of Public Safety. This is to underestimate the scope of his achievement. The Grand Monarch did not leave an imprint on French institutions that can be compared with the heritage of the Emperor. His immediate successors might repudiate his work, they could not undo it, and the Napoleonic state was long to outlive its author and the ends to which he had directed it.

4. THE NAPOLEONIC EMPIRE: RISE

THE Consulate was more important in the history of France, though not of Europe, than the Empire. What remains is a ten-years wonder, the history of conquests as dazzling as they were ephemeral, of armies marching and counter-marching from Lisbon to Moscow, and peace a brief breathing-space between wars. If we ask, as the Greeks would have done, what was the end of the Napoleonic state, the answer must be war. In war it had begun, war remained its *raison d'être*, and by war it was to end.

The Treaty of Amiens could not in the nature of things be more than an armistice, but it provided an opportunity for extra-European policies to be developed by Bonaparte. With France's position in Europe consolidated, he looked to the restoration of her overseas empire. Louisiana and the colony of St Domingo had been gained from Spain; and the colonies which had been conquered by Great

The First Empire

Britain during the Revolutionary War were restored to France, which thus had in 1802 a larger colonial domain than in 1789. The position was less favourable than it might seem, but to understand the reason for this we must briefly look back over developments in the West Indies since 1789.

The Revolution had at first seemed a golden opportunity for the wealthy planters of the French Antilles, the Grands Blancs, in the name of self-government (the usual demand of those who want to oppress others) to relieve themselves of the control of the authorities in Paris. At the same time, to prevent the liberal ideas of the Constituent Assembly from being applied to the colonies, a number of big colonial proprietors had formed in Paris, in June 1789, a club to defend their interests, called from its meeting-place the club Massiac. On the other side, the Société des Amis des Noirs rallied anti-slavery opinion. The liberal tendency was the stronger in the Assembly, and it was joined to a belief in centralized control. The principle that the colonies are an integral part of France was first enunciated by the Revolution in a decree of March 1790; it was repeated in August 1792 and again in the Constitution of the year III. The extension of civic rights was much slower and more reluctant. In May 1791 coloured men who were sons of a free father and mother were given the vote. This was only some 5 per cent of the whole black or mulatto population, but both white and black now began to take up arms. In an attempt to restore peace the Legislative Assembly gave political rights to all free men, and sent over to St Domingo, in September 1792, commissaires and 6,000 troops to enforce its policy. The planters resisted and their leaders signed a treaty temporarily delivering the islands to the British, in return for military and naval assistance. The commissaires, in desperation, proclaimed the enfranchisement of all blacks who would join them. Meanwhile, in July 1793, the Convention had abolished the slave trade, and in February 1794 was to vote the abolition of slavery. In the confused triangular struggle of English, French, and coloured that followed, the chief victor was the yellow fever. But by 1798 the great Negro general Toussaint-Louverture was undisputed ruler of St Domingo; while in Guadeloupe a revolutionary commissaire with the aid of the Negroes had driven out a British force of occupation.

The legislation of the Revolution had, in spite of everything, made important reforms, but the French colonists, supported by Bonaparte, had no intention of accepting them. The Constitution of the year VIII laid it down that the colonies should be ruled by special laws; in 1802 they were placed under executive regulations and exempted from legislative control. The department of the Colonies in the Ministry of the Marine, staffed with *ancien régime* officials from whom Bonaparte took his advice, willingly abandoned all the reforms of the Revolution. The French trading monopoly was restored in the West Indies. Slavery was re-established where it had been abolished, Negroes were excluded from France, and mixed marriages prohibited. It is reasonable to suppose that the influence of the creole Josephine reinforced Bonaparte's native illiberalism in his dealings with the colonies. In the lesser islands small military expeditions from France restored French authority without difficulty. St Domingo, where Toussaint-Louverture had established an autonomous authority with himself as Governor though recognizing French suzerainty, presented a more difficult problem. To solve it Bonaparte despatched an army of 30,000 under General Leclerc, with instructions to gain the confidence of the Negroes and arrest their leader. Toussaint was seized and sent to France, where he died within a year in prison, to be remembered in one of Wordsworth's greatest sonnets. The removal of the one Negro leader with authority and statesmanship intensified the ferocity of the servile war against France. Those of the French who were not killed by the Negroes were exterminated by disease, and the pearl of the Antilles passed for ever out of French possession.

Louisiana was lost in a different way. Officially annexed in March 1803, it was sold to the United States in Decem-

The First Empire

ber. The remaining scattered colonies fell to English naval expeditions in the course of the following years. The loss of the first French Empire, begun in 1763, had been completed by Bonaparte. He was too much a man of the *ancien régime* to be really interested in colonies save as pawns in the military struggle, and his imagination turned more easily to the East than to the West. There, the army he had left behind in Egypt, defeated by a British expeditionary force in 1801, had capitulated; but Napoleon's eyes still saw the Mediterranean as the route to India, where French agents were hard at work. His troops remained at Leghorn and Ancona on the west and east coasts of Italy; treaties were concluded with Tripoli and Tunis; Algiers, after the pillage of a French ship, was threatened with attack; French diplomacy was active at Constantinople; and a French agent, Sébastiani, was sent on a mission to Syria and Egypt. All this, while perfectly within French rights, was not likely to reassure her recent enemies.

Military movements on the Continent were also a source of alarm to Great Britain. French control over the satellites was strengthened. In Italy, Piedmont was divided into six departments and its army amalgamated with the French; the Ligurian Republic became a French military division; and Bonaparte appointed himself president of the Cisalpine Republic. In the north, French troops continued to occupy the Dutch ports. By an Act of Mediation the Swiss cantons were re-organized and French control was established over the Alpine passes. Italians, Swiss, and Dutch were all called on to furnish contingents of conscripts for the French army.

None of these measures, except the retention of troops in Holland, was an infringement of the Treaty of Amiens. The new *casus belli* was to arise in the Mediterranean, where Great Britain had undertaken by the Treaty of Amiens to restore Malta to the Knights of St John, but on second thoughts, despite her treaty obligation, could not bring herself to abandon such a valuable strategic position. British intransigence was encouraged by secret negotiations with Russia, also alarmed at the evidence of Bonaparte's interest in the Near East. On 30 January 1803 the *Moniteur* published Sébastiani's report on his tour there, in which he seemed to be putting forward, in language referring to the British in terms of contempt, proposals for a French reconquest of Egypt.

Why did Bonaparte, although he toned down the report slightly, publish such a provocative document at a moment when – though we need not attribute any noble dreams of permanent peace to him – he was not yet ready for a renewal of war? The answer seems to lie in the natural incapacity of a dictator for understanding the politics of a parliamentary country. The vulgar and immoderate personal attacks of the British press, which he attributed to the inspiration of the British government, drove him to fury; and the language of the parliamentary opposition led him to believe that the country was too divided by political conflicts to react strongly to his provocations. British opinion, on its side, had now overwhelmingly decided that Bonaparte was merely using the peace as an armistice during which to prepare for further aggression. The British government was determined to obtain further securities. Bonaparte, who had given hostages to fortune overseas and had not yet rebuilt French naval strength, was also suspicious of the reliability of his Russian alliance. He therefore temporized and even offered concessions. A British ultimatum on 23 April insisted on the continued occupation of Malta for ten years, the cession of the neighbouring island of Lampedusa to Great Britain, the evacuation of Holland by French forces, and the recognition of the Italian satellites only on condition of compensation for Sardinia and Switzerland. This was in effect a repudiation of the terms of Amiens. Bonaparte offered more concessions but the British government would be satisfied only by the integral acceptance of its ultimatum. Failing this, negotiations were broken off and the war renewed in May 1803, after fourteen months of uneasy peace.

The Treaty of Amiens had not contained the conditions of a lasting peace. Bonaparte was not prepared permanently

The First Empire

to accept a situation in which Great Britain outweighed France in naval power and in overseas empire; Great Britain, for her part, did not regard French military hegemony in Europe as compatible with her own security. War was inevitable in these circumstances: the problem was how it could be waged, how the land and the sea power could measure their strength against one another. The British could seize French shipping and mop up the French colonies again one by one; but they could only intervene in Europe by means of alliances. Bonaparte's problem on the other hand was to find some means of bringing his far greater military power to bear directly against England. His solution was the Boulogne Camp and invasion across the Channel.

All through the wars of the eighteenth century plans for the invasion of England had accumulated in the dossiers of the French ministries. Bonaparte put these into practice on an unprecedented scale. No attempt was made to conceal his preparations. The Bayeux tapestry was brought to Paris for exhibition as a reminder of a previous successful invasion of England from France. By the summer of 1804 there were six to seven hundred invasion barges and a Grand Army of over 100,000 men gathered on the coast at Boulogne. A year later they were still there. The French admiral Villeneuve's manoeuvre to entice the British fleet to the West Indies had failed to produce that temporary French control of the Channel which was necessary for the invasion. The battle at Trafalgar, into which Villeneuve was driven by Bonaparte's reproaches, brought about the destruction of the French and Spanish fleets and guaranteed British control of the seas for the rest of the war. But even before the battle Napoleon had – he believed temporarily – abandoned his invasion plan and struck camp at Boulogne.

Russia, which had decided on war with France, and Austria, under pressure from Russia and alarmed at the growth of French power in Italy and Germany, joined Great Britain to form the Third Coalition in July 1805. By the

A History of Modern France

end of August the Grand Army was marching across southern Germany in seven columns. By agents and informers Napoleon already knew exactly the dispositions of the Austrians. He fell on the incompetent Austrian general, Mack, at Ulm and routed him. The Russian allies, with another Austrian army, barred the French advance at Austerlitz where, on 2 December, in turn they were overwhelmed. Twice defeated, Austria concluded a humiliating peace at Pressburg.

Prussia, alarmed at the continual growth of French power in Germany, which it had so far done much, passively and even actively, to promote, now belatedly took to arms – the most highly polished, as well as the most antiquated, in Europe – to be humiliatingly crushed at Jena in November, 1806. Russia, which alone remained of the European allies, was defeated in the bloodiest and most hard-fought battles Napoleon had so far been engaged in, at Eylau and Friedland, in 1807.

The sequel was the meeting of Napoleon and Alexander on the raft at Tilsit, on 25 June 1807, when Napoleon dictated the terms of peace. Prussia was reduced to a mere torso. Russia had to make major concessions in the Near East, abandoning the Ionian Islands to Napoleon, evacuating the Turkish provinces of Moldavia and Wallachia on the Danube, accepting the Continental System, and, if Great Britain did not agree to Russian mediation, concluding an alliance with France. Napoleon was master of Europe west of the Russian border. The frontiers of France were extended to the Rhine in the north-east and to take in Piedmont, Parma, Genoa, and Tuscany in Italy. They were bordered by a glacis of satellite states – the former Batavian Republic, now the Kingdom of Holland, under his brother Louis; the Confederation of the Rhine, with Bavaria, Württemburg, Baden, and other states, and the electorate of Saxony promoted to be a kingdom; the kingdom of Westphalia, formed out of the territories of the deposed rulers of Brunswick and Hesse-Cassel, with the subsequent addition of part of Hanover, placed under Napoleon's younger

The First Empire

brother, Jerome; Prussian Poland, formed into the Grand Duchy of Warsaw, under the King of Saxony; the Helvetic Republic; the Kingdom of Italy, based on Lombardy-Venetia and stretching down the coast of the peninsula through the eastern part of the Papal States to Ancona, with the privilege of having Napoleon himself as its king, crowned in 1805 with the iron crown of Lombardy at Milan, his step-son, Eugène Beauharnais, being Viceroy. The western half of the Papal States, surrounded by French power, still had a precarious and short-lived independence; but to the south the Kingdom of Naples – not of the Two Sicilies, for sea-power and a British force under General Stuart which won the small but significant battle of Maida in 1806, kept the French armies on the landward side of the Straits of Messina – was given in 1806 to Joseph Bonaparte, who was succeeded, when he was transferred to the throne of Spain, by Murat, not so much in his capacity of cavalry general as in that of husband of Caroline Bonaparte. Napoleon had done well by his clan. This was not to be the farthest limit of his empire, but already Russia and Austria were the only continental powers not dominated by him.

How was it that France, which under Louis XIV had known no such success, which since Fleury had had no luck in its foreign policy and known hardly anything but defeat, within fifteen years had acquired the hegemony of Europe? The military genius of Napoleon is part of the answer; the improved weapons, which he inherited from the reforms of the later years of the *ancien régime*, another part. But neither leadership nor material would have won victories without the men, the armies which had grown out of the ragged battalions of the Republic. What the Revolution had bequeathed to Napoleon was a large body of veterans, by now all really professional soldiers, many of them trained in the army of the line before 1789 and all blooded in the battles of the Republic. Young men of adventurous spirit, ability, and ambition from all ranks of society, seeking the quickest path to advancement, furnished the officers. The wars of the Revolution provided a supply, though a wasting one, of able generals. The masses that were required to be poured into and amalgamated with these cadres to fill out the armies of the Empire were provided by conscription. Although there were many exemptions and evasions, between 1800 and 1812 Napoleon raised well over a million men from France; a week at the depot to equip them and give them a rudimentary notion of military discipline, and they could be sent to the front, to be fused with trained men and learn the art of war on the field of battle. The brutal punishments which were regarded as necessary to discipline in British and other armies had been abolished by the revolutionaries. *Esprit de corps*, honours, and the spirit with which Napoleon inspired his soldiers from top to bottom, were a better substitute.

To picture a French army, using French resources, as conquering Europe, would, however, not be correct. From the beginning of the Revolutionary War the French armies had lived off the country, and as their wars were always, until 1813, fought on foreign soil, the main burden did not fall on France. The numbers of men raised from France, though large by *ancien régime* standards, were not excessive. Up to 1812 the annual average works out at some 85,000, and this from a France which was steadily expanding its frontiers. As well as Piedmontese, Belgians, Dutch, and inhabitants of some German states, which were subjected to the laws of conscription when they were annexed, levies were raised from the satellite states. The army that invaded Russia in 1812 had contingents from every nation of Europe: of its 700,000 men only a third were French.

It was in moving the huge bodies of men he commanded across the map of Europe and concentrating them on the chosen field of battle that Napoleon showed his greatest military genius. The battle engaged, solid columns were flung at the enemy, a method that was costly in lives but the most efficient way of using masses of half-trained or untrained conscripts; it was successful until it met the concentrated fire of the English regiments of the line.

The most important factor of all in the Napoleonic

The First Empire

conquests was the result of a technical change. The art of war seems to progress through alternate periods in which the defence and the offensive predominate. At the end of the eighteenth century the mobility of armies was greatly increased; the French were the first to exploit this and Napoleon was the first great master of the new techniques. Improved road surfaces, light field-guns, organization of armies in divisions, moving along different roads and therefore able to live off the country and dispense with cumbersome baggage-trains, the concentration of artillery fire and infantry attack – these methods, learnt from the military theorists of the *ancien régime*, especially Guibert, author of the *Essai général de tactique* of 1772, were put into practice by Napoleon, with such effect that by 1807 all Europe, except Russia, was at his feet.

After Tilsit it might have been thought that Napoleon would rest on his laurels, content with his unchallenged military supremacy. The capacity for accepting a limit to his ambition was against his nature, but we need not resort simply to an explanation in terms of personal character; the perpetuation of war was in the nature of his régime, but in a more subtle way. England remained unconquered and after Trafalgar could apparently only be conquered by a restoration of French sea-power to the level at which it could challenge and defeat the might of the British navy. With the resources of France and all the satellite states to draw on, one might have thought that the creation of a new navy would not have been beyond Napoleon's power. If he chose another way of attack it was not, perhaps, because he recognized the restoration of French naval strength as impossible, but because he believed implicitly that this other way, while ensuring the collapse of British power equally, and perhaps more expeditiously and certainly, possessed also other and inherent attractions which made it desirable in itself. The Continental System was a device for bringing Great Britain to her knees, but it was also, quite apart from this, a method of increasing and consolidating the wealth and therefore the greatness of

A History of Modern France

France. Moreover the Continental System was not invented out of nothing by Napoleon: it was a development of the policies of the Republic and the *ancien régime*.

The use of economic weapons in the struggle for power was not new. The revolutionaries had used them in their war against Great Britain. The hated commercial treaty of 1786 was annulled immediately after the declaration of war in 1793. All British goods were excluded from France; all shipping entering French ports had to be French or that of the country from which the goods came. 'Let us decree', cried Barère, 'a solemn navigation act and the isle of shop-keepers will be ruined.' As early as 1795 there was a proposal to use the alliance with Dutch naval power to exclude British trade from the Continent. Napoleon did not have to invent the Continental System; as in so many other fields, he found an idea already in existence and merely applied it with his own method and whole-heartedness. It was generally believed that British power rested on her naval strength and her subsidies – the guineas of Pitt; and both these on the profits she derived from trade. To destroy that trade by cutting off its markets would ruin her finances and rob her of her power as effectively as if every port in the British Isles were sealed: thus could the sea power be blockaded from the land.

This, however, is only one side of the Continental System. There was also the thought that what England lost France could gain, taking the place of her rival as the great industrial nation of Europe, and drawing in by her exports the wealth that would be barred to England. The Treaty of Amiens gave Napoleon the respite he needed to begin his policy of Bonapartist Colbertism by injecting a stimulus into French industry. His efforts were vigorous and at first not unsuccessful. Schools were set up for technical training, prizes offered for inventions, industrial fairs organized, Jacquard's machine for silk weaving was brought into use. Great French chemists, Lavoisier, Fourcroy, Berthollet, discovered new methods of dyeing, bleaching, and tanning. Industrialists and technicians visited the factories of Great

The First Empire

Britain, and British machines and workers were imported into France, where they were put into operation with the aid of government credits and patronage. The French industrialist, Richard Lenoir, by 1810 had six cotton spinning mills with 3,600 workers in Normandy. Ternaux, a wool manufacturer of Sedan, employed 24,000 workers. Between 1788 and 1812 the number of looms increased from some 7,000 to 17,000 and the workers from 76,000 to 131,000. Such details, however, must not be allowed to give the impression of rapid industrial progress. The Revolution and the Empire may have provided a stimulus in some directions, but it is doubtful whether the pace had in fact increased. By 1815 French industry, it is estimated, was at the level of mechanization reached in Great Britain by 1780. Domestic labour was still the norm. Little workshops, with a master man and a few *compagnons*, working from one to five looms, still overwhelmingly predominated even in the textile industry. The small scale of industry is revealed by a few figures: 452 mines with 43,395 workers, 41 ironworks with 1,202, 1,219 forges with 7,120, 98 sugar refineries with 585. At Marseille the soap industry had 73 workshops and 1,000 workers. The industrial revolution in France, of which there were notable signs before 1789, was progressing very slowly. The energy of the nation had been diverted first to civil strife and then to conquest.

The authoritarian and hierarchical spirit of the Emperor, as well as the victory in the Revolution of the men of property, was reflected in the labour laws of the Empire. In 1803 was introduced the *livret*, a kind of passport and police visa, which every worker had to possess and in which were recorded all his changes of employment, reasons for leaving each job, and wages. It was kept by the employer and without it a worker could not be employed and would be regarded as a vagabond. Strikes were vigorously prohibited under severe penalties. The *compagnonnages* only survived clandestinely. Working conditions were miserable, though there seems to have been a modest rise in real wages up to 1810 and a fall after this.

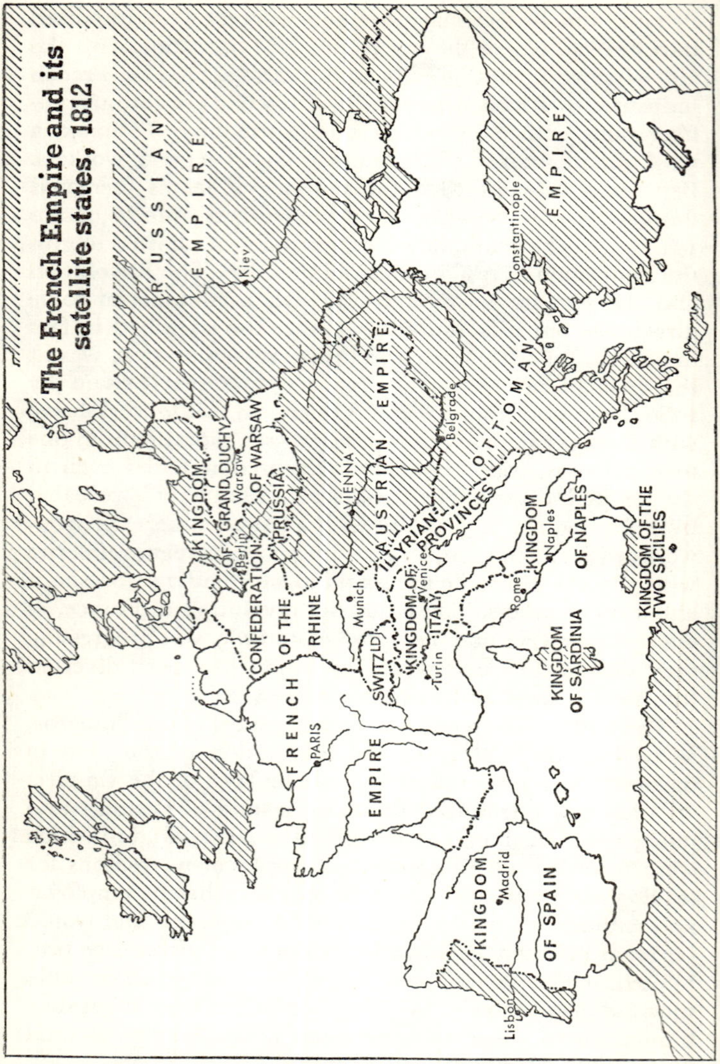
The French Empire and its satellite states, 1812
RUSSIAN EMPIRE
Kiev
KINGDOM OF PRUSSIA
GRAND DUCHY OF WARSAW
Warsaw
Berlin
CONFEDERATION OF THE RHINE
VIENNA
AUSTRIAN EMPIRE
Belgrade
OTTOMAN EMPIRE
Constantinople
ILLYRIAN PROVINCES
Munich
SWITZLD
KINGDOM OF ITALY
Venice
Turin
Rome
KINGDOM OF NAPLES
Naples
KINGDOM OF THE TWO SICILIES
KINGDOM OF SARDINIA
FRENCH EMPIRE
PARIS
KINGDOM OF SPAIN
Madrid
Lisbon

The First Empire

Napoleon, like his predecessors, was chiefly interested in power, and in prosperity only as a means to power. His commercial policy was therefore at the service of his political ends. His conquests gave him ample opportunity to exclude British trade from the Continent, beginning with the occupation of Hanover in May 1803, which enabled him to close the mouths of the Elbe and the Weser. These measures, along with the prohibition of, or heavy duties on, colonial produce, increased the cost and diminished the supplies of raw material for French industry. This policy was intensified and systematized by the Berlin Decrees of 1806. By the Milan Decrees of December 1807 any ship which had called at a British port, paid a duty to Britain, or even been examined at sea by the British, was made a lawful prize. The result was in effect to exclude neutral shipping, on which Europe now depended for its supplies from overseas, from ports under French control. The British Orders in Council, blockading all French ports, were imposed more effectively by a fleet which swept the seas, and by raiding privateers. French privateers, the most successful of whom was the famous Surcouf, took a heavy toll of British shipping, at a rate of nearly 450 losses a year; but a high percentage of British exports (from 25 to 42 per cent, and re-exports (71 to 83 per cent) continued to go to the Continent. In the attempt to prevent this, Napoleon organized an army of customs officials round the coasts of Europe. The extent to which the Continental System dictated the aggressions of the Empire, such as the invasion of the Iberian peninsula, has perhaps been exaggerated; but annexations were at least influenced by the needs of the System. Napoleon's aim was, in his own words, to close every port from the Sound to the Hellespont to British shipping.

To portray the Continental System, as it has been portrayed, as an attempt to create a great pan-European economic union, is to attribute to Napoleon a degree of enlightenment in the pursuance of his ends which dictators do not usually possess. If it had been this the System might

A History of Modern France

conceivably have aroused less resentment in the rest of Europe. On the contrary, it was, as I have already said, a device not only for defeating England, but also for ensuring French economic supremacy. The economies of the other nations were subordinated and geared to that of France. His object, Napoleon declared in 1810, was to encourage the export of French goods and the import of foreign bullion. Thus, new frontiers in Italy, with high customs barriers between them, were devised to enable French industrial products to capture the Italian market. The Grand Duchy of Berg, centred on the Ruhr valley, already a growing industrial area, was cut off from its markets in the Netherlands and the Baltic by high tariffs. The export of Italian textiles to southern Germany was prohibited. Raw silk from Piedmont was directed to Lyon and away from the silk workers of Lombardy by means of tariff adjustments. French manufactures could be exported freely into Holland, but Dutch goods had to pay customs dues to enter France.

As has already been indicated, these efforts to turn France into the great industrial nation of Europe failed. The loss of colonial raw materials was incompatible with their success, though desperate efforts were made to improvise substitutes. The growing of woad was promoted in the south-west of France, where its production had flourished in the Middle Ages, to replace colonial indigo; chicory provided a substitute for coffee and beet for the sugar cane. Attempts were made to introduce the growing of cotton in southern Italy, but the cotton industry languished for lack of raw materials. The substitutes had at the time only mediocre success.

The decisive factor in Napoleon's attempt to create a French industrial empire was that he was not merely setting land power against sea power, but land communications against sea communications, at a time when transport by water was immeasurably cheaper than transport by land. If the rivers of Europe had flowed in a different direction the prospects might have been brighter, but the great

The First Empire

strategic roads that were driven across France and stretched out to the French Empire could not materially diminish the cost of land transport. Despite all Napoleon's efforts, French foreign trade under the Empire never regained the level it had reached in 1789. In Bordeaux, wrote the American consul in 1808, grass was growing in the streets and at the great quays a mere handful of vessels with cargo swung in the tide.

When the economic crisis of 1811–13 burst on Europe, though the contemporary crisis in Great Britain would suggest more general causes, Europe naturally attributed it to the Napoleonic system. In France itself, at Mulhouse 40,000 workers out of 60,000 were unemployed, and 20 to 25,000 at Lyon. Napoleon, who had learnt during the Revolution to fear starving urban mobs, modified and opened loop-holes in his economic legislation, and this was the effective end of the real enforcement of the Continental System, though it had already broken down largely in practice. Round the coastline of Napoleonic Europe, from Gotenburg in Sweden, Heligoland, Gibraltar, the Balearics, Malta, after their capture in 1809 the Ionian Isles, a flood of contraband goods seeped into Europe. Smuggling became one of the most remunerative and by no means the least numerous of professions. It was conducted sometimes by official subterfuge, sometimes by force of arms. Administrators and generals, and the customs officials themselves, made a regular trade of corruption. Against universal smuggling the Napoleonic machine of repression that had been created was powerless. When confiscated goods were ordered to be burnt, valueless rubbish was destroyed in their place. Smuggling became so much an organized trade that smuggled goods were even insured against seizure. The rate at Strasbourg on illicit goods destined for France was 30 per cent. Napoleon himself connived at the infringement of his own laws. He wrote to his brother Louis to fix the point where English smugglers were to land to purchase Dutch gin: what was essential, he believed, was that they should be made to pay in bullion and not in goods. But at

Hamburg, English clothing and shoes were being bought for the French army.

It was only after the economic crisis of the latter years of the Empire that Napoleon had recourse to the organized breach of the Continental System by the method of licences. Since Great Britain was doing the same, an interchange of goods developed between the two countries at war. French ships were allowed to trade with England under a neutral flag; unfortunately, once outside Napoleon's clutches they generally stayed outside, to swell the merchant marine in British service. The licences were, of course, expensive, and there were heavy duties on the imported goods, so that fiscal motives were not absent from Napoleon's mind. Finally, the opposition that his economic policies had always aroused in the rest of Europe spread to France. The commercial and industrial classes began to detach themselves openly from a régime the burden of which went on increasing and the benefits diminishing.

Empire and military glory were in the end as incompatible with economic progress as the political chaos of the Revolution had been. And the Emperor himself, if he had started as the heir of the Revolution, was turning in his social policy into something more like the restorer of a pseudo-*ancien régime*. The creation of the Legion of Honour in 1802, against the advice of many of his supporters, was an early sign of his anti-egalitarian tendencies. Once he was Emperor he needed a Court, the nucleus of which was provided by the six Grand Dignitaries of the Empire – Grand Elector Joseph Bonaparte, Grand Constable Louis, Arch-chancellor of State Eugène de Beauharnais, Grand Admiral Murat, Arch-chancellor Cambacérès, and Arch-treasurer Lebrun – four relations plus the former second and third consuls. For the ceremonies of the new court a series of Grand Officers of the Crown, drawn from the *ancien régime*, provided the correct tone. Mme Campan was there to explain to the Ladies of Honour and the Empress how Marie-Antoinette used to do things. A whole gamut of titles, from duke to chevalier, was recreated and made

The First Empire

hereditary on the granting of an appropriate entail. Sons of ministers, councillors of state and the like, and the nephews of archbishops, became counts. Prefects were barons or counts. Altogether Napoleon created over 3,000 nobles. Of course, a real noble was even better. Those among the *ancien régime* nobility who rallied to the imperial banner were singled out for favour. They came increasingly to dominate the Court and the administration as the Empire reached its zenith.

5. THE NAPOLEONIC EMPIRE: FALL

IN 1807, after Tilsit, there was a reorganization of the ministries, in which Talleyrand lost the Ministry of Foreign Affairs, though he was made a Grand Dignitary. He had already decided that Napoleon's ambition would bring him to ultimate ruin, and having served him well and gained a huge fortune by the acceptance of bribes, he was now secretly negotiating with Napoleon's enemies. He had never believed in the wisdom of the humiliation of Austria. In the course of 1808 Talleyrand and Fouché, when Napoleon was absent in Spain, began to make plans for the choice of a successor, who was apparently to be Murat. Napoleon did not remain in ignorance of this. When he returned he dismissed Talleyrand with a torrent of abuse; but the ex-bishop, ex-revolutionary, ex-minister of Foreign Affairs, ex-Grand Chamberlain, continued to haunt the Court like a vulture of ill omen biding his time. Fouché, former terrorist and regicide, minister of police since 1799, and a particular friend of Josephine, had been useful to Napoleon as a link with the revolutionaries, but subsequently established a position also as a kind of patron to many royalists. During the Revolution, while a leader of the anti-religious party, he had protected priests, especially members of his old order of the Oratory. His contempt for the Concordat was unconcealed, not for lack of a clerical capacity for dissimulation but from a natural independence of mind. He was the least servile of all Napoleon's servants and the humanest minister of police a dictator ever had. But when, in 1810, Napoleon discovered that Fouché had been engaging for the past year in secret negotiations with England, his dismissal was inevitable. Though Talleyrand and Fouché waited to be dismissed – and it is a sign of their confidence that they feared no more – it is evident that they had deserted Napoleon by their own choice and were preparing for a future in which they foresaw his inevitable defeat. It was an ominous sign. Their successors, often former royalists, were men of inferior calibre and untried loyalty. Whereas at first Napoleon had gathered round him a collection of the ablest men in France, his later appointments were increasingly influenced by favouritism and Court intrigue. He now wanted flunkeys, says Chaptal bitterly, not advisers.

Intolerance of criticism was only one sign of the degeneration that was beginning to come over the Emperor, both physically and mentally. His decline may be said to have begun even before the Empire had reached its height. His aggressions were increasingly irrational. Thus the Pope had not realized the nature of the relationship which Napoleon assumed to have been created by the Concordat. 'So far as the Pope is concerned', he wrote, 'I am Charlemagne'; if the Pope did not behave he would be reduced to the status of bishop of Rome. For military purposes, French troops had already occupied the Adriatic coastline of the Papal States and the port of Ancona. In 1809 the Papal States were annexed to the French Empire and the Pope was arrested and carried off to captivity. His subsequent refusal to collaborate with Napoleon, though inconvenient, especially because it prevented the filling of vacant sees in France, had surprisingly little practical result.

The French intervention in Spain was to have more momentous consequences. Under Godoy, Prince of the Peace, an adventurer who had made the Queen his mistress, Spain had become a French satellite. To extend French control over the whole peninsula, a joint Franco-Spanish army invaded Portugal in 1807. Napoleon, however, was

The First Empire

not satisfied with the aid he was getting from Spain. Under direct French rule, he believed, this backward and priest-ridden nation could be modernized and so contribute far more to the strength of the French Empire. The sordid intrigues which followed in the Spanish Court need not delay us. In May 1808 the King and Queen and the heir Ferdinand were summoned to Bayonne and by threats made to sign away their rights over Spain. Godoy was imprisoned, regretted only by the infatuated Queen and a few other mistresses. Joseph Bonaparte, brought from the throne of Naples, was put on that of Madrid.

Even before Joseph entered his new capital, where he was able to stay on this occasion only for eleven days, a spontaneous insurrection all over Spain had imperilled some 150,000 French troops dispersed over the whole peninsula. In July one force had to capitulate at Baylen and in August another, beaten at Vimiero by a hurriedly dispatched British expeditionary force under Wellesley, signed the Convention of Cintra and was shipped back to France. Joseph and the remaining French troops withdrew behind the Ebro. All this was unprecedented. If allowed to succeed it might set a fatal example. The veteran corps of Victor, Mortier, and Ney were called from Germany and a great French army was assembled under Napoleon on the Ebro. The Spaniards were routed and driven back. A small British force under Moore retreated to Corunna and was evacuated by sea. Joseph was reinstated in Madrid. However, the diversion effected by Moore's army had drawn back the French forces from their triumphal sweep through the peninsula. After this Napoleon returned to Paris and never came to Spain again. During the remainder of the wars of the Empire, Wellington from his base in Portugal, and the Spanish guerrillas, were to tie down a large French army permanently. In Napoleon's winter campaign of 1808 he had over 300,000 men in Spain; in the spring offensive of 1810 the number rose to 370,000; in the crisis of the Empire in 1812 there were 290,000 and in 1813 still 224,000. The wastage by battle and disease was heavy all through. If it was a side-show it was a very expensive one: henceforth Napoleon was to have to fight on two fronts.

The French reverses in Spain may have played some part in the resurgence of Austria, which had remained unreconciled to the humiliation of Austerlitz and had since been reorganizing her military forces. A hard-fought campaign from April to July 1809 ended in another Austrian defeat, at Wagram; but Napoleon's position was still not secure. The Tyrol had revolted, Venetia had been captured by the Austrians, Prussia and Russia were hesitating on the brink of war, far away to the West Soult had been driven out of Portugal, and a British expedition had landed in Walcheren. Even Wagram, though an Austrian defeat, was not a rout, and was only worth an armistice. But when it became clear that Russian aid was not coming, and that Vienna itself was exposed to attack, the Austrian Emperor gave up the struggle and bought peace with more territorial concessions – a large part of Galicia to the Duchy of Warsaw, Salzburg and the Tyrol to Bavaria, the Illyrian provinces, in accordance with the requirements of the Continental System, to direct French rule.

Victory still followed the imperial eagles but one thing was lacking to Napoleon's ambitions. The intrigues of Talleyrand and Fouché had made the insecurity of his position clear. His clan evidently depended entirely on himself: there was no hope in it for the establishment of a Bonapartist dynasty. Josephine would now never give him a child, but he knew through a mistress, in 1807, that he was capable of getting one. For some time schemes for a divorce and re-marriage had been mooted, and after a few unsuccessful approaches to the old dynasties, the Habsburgs, unlucky in battle, remembered their tradition – *Bella gerant alii; tu, felix Austria, nube.* They had an available princess, Marie-Louise, ready for the sacrifice, and as the young Austrian minister Metternich wrote, the Austrian Emperor 'will shrink from nothing that may contribute to the welfare and peace of the state'. He would however have shrunk from a civil marriage, which in any case would not

The First Empire

have been adequate for Napoleon's purpose. Josephine therefore had to be got rid of, not by a divorce, but by a declaration of the nullity of her marriage. This involved proving the invalidity of the religious ceremony which she and Napoleon had gone through on the eve of the coronation in 1804. Though performed by a cardinal – Napoleon's uncle, Fesch – this marriage had been clandestine, it was argued, and without adequate witnesses. To complete the conviction of the religious court that tried the case, it was established that Napoleon had acted under compulsion from Josephine. The religious requirements of the Church were thus met, and it was disappointing – seeing that everything was in order – that thirteen cardinals out of twenty-seven should have stayed away from the marriage ceremony with Marie-Louise in 1810. Napoleon in revenge assigned to them compulsory residences and forbade them to wear their robes of office. Hence they became known as the black cardinals. In 1811 was born the little boy who was proclaimed King of Rome but never to inherit an Empire in which the cracks were already visible.

Now that Austria had been once more defeated, and by the dynastic alliance had apparently accepted defeat, Russia remained the only continental power that was not subordinate to France. The nominal ties of Tilsit could not prevent the growth of mutual suspicion and conflict of interests. Alexander and Napoleon suspected each other – and rightly – of preparing an attack when the opportunity came. They had more concrete grievances. Napoleon strengthened his position in the Baltic by the annexation of Oldenburg in December 1810, although Alexander's sister was married to the heir to the Duchy, and despite the guarantees of Tilsit. He began to move his troops eastwards, garrisoning Danzig, turning the Grand Duchy of Warsaw into a great military base and gathering huge magazines of supplies there. Meanwhile Russia, like the rest of Europe, was suffering from the economic crisis. To cope with the consequent discontent Alexander imposed heavy duties on French imports and opened his ports to neutral shipping. In effect he was withdrawing Russia from the Continental System, and although British trade with Russia was insignificant, this may have influenced Napoleon. More alarming was the fact that in May 1812 Russia concluded peace with the Turks. This was perhaps the decisive event, for Napoleon knew that it freed Alexander's hands in a way that nothing else could have done. Alexander had also concluded an agreement with Bernadotte of Sweden, received promises from Austria that her support for Napoleon would be only formal, and was negotiating secretly with Great Britain. Of all this Napoleon was not unaware. A defensive reaction would have been against the nature of the man and his system. War it had to be.

On 24 June 1812 the Grand Army began to cross the Niemen. Napoleon had gathered in the Grand Duchy of Warsaw 675,000 men and 1,350 cannon. Poles, Prussians, Austrians, Dutch, Swiss, Italians, all the nations of Europe had sent their conscripts tramping across Europe. Russia was to be overwhelmed by sheer weight of numbers. Instead it was Napoleon's own military machine that, in the long barren distances of Russia, was to collapse under its own weight. As the Russian armies avoided battle and withdrew, Napoleon moved forward, his armies struggling on through the heat of summer. At last, in front of Moscow, the Russians stood and Napoleon could fight the battle for which he had been longing. But it was not the *coup de grâce* he needed to deliver. At Borodino some 30,000 of his troops were killed, and though the Russians lost more they retreated in order. The occupation of an empty Moscow, the burning of the city, the retreat after five weeks waiting for peace emissaries who never came, with an army already reduced to about 100,000, with officers and men, baggage-trains, horses, carriages loaded down with the spoils of Russia's conquered and looted capital, across a region that it had already desolated, in the rain and mud of autumn, turning to the snows of winter – all this is a many times told tale of greed and cruelty, heroism and despair. After the tragic crossing of the Beresina on 27 November, famine and

The First Empire

frost and the pursuing Russians completed the annihilation of the army of the Empire. It was not beaten in battle; under the stress of a long, starving retreat, the great cosmopolitan military machine collapsed and disintegrated, leaving behind it a legend in history. Some 1,000 of the Guards, out of the great host that had set out, held together when Ney re-crossed the Niemen on 14 December.

Napoleon had already, on 6 December, deserted an army that no longer existed and was hastening back to Paris, where the essentially ephemeral nature of his *régime* had just been demonstrated by the Malet conspiracy. In this extraordinary episode a republican general, Malet, and a royalist priest, Lafon, both in custody as political prisoners, came near to overthrowing the Empire in its capital by the simple device of forging a document announcing the death of Napoleon and the constitution of a provisional government under the banished general Moreau. In his name Malet assumed command of Paris, and arrested the Minister of Police, the War Minister, and the Prefect of Police – all in the space of a single morning. Only when the commander of the Paris garrison challenged the news, and the little band of conspirators failed to keep up the pretence of Napoleon's death successfully, were they resisted. Then, of course, they were easily seized and after a rapid trial executed. It was a gallant adventure and deserved a better sequel. It was also clear evidence that the whole government of Napoleon rested on the cohesion of the military and administrative machine he had created and that this in turn depended exclusively on his person.

Back in Paris, Napoleon set the administration to the task of raising conscripts from France, for the first time really ruthlessly. Europe was now rising everywhere against his domination, but there were still Napoleonic armies and garrisons far and wide. Indecisive battles against Russians and Prussians, at Lützen and Bautzen, in May 1813, were followed by an armistice. If Napoleon had been capable of concessions, he might now have kept the Austrians out of the war and disintegrated the alliance; but such moderation

A History of Modern France

had long since ceased to be possible for him and the struggle was resumed. He had some half a million men in the field, the allies rather more. Moreau was advising them and Bernadotte bringing an army down from Sweden. A French victory at Dresden in August was followed, in October, by the battle of the nations at Leipzig. After this, with its soldiers dead in battle or by disease, deserters or prisoners, or uselessly shut up in fortresses scattered about Germany, the Army of 1813 followed that of 1812 into the void. Only a fragment retired across the Rhine.

More conscripts were called up from France: there were no foreign allies or dependents left to exploit. Still, in December 1813, Napoleon refused to negotiate in time for a recognition of the 'natural frontiers' of France. By now the armies of the coalition were in Switzerland and on the Rhine, and Wellington had crossed the Pyrenees. In January 1814 Murat deserted Napoleon and Italy was lost. In France itself his régime was patently breaking down. It had entered the winter of its discontent. Under the frozen surface of dictatorship resentment brooded. Conscription had reached the point at which it was meeting open resistance even from the inert peasantry. They were touched more closely when Napoleon's armies, fighting for the first time on French soil, supplied themselves by the normal method of requisitioning which had carried them all over Europe. The *droits réunis*, the hated taxes on alcoholic drinks, tobacco, and salt, were a long-standing grievance of the peasantry. Industry had lost its markets with the collapse of the Empire and unemployment was widespread in the towns. Commerce was languishing and the finances in disorder. The clergy, who had never quite forgotten their loyalty to the Bourbons, were a centre of opposition everywhere. All those who had acquired wealth and jobs saw the need to insure against the future. An underground royalist movement, a kind of royalist and catholic free-masonry, which had been created in 1810, was reviving the memory of the Bourbons in a country that had begun to forget them. But though the royalists were active and beginning to

The First Empire

emerge above ground, the nation as a whole remained passive.

When the allies invaded France, it accepted the foreign invaders as passively as it had borne the rule of Napoleon. Épinal surrendered to fifty cossacks, Reims to a platoon, Chaumont to a single horseman. The one demand of the country was peace. The Senate, called together by Napoleon in December 1813, performed its last act of homage towards the man to whom so many of its members owed fame and fortune. But the Legislative Body, that collection of insignificant yes-men, voted by 223 to 51 an address of unprecedented independence: 'Our ills are at their height. The *patrie* is threatened at all points of the frontier; we are suffering from a destitution unexampled in the whole history of the state. Commerce is destroyed, industry dying ... What are the causes of these unutterable miseries? A vexatious administration, excessive taxes, the deplorable methods adopted for their collection, and the even crueller excesses practised for the recruitment of the armies ... A barbarous and endless war swallows up periodically the youth torn from education, agriculture, commerce, and the arts.' This was strong language, and the Legislative Body ended with an appeal for abandoning the ambitious schemes which had been for twenty years 'so fatal to all the peoples of Europe'. No wonder that Napoleon banished the authors of the address, forbade its publication, and prorogued the Legislative Body.

If he had been willing to buy peace by renouncing the Empire he might still have got it and remained the ruler of France. In February and March 1814 negotiations with the allies at Châtillon proved that he could not bring himself to do this. Instead, with a small army of some 60,000 men, largely untrained conscripts, he manoeuvred brilliantly between the invading armies in the East of France and inflicted reverses on them. The requisitions and brutalities of the invaders aroused patriotic feeling in the occupied areas, but this did not spread to the rest of France. The allies, realizing the scarcity of Napoleon's troops, ceased to play his game, by-passed his forces, and advanced on Paris. On 29 March, in accordance with orders from Napoleon, Marie-Louise and the King of Rome left the capital. All the higher officers of state were commanded to leave with them but many found means of remaining. On 31 March Paris capitulated and the troops garrisoning it moved to Fontainebleau, where Napoleon established his headquarters. The same day the allied forces entered through the porte Saint-Denis, marched across Paris amidst curious crowds and bivouacked in the Champs Élysées.

A provisional government, of which Talleyrand was the leading member, was set up. The Senate and the Legislative Body voted the deposition of Napoleon. But what was to take his place? Talleyrand, who had established close relations with the Czar, had largely won him over to a restoration of the Bourbons. The Paris press, now under royalist control, agitated for a restoration. But the allies were still hesitant. Europe had been conditioned to fear the French nation and was still alarmed at what it might do if an unpopular régime were forced on it. At this stage what was happening in the South-west was perhaps decisive. The army of Wellington, having crossed the Pyrenees, was advancing towards Toulouse in pursuit of Soult. A small British force, detached from the main army, was sent off to occupy Bordeaux. The imperial authorities fled across the Gironde, and on 22 March the British advance-guard, to which a squadron of young royalists had attached themselves, entered the city, to be welcomed by the Mayor of Bordeaux, a member of the royalist secret society of the Chevaliers de la Foi, with a white cockade and the cry of *'Vive le Roi'*. In the afternoon arrived the duc d'Angoulême, greeted with wild demonstrations of joy. The influence of this spontaneous French rejection of Napoleon and proclamation of the Bourbons, on both the allies and the French leaders in Paris, was considerable. Napoleon himself, faced with the refusal of the marshals to engage in another battle, had abdicated in favour of the King of Rome and sent plenipotentiaries to Alexander. It was already too late to

The First Empire

save even this from the wreck. Marshal Marmont, despite a short-lived mutiny among his troops, marched them to the enemy lines and surrendered. On 6 April Napoleon abdicated unconditionally. Four days later, so slow did news travel, the last battle of the allied invasion was to be fought, a bloody assault in which Wellington overcame Soult's entrenchments before Toulouse.

On 12 April the comte d'Artois, as lieutenant-general for his brother, Louis XVIII, entered Paris in triumph. Through decorated streets and applauding crowds, he went to Notre Dame where the *Te Deum* was sung. Louis XVIII himself landed at Boulogne on 24 April and, received everywhere with enthusiasm, moved slowly to Saint-Omer where he met a delegation from the Senate and issued a royal proclamation. 'Louis, by the grace of God, King of France and Navarre', recalled by the love of his people to the throne of his fathers, promised France representative government in a Senate and Chamber of Deputies, taxation only with consent, public and individual liberty, freedom of the press, freedom of religion, responsible government, judicial independence, a career open to talent, and – not least – that no one should be punished for opinions or votes during the fallen régime, the recognition of the national debt, of pensions, grades, and military honours, of titles of both the old and new nobility, and of the sales of national property. It was a compromise between divine right and the Revolution, rather to the advantage of the latter. On 3 May Louis XVIII and the royal family made their ceremonial entry into the capital.

Napoleon, largely by the mediation of Alexander, was meanwhile journeying to a smaller kingdom in Elba. While he travelled through country that had experienced the allied occupation his reception was favourable, but as he moved south, according to the Prussian commissioner who accompanied him, it became increasingly hostile. He got through Lyon at night. At Orange there were shouts of '*Vive Louis XVIII*', and at Avignon '*À bas le tyran*'; he saw himself hanged in effigy and after this disguised himself in

A History of Modern France

an old blue coat, put up a white cockade, and preceded his carriage in the guise of a courier. Later he dressed himself as an Austrian officer. He embarked from Fréjus, where he had landed fifteen years earlier on his way home from Egypt, leaving then also a defeated army behind, but with the triumphs of *brumaire* and the Empire before him. Fearing assassination he refused to embark on the French ship provided for him and sailed to Elba in a British frigate. He left a France which, it has been estimated, had lost in his wars 860,000 men between the ages of 23 and 44, half of them under 28.

The Restoration did not begin well. Talleyrand confined himself to foreign affairs. The old system of government by a *conseil d'en haut*, with no chief minister, no unity, and therefore no policy, was revived. The two most important ministers were baron Louis for Finance, and Dupont, remembered only for his defeat at Baylen and perhaps unmerited disgrace, at the Ministry of War. By an austere financial policy Louis put the budget into better shape, but at the price of maintaining the unpopular *droits réunis* and of economies which cut down pensions and salaries. Dupont's policy demoralized the army. He retired many officers and put many more on half-pay, brought into it, over the heads of Napoleonic veterans, a host of *émigrés* who had never seen a battlefield or commanded a man, recreated the Household Guard – the Light Horse, Grey and Black Musketeers, the Cent Suisses, and the rest, crammed with dissatisfied royalists, expensive, intriguing, and useless – 6,000 men, all with the rank and pay of officers, costing twenty million francs a year. 'The indignation and exasperation of the army', wrote Philippe de Ségur, himself a noble of the *ancien régime* but one who had acquired other ideas and other loyalties in the Imperial Army, and a veteran of the Moscow campaign, 'had become so violent that at the Tuileries, among the officers of the Old Guard on half-pay, spectators like myself of the reviews which were held, I had difficulty in preventing an outburst.' The flag also was already a burning issue. 'They imposed on us', wrote de Ségur, 'the

The First Empire

flag under which they had fought us.' At the same time, the old court ceremonies and the King's household were recreated as though nothing had happened since 1789.

Napoleon at Elba was not uninformed of the dissatisfaction in France, and at the end of ten months was sufficiently dissatisfied himself with ruling a tiny island in place of half Europe to be ready to set out on his last and most reckless venture. On 1 March 1815 he landed with 1,050 troops, once again at Fréjus, and avoiding this time royalist Provence, took the mountain road from Cannes to Grenoble. Opposition melted away wherever he appeared. By itself the march from Fréjus to Paris is sufficient evidence of his magnetic personality. It is clear, however, that what he could appeal to now was primarily the loyalty of the old soldiers to a great leader, and their habit of obedience. The survival of revolutionary sentiments, and the possibility of their re-awakening, was shown at Lyon, where enthusiastic crowds added to cries of *'Vive l'Empereur'* those of *'À bas les prêtres'*, *'À bas les nobles'*, *'Mort aux royalistes'*.

The news of Napoleon's landing reached Paris on 5 March. Before anything could be done, on the next day he was at Grenoble, and in the capital complacency was rapidly being succeeded by frantic and futile orders and counter-orders, and something approaching panic. The defection of Ney, in command of the royal troops in Franche-Comté, was decisive. At midnight on 19 March, Louis XVIII, accompanied by a few horsemen only, took the road for Lille. Finding the garrison there hostile, he crossed the frontier to Ghent.

Napoleon was once again master of France, but what use would he make of his revived authority? He announced that he had given up the Grand Empire, but was alarmingly ambiguous as to the scope he envisaged for the French Empire to which he now promised to limit himself. No promises could have disarmed the enmity of the other Great Powers. They declared Napoleon outside the pale of civilized society and had 7–800,000 men under arms to back up their ban.

To give the new régime a more liberal cloak, Napoleon issued, with the advice of Benjamin Constant, an *Acte additionel*, proposing a constitution not so very dissimilar from that adumbrated in Louis XVIII's *Charte*. Either believing in Napoleon's professions of liberalism, or thinking him a lesser evil than the Bourbons, Carnot emerged from retirement to become Minister of the Interior. But even if Napoleon had been sincere, and there is little reason to suppose that he was, he could not give France what its people still wanted more than anything else – peace, or its ruling classes what they wanted – stability, and security for their property and jobs. The chief reason for his successful return, after the loyalty of the old army, was the passivity, the political inertia of the nation. Of course, protestations of loyalty flowed in from the same officials who a year earlier had hastened to offer their allegiance to Louis XVIII and were to repeat the performance once the Emperor had been defeated. The weakness of the royalists was shown by their inability to offer serious resistance, except in the Vendée, where a rising pinned down 30,000 men whom Napoleon could well have used in Belgium.

The thought of an appeal to the masses, if it ever entered Napoleon's head, was rejected. There is no evidence, of course, that the masses would have risen, or what they could have done if they had. Instead, the governmental machine was put into operation in the orthodox way to raise a new conscript army. 600,000 men were called up, but when Napoleon invaded Belgium he could only assemble an army of 125,000, though these included many veterans, gathered back in France from the scattered remnants of his former armies. He marched off, leaving treachery behind him in the person of Fouché, once again Minister of Police, working with the liberals, protecting royalists, in secret correspondence with Metternich and Talleyrand at Vienna and Artois at Ghent, and revealing half of what he was doing to Napoleon, with a foot in every camp. He calculated on Napoleon's survival for some three months, in the course of which the duc d'Otranto reckoned to make himself – as

The First Empire

for a short while he was to be – indispensable to all parties.

In Belgium, the only forces ready to oppose Napoleon were 120,000 Prussians under Blucher, and a mixed force of Belgians, Dutch, Hanoverians, and English under Wellington. The Prussians were driven back at Ligny and Wellington's forces, held by Ney at Quatre Bras, retreated on the hill of Mont-Saint-Jean near the village of Waterloo. There, on 18 June, Napoleon flung his massed columns at them with little attempt at manoeuvre, in increasingly desperate attacks as the threat of the Prussian army, coming up on his flank, became greater. In the later stages of the battle only a retreat could have saved the French army, but Napoleon knew that farther off were the Austrians and Russians, and that if he did not win his first battle his chance was gone for ever. The retreat therefore became a rout and his last army vanished.

> *Comme s'envole au vent une paille enflammée*
> *S'évanouit ce bruit qui fut la grande armée.*

Back in Paris, on 21 June, Napoleon still talked of fighting on, draining the country of men, but there were none now to follow his frantic egoism. He signed his second abdication. If he had not done so the Chambers would have done it for him.

The liberals in Paris, being rid of the Emperor, did not want to replace him with a king, least of all a Bourbon. The man of the moment, however, was Fouché, who had turned to the royalists. He secured the withdrawal of the French army covering Paris and by a series of masterly manoeuvres was able to present to Louis XVIII, returning as rapidly from the frontier as he had fled there, a peaceful and unopposed restoration, and himself as his Minister of Police.

Meanwhile, Napoleon was *en route*, by way of Rochefort, though he did not suspect this as yet, to St Helena. From the *Bellerophon*, on which he had taken refuge, he wrote to the Prince Regent in a last fine gesture, 'I come, like Themistocles to seat myself at the hearth of the British people.' The hearth of the British people was a very cold one but we need not waste too much sympathy on Napoleon. The last fling of his ambition had to be paid for, like the earlier ones, by France; not only in the loss of life and the expense of war, but in a severer treaty of peace. France was reduced to the frontiers of 1789, with the additional loss of one or two small areas for strategic reasons, the most important being the Saar, its future economic importance not yet suspected. An indemnity of 700 million francs was extorted. The works of art looted from Europe were to be returned. The fortresses of the North and the East were to be occupied by 150,000 allied troops for a period of from three to five years. The price of the Hundred Days in the terms of a treaty can easily be stated: its price in terms of the subsequent history of France remains undefinable.

II

THE CONSTITUTIONAL MONARCHY

1. THE RESTORATION

The Second Restoration was to take place under very different auspices from those that had presided over the First. Fouché prepared the way for it in Paris. Talleyrand, hurrying back from Vienna, met the King at Saint Denis – where the kings of France had been buried for centuries, until the revolutionaries dug them up – and presented Fouché, vice leaning on the arm of crime Chateaubriand said, to Louis XVIII, who accepted the regicide as his Minister of Police. It was a very different homecoming from the first. Even if Wellington and the King's advisers, who urged on him the necessity of accepting Fouché and Talleyrand as his ministers, were mistaken in believing that this was the only way to a peaceful second restoration, the fact that they believed it, and that the King yielded to their opinion, is in itself significant of the latent weakness and even contradiction in his position; for despite his ministers Louis XVIII did not intend to return the second time, any more than he had come back the first, as the king of a crowned Revolution. When, on the news of the abdication of Napoleon in 1814, a courtier announced to him, 'Sire, you are King of France,' he had replied, 'Have I ever ceased to be?' His sense of indefeasible, hereditary, divine right, which supported him in the years of exile, had become second nature. It gave him a dignity which his physical appearance might otherwise have prohibited. Immensely fat and walking only with difficulty, he occupied the throne like an old idol, self-sufficient in divinely sanctioned egoism. If he compromised with new conditions it was without faith and with very little hope.

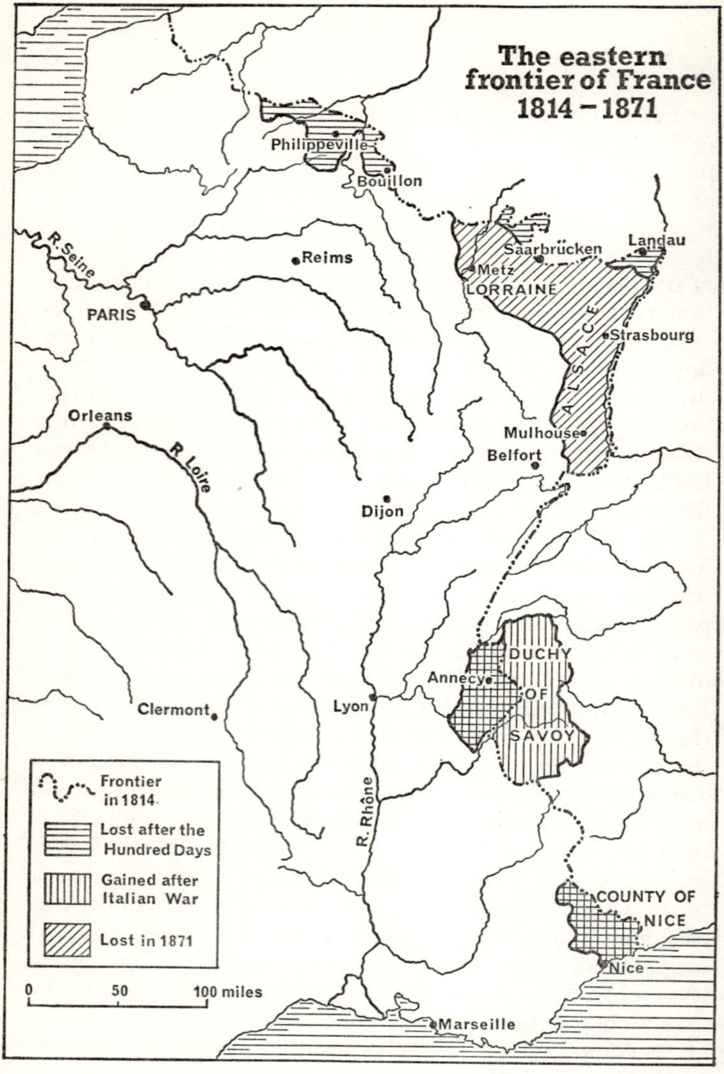

The eastern frontier of France 1814 – 1871
Philippeville
Bouillon
R. Seine
Reims
Saarbrücken
Landau
Metz
LORRAINE
ALSACE
Strasbourg
PARIS
Orleans
R. Loire
Mulhouse
Belfort
Dijon
DUCHY OF SAVOY
Annecy
Lyon
Clermont
R. Rhône
COUNTY OF NICE
Nice
Marseille
Frontier in 1814
Lost after the Hundred Days
Gained after Italian War
Lost in 1871
0
50
100 miles

The Constitutional Monarchy

Louis XVIII's English exile had not taught him the virtues of parliamentary government. At bottom he shared the views of his younger brother, who once declared that he would sooner earn his living as a wood-cutter than be King of England. This did not mean that the restored Bourbons intended, even if they had had the power, to bring back the absolute monarchy. The question is often discussed as though there were no other choice, at least in ideology, than that between the absolutism of a Louis XIV and the principles of the Revolution. This is to forget that it was not the ministers of Louis XVI but the *émigrés* who returned in 1814, and that the kings of the Restoration had formerly been, when they were Provence and Artois, the leaders of the Counter-revolution. Their programme had been that of the aristocratic revolt, of the Assembly of Notables and the Royal Session of 1789. These were the political ideas that Louis XVIII and his advisers embodied in the Charter of 1814.

The concessions it offered should not be underestimated. The recognition of the principles of liberty and equality, with which it commenced, perhaps meant less, but not in practice so much less, than it had in 1789. More important was the assurance that a curtain of forgetfulness was to be dropped over opinions and votes expressed before the Restoration: this was necessary if the political, administrative, military, and religious personnel which had served the Empire was to continue to serve the restored monarchy. The Civil Code and all existing laws which were not contrary to the *Charte* were maintained in force: this was to retain the administrative and social structure given to France by Napoleon, and here the fundamental contradictions of the Restoration begin. To superimpose the pseudo-Gothic of an aristocratic reaction on the pseudo-classical pillars of the Napoleonic system was to create a piece of wedding-cake architecture, essentially ephemeral.

A second problem was that of land ownership. It was met by a recognition of the inviolable right of all existing property, including specifically all the lands of the Church and the *émigrés* which had been confiscated by the Revolution and had passed to new possessors. Legal recognition of the changes in land ownership was doubtless inevitable, but could those who had been despoiled reconcile themselves to the fact that even if the King was enjoying his own again, they were not?

Thirdly, religious toleration was proclaimed. This was an achievement of the eighteenth-century Enlightenment, consolidated by the Revolution; but Roman Catholicism, a declining, emasculated force in the eighteenth century, was now moving towards a new militancy on the crest of a wave of religious revival. The immediate question was whether it would continue passively to tolerate its enemies. A more fundamental issue was whether the anti-clerical spirit, now deeply rooted among the educated classes, would ever be prepared to accept willingly the recognition in the *Charte* of the Catholic, apostolic, and Roman religion as the official religion of France, and the close alliance between Church and State that was the natural corollary. A minor problem, but one which was to give the Restoration much trouble, was slurred over in the clause which recognized both the liberty of the press and the right of the government to repress its abuse.

When we turn to purely political issues, contradictions are equally apparent in the *Charte*, though here there was more scope for a compromise to be worked out in practice. The aim was to establish a constitutional but not a parliamentary monarchy. The King embodied the executive power and had the initiative in legislation; but a parliament composed of two chambers was to discuss and vote the laws and the taxes, and the Chamber of Deputies had the right of impeaching the King's ministers before the upper chamber. These provisions were illogical but reasonable. They were to prove quite workable and to give France a valuable apprenticeship in parliamentary government. The issue that had divided the *noblesse* in 1789, the creation of a house of peers, was settled without any dispute, and here perhaps the example of Great Britain and of the institutions

The Constitutional Monarchy

of the Empire were not without influence. An assembly of the highest dignitaries, lay, ecclesiastical, and military, of both the old régime and the Empire, nominated by the King, formed a decorative, impressive, and workable upper chamber.

The fundamental problems of the Restoration were, however, essentially extra-political in the narrower meaning of politics. Louis XVIII recognized clearly what they were when he wrote to his brother, in 1817, that he did not intend to be the King of a divided people. 'All the efforts of my government', he said, 'are directed to the effort to fuse the two peoples, who exist only too much in fact, into a single one.'

Unhappily the Hundred Days had broken the spell of general reconciliation which seemed for a moment to be operating in 1814. A White Terror raged in the South before the central government was able to regain control. La Bourdonnaye, in the Chamber at Paris, demanded chains, executioners, tortures. 'Defenders of humanity', he cried, 'learn how to shed a few drops of blood to spare a torrent of it.' Doubtless to the disappointment of such real enthusiasts, the legal proceedings resulted only in a few thousand imprisonments. Fouché connived at the escape of many of those who had compromised themselves during the Hundred Days. Ney, bravest of the brave, whose execution was undoubtedly a political blunder, was given every opportunity of escaping before his trial, even though his desertion to Napoleon had been flagrant.

The first step out of the provisional for the Second Restoration was the election of a Chamber of Deputies. The government of Talleyrand and Fouché appointed the prefects and the presidents of the electoral colleges, and perhaps assumed that having chosen the makers of elections, the election was as good as made. But, not for the last time in the nineteenth century, it was shown that there were limits to what the administration could achieve by electoral management. Local notabilities dominated an election which took place in two stages, the primary electors having the task of choosing the actual electoral colleges. Out of a total electorate of 72,000, those who voted numbered 48,000. The result, which has never received a fully satisfactory explanation, was an overwhelmingly reactionary and royalist assembly, the famous *Chambre introuvable*. In the face of this striking repudiation by the electorate even the cleverness of Talleyrand and Fouché could do nothing and they faded from the scene. In their place Louis XVIII called on the duc de Richelieu, whose disinterested loyalty was well known, who had proved his capacity as an administrator in the service of Russia, where he had been governor of the newly conquered territory on the Black Sea, and who because of his long absence was uninvolved in any of the factions of the Emigration. Wellington said of him that his word was equal to a treaty. His colleagues, however, were weak, and the *Chambre introuvable* ungovernable. Louis XVIII has been praised for breaking with the reactionary elements which dominated it and at the same time blamed for rejecting, at the outset of his reign, the principle of parliamentary government; but the former was probably inevitable and the latter he had never accepted. The Chamber was dissolved in September 1816 and in the new elections the government of Richelieu obtained a working majority. Under him, by one of those remarkable financial recoveries which are a feature of French history, the indemnity imposed after the Hundred Days was paid off and the occupying armies withdrew in November 1818. Richelieu resigned in December 1818 but he had brought France back into the comity of nations.

The resignation of Richelieu, much more than the dissolution of 1816, was the proof that the régime was still a monarchical and not a parliamentary one, and that a minister could not hold office without the favour of the king. Louis XVIII was not ill disposed to the minister, but behind the scenes he was taking the advice of a personal favourite. This was Decazes, son of a notary of the Gironde. Decazes had become prefect of police for Paris after the Hundred Days, as such obtained access to the King, and

The Constitutional Monarchy

completely won his devotion. 'Come to receive the tenderest embraces of thy friend, thy father, thy Louis', the King would write to him. Decazes has perhaps been unduly written down because of the way in which his political fortune was built up. If he had not an elevated character and was no great statesman, he was successful in reconciling the rôle of royal favourite with moderate concessions to the left. In the new government, of which he was virtual though not nominal head, he combined the offices of Police and the Interior. Where Richelieu's administration had rested on the centre but looked for support towards the right, Decazes, equally with a centre government, relied on the support of the left.

The difficulty for any such government was that the one strongly organized and coherent party in Parliament belonged to the right. This was the party of the Ultras or pure royalists. It looked towards the King's brother, Artois, and represented the purest ideas of the Counter-revolution. Its strength in the country came from the support of the secret society of the Chevaliers de la Foi. Its leader in the Chamber of Deputies was the able parliamentarian, Villèle, and in the Chamber of Peers it had Polignac, Montmorency, and Chateaubriand to speak for it. The paradox was that the pure royalists from the beginning found themselves in opposition to the King; the less pure royalists who supported him formed the political centre, with a right wing represented by Richelieu and a left wing by Decazes. The left proper, only gradually returning to the political arena after the fiasco of the Hundred Days, took cover under the title of Independents.

With the revival of political life had come also that of political thought. The chief theorist of the left was Benjamin Constant, who saw the safeguard of the liberal principles to which he was devoted in a parliamentary monarchy after the English fashion, and whose political thinking, possibly for that reason, has lacked in France the recognition it deserves. The centre-left found its theorists in the doctrinaires Royer-Collard, Barante, Guizot, de Broglie,

Charles de Rémusat, who saw political life as a careful balancing of interests, and recognized no authority but that of law, or impartial reason, which however they tended to identify in practice with the interests of the socially dominant classes. The Ultras obtained doctrinal support from the writings of the theocrats, Joseph de Maistre, de Bonald, and Lamennais, for whom politics was the handmaid of religion and kings were the servants of the Pope, in whom was embodied the divine will on earth.

Political realities were far below this realm of high theory. They have to be discussed in terms of the membership of parliaments and cabinets, of party manoeuvres, franchise adjustments, and electoral wangling. The *pays légal*, those who had the vote, was restricted to some 90,000 electors in a nation of well over twenty-six millions, the qualification being the payment of 300 francs in direct taxation. Since by far the greater proportion of the wealth of France was in the form of land, and it was in land that those who had made money chiefly tended to invest it, this was primarily a landowners' franchise. To be eligible to stand as a candidate it was necessary in addition to be subject to a tax of 1,000 francs and to be over forty years of age. The number of possible candidates in the whole of France was some 15,000 of the wealthiest men. Nothing very revolutionary, it might be thought, could emerge from such an electorate. An analysis of the last Chamber of Deputies of the Restoration gives 38·5 per cent higher officials, 14·8 per cent engaged in trade, finance, or industry, 5·2 per cent belonging to the liberal professions, and 41·5 per cent large landowners, apart from such members of the previous categories as were also landowners, as probably most were.

The large proportion of the deputies who had played a part in public life under the Revolution and the Empire is an indication that the Restoration assemblies were not likely to be wholly swayed by Ultra views; nor was there much chance for the left in the elections. But to obtain a reliable body of supporters the government had to resort to methods of electoral management such as had been used

The Constitutional Monarchy

experimentally under the Directory and were to become classic in nineteenth-century France. Reducing the taxes of known opponents for the purpose of robbing them of the franchise was a common device. To prevent appeals against exclusions, the lists of electors might be posted up only at the last moment, at night, not in alphabetical order, and at a height which made them unreadable without a ladder. The prefects who managed the elections for the government saw to it that all government servants voted for the right candidate. Electoral meetings were prohibited. The electoral colleges were presided over by officials, and although the ballot was in theory secret, supporters of the government took care not to conceal their votes.

Once in the Chamber, the functions of the deputies were limited. The choice of ministers rested in the hands of the King, and the cabinet system was as yet only imperfectly evolved. Under Talleyrand, Richelieu, and Decazes there was an effective President of the Council, who coordinated the policy of the ministers. Villèle, on the other hand, when he became head of the government, adopted the practice of working alone with the King, and Charles X aspired to be himself the real leader of the ministers. The identification of the last of the Bourbons with the policy of his government was so close that it was impossible to prevent the fall of the government from bringing with it the abdication of the monarch.

In spite of the narrowness of the franchise and the control exercised by the government over elections, the multiplicity of parties stood in the way of stable administration during the Restoration. Decazes tried to conciliate the opposition, but when he went to the country in 1819 the result was merely an electoral victory for the left, in which even the former constitutional bishop and regicide, Grégoire, was returned, it is true with the aid of ultra-royalist votes. This was a blow to Decazes, but the fatal event for him was the assassination, in February 1820, of the duc de Berry, as he was leaving the Opera. It was an isolated crime but it gave an opening to all the enemies of the minister, and enabled them to force Louis XVIII reluctantly to abandon his favourite and recall Richelieu to office. To bring under control the reviving political activity, laws permitting the arrest of suspected persons, extending the censorship of the press, and conferring a double vote on the wealthier members of the electorate were passed. In September 1820 the birth of the posthumous son of the duc de Berry guaranteed the continuance of the Bourbon line.

The left now began to flirt with revolutionary movements. Representatives of small secret societies met under the chairmanship of Lafayette to discuss insurrectionary plans; but Richelieu, who was as well informed of these plans as the left-wing leaders themselves, took steps to make them aware of this fact and the embryo revolution was still-born. The international secret society of the Carbonari, which had perhaps as many as 40,000 members in France, was stirred into activity by the revolutions in Spain and Naples, but achieved nothing beyond a few petty local disturbances. The best known was the attempt of the four sergeants of La Rochelle to subvert their regiment. Denounced, they were arrested, tried, and executed. The left, however ineffectively, was thus abandoning the policy of compromise; the right was preparing to take over power; and the centre, on which Richelieu based his government, was fast disappearing.

France under the Restoration was not yet a parliamentary monarchy, and when the second Richelieu ministry fell, in 1822, it was again not because of a change in the balance of power in the Chamber but because the King had acquired a new favourite. Some years earlier a young woman named Zoë, Countess of Cayla, had sought the royal protection in a lawsuit against an 'unworthy spouse'. Beautiful, witty, and aged twenty-seven, Mme du Cayla won her suit and the royal affections at the same time. Given the age and infirmity of the King she could hardly become a royal mistress in the full sense of the term; but every Wednesday she visited the Tuileries for a private game of chess with the King, during which the doors of the royal apartment were

The Constitutional Monarchy

guarded; and every day she wrote the King a letter, in composing which she was assisted by Villèle. Not surprisingly, Villèle, who had entered the government in 1820, in September 1822 became President of the Council.

Villèle, a minor noble from Toulouse, short, ugly, intriguing, and ambitious, was the leader of the ultra-royalist party in the Chamber of Deputies, so that even without Mme du Cayla he would have been the appropriate minister for the royalist reaction. He was inexhaustible in his capacity for work, a master of detail, and unwilling to share his authority with anyone. Louis XVIII, now completely preoccupied with his health and Mme du Cayla, left the control of affairs almost entirely to his brother and successor, Artois, along with Villèle, whose great achievement was in the field of finance. Between 1822 and 1827 he put public finances in France on foundations which kept them sound and stable until the crisis of the twentieth century. The task of establishing a budgetary system and strict control of governmental expenditure, which had proved beyond the powers of the Controllers General of the *ancien régime*, but to which the Finance Ministers of Napoleon had made an important contribution, was now completed. This was perhaps the most important service of the Restoration to France. It was the return to peaceful international relations which made financial stability possible, of course. It is no accident that while the eighteenth and twentieth centuries, which were centuries of large-scale wars for France, were marked by instability in the national finances, the nineteenth century, with no really great and prolonged war between 1815 and 1914, was one of balanced budgets.

Peace after 1815 also brought with it a marked improvement in trade. According to one set of statistics French foreign trade more than doubled between 1814 and 1825. It is true that according to another set it remained stationary, but the former seems on the face of it the more likely. Altogether the Restoration gave France efficient and honest government, and, so long as Louis XVIII lived, moderation and a reasonable degree of stability, which endured long

81

2. CLERICALISM AND ANTI-CLERICALISM

THE failure of the Restoration was not primarily in the field of government, where it was weak, but in that of religion, where it was strong. Although the succession of Charles X may have precipitated the crisis, its beginnings can already be seen under Louis XVIII. Europe, in the early years of the nineteenth century, witnessed a widespread religious revival. This strongly affected the French church, in which there was now a zealous episcopate and a lower clergy gradually growing in number and unexceptionable in devoutness. Religious houses for women increased from 1,829 in 1815 to 2,875 in 1830. Orders for men were tolerated, though only in the case of three missionary orders were they authorized by law, but these also were increasing in number. The Jesuit-inspired Congregation engaged in energetic religious propaganda throughout France. An attempt was even made to annul the Napoleonic Concordat and return to the relations between Church and State that had prevailed under the *ancien régime*; but the terms of the Concordat – and this is perhaps the ultimate judgement on it – were too favourable for the Papacy to abandon and the negotiation for its revision proved abortive.

The Gallicanism of the Restoration was an anachronism, as became quite evident after 1830, when there was no longer a king with the sanctity of hereditary divine right on the throne. With Bonald, de Maistre, Lamennais, force of argument and literary talent were both on the side of the Ultramontanes. The religious revival naturally worked to the benefit of Rome. Gallicanism now stood for the authority of the French bishops, authoritarian and often aristocratic, with all the enhanced power conferred on them by the Concordat over the lower clergy, who could be transferred from parish to parish, or deprived of their office, at the

The Constitutional Monarchy

bishop's arbitrary will. No wonder that a habit of looking, or even appealing, to Rome grew up among the clergy: they had no one else to appeal to.

Napoleon had attempted to use the Concordat to reduce the Church to the rôle of an instrument of the State: under the Restoration there seemed a danger that the State might be made the instrument of the Church. In the interests of religion the episcopate did not hesitate to call on the support of the administration. With the Ultras in power this tendency was intensified. The Panthéon, purged of the infidel remains of Voltaire and Rousseau, was given over to religious uses. Secondary education was placed, in 1821, under the supervision of the bishops. A high ecclesiastic, Mgr Frayssinous, was appointed Grand Master of the University. In 1824 the appointment of all teachers in primary schools was given to the episcopate. In 1822 two new press offences were created – criticism of the divine right of kings and outrage on religion. A law against sacrilege made the profanation of sacred vessels punishable with imprisonment for life, and, in the case of profanation of the consecrated host, with death, though in fact the law was never applied.

When Charles X, who succeeded to the throne in 1824, was crowned in the cathedral at Reims, it was with all the apparatus of the religious revival. The assembled multitude cried *Vivat Rex in aeternum*; but it was noted when the King returned after the ceremony to Paris that his reception in the capital was distinctly lukewarm. Eternity was to last for five years.

While the depth and seriousness of the religious revival in France must not be underestimated, its limitations also should not be forgotten. Rationalism and anti-clericalism had driven too deeply into French soil to be easily uprooted. The intellectual life which had flourished under the *ancien régime* had been blighted but not killed by the frosts of the Revolution and the Empire. Now, in a milder, if still somewhat austere, climate, it reburgeoned as in a new spring. Science continued its progress, uninfluenced by, and unin-

A History of Modern France

fluencing, the changing political scene. Lamarck, who had studied under Buffon, links the zoology of the encyclopedists with the evolutionary theories of the nineteenth century. Cuvier practically created palaeontology, and Ampère has been called the Newton of electricity. The son of the great Carnot, Sadi Carnot, founded thermodynamics and Fresnel produced the wave theory of light.

History experienced a remarkable revival, amounting almost to a rebirth, under the Restoration. The famous École des Chartes was founded and the publication of the great collections of memoirs relating to the history of France was begun. Barante's *History of the Dukes of Burgundy* (1824-6) was as successful as a novel, and Augustin Thierry wrote a notable history of the Norman Conquest of England (1825). Guizot's *Essais sur l'histoire de France* (1823) was followed by the six volumes of his lectures on modern history at the Sorbonne in 1828-30. As opposition became bolder, historians turned to more recent times with the histories of the French Revolution by Thiers in 1823-7 and Mignet in 1824.

Above all this was a period of rebirth in literature. The new romantic spirit which crossed the Channel with Walter Scott and the Rhine with Mme de Staël's *De l'Allemagne* (1810) was in the beginning religious, monarchical, hierarchic, its eyes turned backwards to the Middle Ages. Lamartine, Victor Hugo, Mérimée, Alfred de Vigny, Stendhal, Chateaubriand raised the flag of romanticism. The paintings of Géricault and Delacroix might have been conceived as illustrations of their writings. The new trend appeared in music with Weber, Rossini, Berlioz.

Literature was not at first hostile to the Restoration, which represented emancipation from the strait-jacket of the Empire and an age of poetry after prose. Louis XVIII, a patron of poetry, impressed by the merit of a young beginner in the art who had determined to do what few dared to attempt – make literature a career – gave him a pension of 1,000 francs, and so eased the first steps of Victor Hugo, whose writings were to be a changing illustration of his age.

The Constitutional Monarchy

He was the son of a general of Napoleon, who had somehow picked up the title of count in the service of Joseph in Spain. After 1815 General Hugo, like so many others, transferred himself to the service of Louis XVIII, and by discovering a noble family of Lorraine with the same name, which had conveniently died out, annexed a more distinguished ancestry for himself. Victor Hugo was not only a poet but a vicomte; and in both capacities Catholic and royalist, writing poems on the death of the duc de Berry, the funeral of Louis XVIII, the war in Spain, attending the *Sacre* of Charles X at Reims.

But despite its initial affiliations the new wine of romanticism was too heady to be confined in the old bottles of Restoration politics or Vatican religion. Literature has during the last two centuries traditionally migrated to the opposition in France. In the years that preceded the revolution of 1830 romanticism deserted Catholicism and monarchism and formed an alliance with liberalism, carrying into the camp of its new partner some of that passionate vigour and anti-rationalist spirit which it had perhaps in part acquired from its former ally. Victor Hugo's *Préface de Cromwell*, a more notable piece of writing than the unplayable drama it introduced, is an invocation to liberty; and in 1830, in the preface to *Hernani*, Hugo denounced the Ultras of all brands.

The clerical reaction continued without the support of many of its former adherents in the literary world. Charles X, who presided over a régime which was now throwing off the hesitations and compromises which had marked the reign of Louis XVIII, had forgotten little; in intellectual goods his mind was so sparsely furnished that there was little for him to forget. At sixty-seven still youthful in manner and child-like in mind, he was determined to be king. However, he continued to support Villèle, whose government had added foreign victory to its financial successes.

The civil war, which had begun in Spain in 1820, could not leave the sister Bourbon monarchy in France unconcerned. Villèle, who was anxious to avoid military intervention, managed to drive the extremer Montmorency out of the ministry on this issue; but his place was taken by Chateaubriand who adopted the same policy. Despite Villèle's reluctance, in 1823 a French army was despatched to restore the Bourbon King of Spain, an ill-omened venture which unexpectedly achieved rapid and complete success. The invasion was little more than a military promenade. By lavish expenditure the financier Ouvrard, in charge of supplies, bought both provisions and an almost unopposed passage through Spain. French intervention re-established the king on his throne without difficulty. Comparisons were drawn, naturally, between this speedy success and the disasters that had encompassed Napoleon's armies in Spain. Villèle was not the better disposed to Chateaubriand because his policy had proved successful, and when the Foreign Minister refused to support a governmental finance measure took the opportunity to secure his dismissal. This was a great mistake, for Chateaubriand flung himself into opposition with vigour, taking the influential *Journal des débats* with him. The Spanish war, thus, though successful, crystallized an incipient split in the ranks of the right, and promoted the growth of a royalist counter-opposition. This is in part attributable to the narrowness and inflexibility of Villèle; but it is difficult not to believe also that the royalists were so unaccustomed to the compromises necessary in government, and the nobility so deeply imbued with the Frondeur spirit, that opposition came naturally to them.

They had a material reason for dissatisfaction. Disappointed under Louis XVIII, with Charles X the *émigrés* expected at last to receive the fruit of their sacrifices in the form of the undoing of the revolutionary land settlement. Villèle gave them the laws on sacrilege, the press, and education, but they wanted something of greater substance. The solution Villèle found was to create 30 million francs in annual new *rentes*, representing the interest at 3 per cent on a capital nominally of a thousand million francs, at

The Constitutional Monarchy

which the value of the confiscated property was calculated, in fact of about 630 millions. The former *émigrés*, or their heirs, now numbered some 70,000 and the indemnity to be divided between them came to an average of some 1,377 francs a year each. It did not satisfy their wishes, while it exacerbated the feelings of the great majority of persons of property who felt that in one way or another they were paying for it.

The propertied men who were aggrieved by the indemnity to the former *émigrés* included also those who were most suspicious of the clerical influences at work in the new reign. The outburst of anti-clerical propaganda which occurred in 1825 has been attributed to the subtle tactics of the liberal opposition, hoping to achieve by this means the electoral success which it had not been able to gain by more legitimate methods. All the measures in favour of the Church and religion were attributed to the influence of the Jesuit Congregation; the existence of the secret Chevaliers de la Foi was unknown to the general public. In fact, while the extent of the clerical reaction was exaggerated, the strength of anti-clerical feeling in France had also been under-estimated. If the liberals were able to use the fear of clericalism to achieve political results that could not have been achieved by more direct methods in a country that was not very interested in politics, this is in itself proof of the strength of anti-clerical sentiment. It was the major current in a rising tide of hostility against Charles X and his government. What two and a half years of Ultra rule had done was shown in March 1827, when the King, reviewing the National Guard of Paris composed largely of the well-to-do middle class, was greeted with cries of 'Down with the Jesuits!', 'Down with the Ministers!', '*Vive la liberté de la presse!*' It was hardly possible to impose any sanction in reply except to dissolve the National Guard.

Meanwhile the extreme Ultras had been becoming increasingly discontented with what they regarded as the excessive moderation of Villèle. A naval intervention in the Greek struggle for independence, which resulted in the successful engagement of Navarino in 1827, had little repercussion in France. If Villèle was to remain in office, he would have to try to secure a change in the composition of the Chamber of Deputies, but after elections held in November 1827 the government found itself with some 160 to 180 supporters in the new house, against an approximately equal liberal opposition, and with a group of 60 to 80 extremists forming a royalist counter-opposition on its right flank. Villèle had now no choice but to resign. The King appointed a ministry of technical experts, without any President of the Council, though the new Minister of the Interior, Martignac, was its spokesman in the Chambers and is often referred to as its head. This government offered some minor concessions, especially in matters of education, to the left; but it was clear that it would not be more than a stop-gap. Charles X was determined not to compromise with the liberal opposition, and if the Villèlists and the royalist counter-opposition could be brought to work together a majority of the right seemed still possible.

The fall of the last Bourbon king of France was so little determined by the nature of things, that in spite of the acute struggle over clericalism it took almost inconceivable imbecility on the part of Charles X and his minister to bring it about. For the new king also had his favourite. This was Polignac, his 'dear Jules'. In secret correspondence with Polignac by the back-stairs of the palace, a new ministry was arranged. Jules de Polignac, a prisoner of Napoleon from 1802 to 1814, was an *exalté* with no grasp of political realities. To him was added La Bourdonnaye, who had been identified with the White Terror of 1815, as Minister of the Interior, and Bourmont, who had deserted Napoleon on the eve of Waterloo, as Minister of War. At the Ministry of Justice was Courvoisier, a recent convert from infidelity to Catholicism, whose chief political guide was the Apocalypse. The government thus oddly constituted took office in August 1829. For six months it proceeded to do nothing, while the opposition prepared itself for resistance. Under the patronage of Lafayette, the society

The Constitutional Monarchy

Aide-toi, le ciel t'aidera organized electoral committees. The students of Paris formed a republican society called *Jeune France*. Inspired by Talleyrand and organized and financed by the banker Lafitte, the Orleanists made their preparations and founded a new paper, the *National*, edited by the liberal historians, Thiers and Mignet.

While the forces of the left were gaining coherence, the ministry was becoming increasingly incoherent. Except for Polignac it was completely renewed, with ministers whose names are not worth recording. The Chamber was dissolved and elections were held in June and July 1830. The customary methods of administrative pressure were employed, and the king issued a personal appeal to the electors to support the official candidates. All was in vain: the opposition won 274 seats against 143 for the government, and 11 of doubtful allegiance. The Polignac ministry had been decisively rejected by the *pays légal*. Everything would now depend on whether the king was prepared to accept the verdict of the electorate and appoint a President of the Council who could work with the new Chamber.

Charles X and Polignac had no such intention. Divine right could not make compromises. Moreover they wore fresh laurels of victory, won in the colonial field, on their brows. After Napoleon the French overseas empire was an attenuated one. In 1815 France possessed five trading stations in India, the isle Bourbon (formerly La Réunion), Saint-Louis and Gorée in Senegal, the small West Indian islands of Guadeloupe and Martinique, Guiana in South America, and the rocky islets of Saint-Pierre and Miquelon off Newfoundland, chiefly valuable because of the fishing rights that went with them. It was not much. The Restoration picked up the scanty and broken threads of French colonial policy, resuming rather the traditions of power politics of the *ancien régime* than the more liberal if muddled policies of the Revolution; there was nothing to inherit from Napoleon. Expansion began in Senegal and a foothold was won in Madagascar; but the major achievement of the restored Bourbons was the result of the Polignac ministry's need for prestige: the expeditions to Spain and Greece were followed, in 1830, by one against Algiers. Efficiently organized and well led by Bourmont, anxious to retrieve his reputation, in three weeks it achieved complete success; the foundation stone of the French North African Empire had been laid under the last and least considered of the legitimate sovereigns.

News of the victory at Algiers reached Paris on 9 July. Charles X and Polignac, encouraged by this success abroad, proceeded to take the steps necessary to reverse their electoral defeat at home. On 10 July Polignac produced the first draft of proposals which, after discussion in the King's Council, were issued on 25 July as the Four Ordinances. These prohibited the publication of any journal or pamphlet of less than twenty-five pages without official authorization; dissolved the Chamber which had just been elected; restricted the effective use of the franchise to the wealthiest 25 per cent of the existing electors; and convoked the electoral colleges to choose a new Chamber.

The first step in opposition was taken by the journalists, led by Thiers and the *National*. They issued a manifesto calling on France to resist. Shops and workshops in Paris were closed on 26 July: the King, as though to model himself on Louis XVI, spent the day hunting. Polignac, who in his blind infatuation did not for a moment expect the opposition to pick up the gage of battle which he did not even realize that he had thrown down, had taken no military precautions. Indeed the best troops, to the number of 40,000, were in Algiers. On 27 July, when it began to dawn even on Polignac that the situation was not quite normal, Marmont was put in charge of the garrison of Paris. On 28 July rioting began in the streets. A number of deputies met and sent a deputation to Polignac which he refused to see. By 29 July, Marmont having found it necessary to concentrate his troops, Paris was in the hands of the rioters, who had lost some 1,800 killed against 200 among the soldiers, in the course of the fighting. The deputies now decided to accept the leadership of the revolution to prevent

The Constitutional Monarchy

it from falling into the hands of extremists, and the Orleanist Lafitte joined other deputies in a self-elected municipal council, the next day to promote itself to the rank of provisional government. Three days of street fighting – *les trois glorieuses* – had been sufficient to overthrow the restored monarchy.

On 30 July Charles X at last recognized that something had happened and that concessions were necessary; but already on the walls of Paris was the placard, drawn up by Thiers and Mignet, calling on the people to place the Duke of Orleans on the throne. The self-chosen provisional government invited him to become lieutenant-general of the kingdom. Orleans, who had been hesitating at a safe distance from Paris, accepted and on 1 August appointed provisional ministers. Meanwhile Charles X, threatened by the populace of Versailles, had taken flight to Rambouillet. There he himself appointed Orleans lieutenant-general and abdicated in favour of his own grandson, *l'enfant du miracle*. Orleans himself still had some legitimist scruples, and if he had accepted this solution it might have been better for France and better perhaps in the long run for himself. The monarchical principle would have been preserved, the fatal cleavage between legitimists and Orleanists averted, and a parliamentary government set up in the name of the legitimate line. But the Orleanists had waited and intrigued too long for this moment to give up the prize at last within their grasp. Orleans convoked the Chambers and announced the abdication of Charles X, without any reference to his grandson. The fallen king slowly made his way with the royal family to Cherbourg, where he dismissed his bodyguard and took ship for England.

The Restoration had failed: this does not prove that it was from the beginning inexorably doomed to failure. On the contrary, the Revolution of 1830 seems at first impression rather the result of a series of accidents, and above all of the obstinacy of Charles X, who went from blunder to blunder as though driven by a blind fate, or as though the little sense there had ever been in that addled pate had entirely vanished with age. He was such a nonentity as to be hardly worth a revolution, and indeed, looking behind the passing events of 1830, one can see that it was not really directed against him; it was against the anachronistic reappearance of a *noblesse* which believed that the eighteenth century had never ended and a clergy which, since the eighteenth century was, so far as the church was concerned, a rather unfortunate episode, looked back to the century of the Compagnie du Saint Sacrement, Bossuet, and the Revocation of the Edict of Nantes. On the other hand, an important section of the educated classes in France, even if they thought that religion might be good for the masses, did not intend that priests should rule, or that their own sons should be educated by them. They turned against a régime in which the influence of the Church seemed to be increasingly dominant.

They also found that the Restoration was robbing them of one of the chief perquisites resulting from the Revolution. The new aristocracy of office created by the Revolution and Napoleon found its ranks swollen after 1815 by an unwelcome accession of strength from *ancien régime* families, who joined in the competition for even the humblest official appointments, and who, because of their ancestry and loyalty to the crown, had what seemed an unfair advantage in the game. The unemployed educated proletariat, searching for a career and especially concentrated in the student population of Paris, which has been wrongly seen as a factor in 1789, was perhaps a reality by 1830. At a higher social level the bankers and businessmen of the chaussée d'Antin looked with jealousy on the aristocratic exclusiveness of the faubourg Saint-Germain. The monarchy, which might have bridged the gulf between ancient names and new fortunes, in the person of Charles X allowed its policies to be dictated and its councils to be monopolized by clergy and *noblesse*. At the same time, inconsistently, it attributed the franchise exclusively to men of wealth. It is true that this was mainly wealth in the form of land, but the extent to which land

The Constitutional Monarchy

had passed into the possession of new men was perhaps not realized. Only this can explain the fact that the Restoration lost the support of even such a restricted electorate.

One thing more was needed to make a revolution possible: a mob to riot in the streets of Paris. Economic conditions supplied the material to fill this gap. The population of France had increased by nearly two and a half million between 1815 and 1830, without any marked increase in agricultural or industrial productivity in these years. After a short economic recession in 1817, a new and severer crisis began in 1826 and was to last until 1832. In 1828, out of 224,000 workers in the department of the Nord 163,000 were receiving some form of charitable assistance. That misery alone does not make revolutions is suggested by the significant fact that the populace provided insurrectionary mobs only in Paris, where the political agitation was concentrated.

Having won Paris with the aid of the mob, the journalists and politicians speedily brought the disturbances under control. The *noblesse* as a whole had perhaps not put up much of a fight in the first Revolution, outside Brittany and the Vendée. In 1830 they offered no resistance at all. In 1789 and the subsequent years at least they fled abroad to start a Counter-revolution; in 1830 they merely gave up their jobs and took refuge in that abstention from public life which has been called *l'émigration intérieure*, which robbed France of the services of a host of families whose position and traditions called on them to contribute to the ruling *élite*, but who had learnt under the bureaucracy of an absolute monarchy to disassociate rights from duties and who had ceased to be a governing class while remaining an aristocracy.

3. THE FOUNDATION OF THE JULY MONARCHY

In 1830 a political movement which had begun as an attempt to force Charles X to dismiss an unpopular minister turned into a revolution. The republican leaders, who now re-entered the political arena with the Paris mob behind them, were determined that the monarchy should disappear with the monarch. They had a ready-made candidate for President of the republic they believed they were about to establish in the person of the Commander of the National Guard, Lafayette, that distinguished relic of 1789, who was far too ingenuous and well-intentioned, and convinced of other people's good intentions, ever to succeed in politics. If a republic had been possible in 1830 he would have made an admirable president, but to the politicians, financiers, and men of property who had led the campaign against clericalism, the *émigrés*, Polignac, and Charles X, the Republic was still a name of terror. Lafayette was to be, in 1830 as in 1789, a mere cathartic agent, who precipitated events without really sharing in them.

The only practical alternative to a republic seems to us so obvious that there is a temptation to believe that the revolution must have been encompassed for the purpose of bringing it about. For the third time the shadow of an Orleanist conspiracy appears on the stage of history, and undoubtedly the Orleanist alternative to the Bourbons had been envisaged by some during the Restoration. There is no evidence, however, of the existence of any real conspiracy. The change in the dynasty was not a consciously calculated result of the 1830 Revolution: it was a pragmatic response to largely fortuitous circumstances.

The incoherence of the July Revolution was demonstrated in its first government. Lafayette and the conventionnel Dupont de l'Eure represented the Revolution, Sébastiani and Gérard, Napoleonic generals, the Empire; Guizot and baron Louis had served Louis XVIII, the

The Constitutional Monarchy

banker Lafitte and the journalist Thiers were active in the Orleanist interest, Casimir-Périer and the duc de Broglie had been less committed opponents of the Bourbons.

There is little significance in this *olla podrida* of a government. More important in the long run than those who were included was the fact of those who were excluded, or excluded themselves. Each of the successive revolutions in modern France has eliminated a section of the political personnel. In the 1830 Chamber of Deputies, 52 members refused to take the oath to the new king and 68 others lost their seats. There was a holocaust in the administration – 20 of the 38 members of the Conseil d'État, 76 prefects, 196 sub-prefects, 393 mayors or deputies, were dismissed. Of 75 generals, 65 were removed from the active list. Practically the whole diplomatic corps was changed.

This was not enough for the more violent revolutionaries, who were determined on revenge for the bloodshed of the streets and called for blood in return. The government would have been very glad to forget all about revenge, but under pressure from public opinion it had to bring the last ministers of Charles X to trial before the peers. While the National Guard, or at least its more advanced members, surrounded the Chamber and threatened lynch law, the accused ministers were got away by a trick to Vincennes. In their absence they were sentenced to life imprisonment and released a few years later.

To the new king and the more conservative among his supporters, the great danger seemed indeed to be the National Guard and its commander Lafayette. Aged as he was, he remained the symbol of revolution, but not for long. When his proposals, including a generous extension of the suffrage and a ministry of the left, were rejected, he resigned. The National Guard was reorganized by a law of March 1831 which confined effective membership to those who paid direct taxation; and although its officers were elected, its administration and finance were put under the control of government officials. It was to be the bulwark of the régime – or so they thought.

The hopes of a great international revolution, which have always accompanied domestic revolution in France, were also to be frustrated. The July revolution had sparked off a Belgian revolt against the Dutch. But if the left saw this as the opportunity to reverse the decisions of 1815 and renew the conquests of the First Republic, Louis-Philippe knew that the other powers would never tolerate a French annexation of Belgium. He believed that Great Britain might be persuaded to accept an independent Belgium, and appointed Talleyrand ambassador in London to implement this policy. He accepted the perpetual neutrality of the new state – envisaged as a safeguard against France – to win British support, and he resisted manfully the temptation presented by the offer of the new throne of Belgium to his son, the duc de Nemours. The success of his policy was demonstrated when, in August 1831, the Dutch king, rejecting the decisions of an international conference, launched his army against Belgium. Louis-Philippe was able, with British approval, to despatch an expeditionary force which preserved Belgian independence.

The conservative nature of the July revolution was marked from the start and embodied in the terms of the new constitutional Charter. It could hardly have been otherwise when the Chamber which drew up the Charter of 1830 was the last elected, on the narrow Restoration franchise, under Charles X, minus the ultra-royalists. There was inevitably a breach with the divine-right monarchy, and if the constitutional changes were more marked in symbols than in positive institutional arrangements, those who made them knew that men are governed by symbols. The new king would have been Philip VII or Louis XIX if he had succeeded legitimately to the throne; instead he became king as Louis-Philippe. In recognition of the fact that he was one of the new national sovereigns of the nineteenth century he took the designation – already given to Louis XVI in 1789 – of *roi des Français* instead of *roi de France*. And that he was the heir of the Revolution and not of the Bourbons was shown by the return to the *tricolore*, in place of the white

The Constitutional Monarchy

flag and the fleur-de-lys, the personal emblems of the dispossessed dynasty. Louis-Philippe had fought under the flag of the Revolution at Jemappes. According to a story, when he first appeared in revolutionary Paris and was greeted with cries of '*À bas les Bourbons!*', Thiers and Mignet rapidly produced a placard announcing, '*Ce n'est pas un Bourbon, c'est un Valois*'. This was nonsense: his ancestry was nothing to the point. His *raison d'être* was to stand between France and a republic.

Yet the principle of popular sovereignty was tacitly admitted. The Charter was not a concession granted (*octroyé*) by the King, as in 1814, but a declaration of the rights of the nation. Apart from this, the changes made in it were significant, but hardly revolutionary. Catholicism was no longer to be the religion of the State', but the religion 'professed by the majority'. The power of suspending or dispensing with laws was specifically taken away from the king, who also had to share the initiative in legislation with parliament. Censorship was to be abolished for ever: which meant that journalists in future were, with certain qualifications, to be allowed to publish before they were damned.

The sessions of the upper chamber were to be public, though when the Charter was drawn up views on its future composition were too contradictory to allow more to be said than that the question of the peerage would be re-examined later. The interests of the king in this matter coincided with left-wing opinion, and a law of December 1831 suppressed the hereditary peerage and made the upper chamber in effect a house of royal nominees. This was a more important decision than might be thought: aristocratic France was doubtless already dead of the kind of pernicious anaemia which had been sapping it for centuries, but this was the last nail in its coffin. The 'Corinthian capitals of polished society' had been finally knocked away, and their removal left the bare structure of power exposed in all its rather unlovely nakedness. Perhaps those, like Guizot and Broglie, who opposed the measure, were not wrong in fearing its social and political implications. The government of France could now be seen to be a combination of bureaucracy and plutocracy. The legitimist gentry and aristocracy withdrew into their manor-houses, or the salons and inner courts of the faubourg St Germain, and abandoned public service of all kinds, though they returned to the Army later in the century. Political power was shared by the king and the Chamber of Deputies. What this meant in practice can be seen from an examination of the electoral laws. The age of eligibility as a deputy was lowered from forty to thirty, and the *cens*, or electoral qualification, to the payment of 200 francs annually in direct taxation. In this respect it seemed that a revolution had been made to raise the total electorate of France to a number estimated in 1846 as 241,000, some 2·8 per cent of the male population over the age of twenty-one. Moreover, since even the great Revolution had never ventured to introduce such a frightful socialistic measure as an income tax in France, direct taxation fell mainly on real estate. Therefore about 90 per cent of the tiny electorate of Orleanist France, it has been calculated, obtained their qualification from taxes on property, the remaining 10 per cent representing commerce, industry, and the professions. The so-called 'bourgeois monarchy' was in fact an oligarchy of landowners. In the absence of a more detailed analysis of Orleanist society, we must not read too much into this statement; but at least it suggests that the landed wealth of the country was no longer mainly in the hands of old legitimist families, but partly in those of a class of new men, who had doubtless made their wealth in many ways in the course of the *ancien régime* and the Revolution. Their figures, like that of père Grandet, dominate the novels of Balzac. Their new wealth had largely been invested in land, and they were now a well-established propertied class, with a sufficiently strong sense of its own interests to use the revolution of 1830 to oust the legitimist-clericalist régime of the restored Bourbons, and at the same time prevent the republicans from acceding to power.

The narrow oligarchical pattern extended from central

The Constitutional Monarchy

to local institutions. The Municipal Law of 1831 established elected councils, but on such a narrow basis that a town of 5,000 inhabitants might have only 300 electors, one of 15,000 could have 700; and towns of 100,000 might reach the figure of 3,000 electors. Even these petty municipal oligarchies were kept under strict government control. The *maires* continued to be chosen by the central government for the larger towns, and by the prefect for the rest.

It was not to be expected that France would at once settle down peacefully after the disorders of 1830. The economic depression continued into 1832, and while in Paris political interests called the tune, in Lyon, always more influenced by economic considerations, industrial disturbances continued. Although the silk weavers of Lyon had not suffered from unemployment, the prices paid by the merchants for their handwork had been greatly reduced and the tariff to which they were accustomed was abandoned. In October 1831 a mass demonstration won the restoration of a minimum tariff of payments, but it was soon repudiated by the merchants. In November, at a review of the National Guard of Lyon, ill-feeling developed between the wealthier members with an elaborate uniform and the artisans in their ordinary clothes. The next day a crowd of several hundred weavers started to go round the town proclaiming, and enforcing, a strike. They were fired on and eight were killed. This was the normal pattern for a revolutionary outbreak in nineteenth-century France. It set fire to Lyon. The weavers rose as a man, barricaded the streets, descended from their quarter on the hillside of the Croix-Rousse. They were joined by companies of the National Guard and in pitched battle with the royal troops captured Lyon. Having won their victory, they policed the city, set guards on the Monnaie and the Recette Générale, and repressed all looting, for these were Lyonnais, sober and serious workers, master craftsmen, men of order. But of course not quite of the prevailing order, as the government realized. A large body of troops was despatched to Lyon, its National Guard was dissolved, the prefect – who had been too reasonable – was dismissed, and the tariff of prices revoked. The workers of Lyon were crushed, but not for good.

In Paris, at the same time, the effervescence assumed a different form. As always, political and ideological motivation was more evident than economic in the capital. There it had not been forgotten that the threat which had stimulated the July Revolution had been clericalism, and the struggle of clericalism and anti-clericalism took a little while after 1830 to settle down. At the outset a group of ardent Catholics had been stirred up by the July Revolution to envisage the possibility of a reconciliation of religion with liberty and to found a journal to advocate this. The leaders – it is not certain if there were any followers – were Lamennais, by now a republican, Lacordaire, a liberal, and Montalembert, a romantic medievalist. Their paper, *L'Avenir*, founded in October 1830, was abandoned in November 1831. While it lasted it had advocated, among other proposals, the abolition of censorship, freedom of education, universal suffrage, and the separation of Church and State. In 1832 the Encyclical *Mirari vos* pronounced the wickedness of all these ideas and the editors submitted to the verdict of the Pope.

Anti-clericalism was less easily brought under control, and it is not certain that all those in positions of power wanted it to be controlled. Whatever its deeper roots, anti-clericalism naturally appears above ground wherever the aspiration of priests to political power and the exercise of control over the life of society brings them into conflict with secular interests. The Church in France had overbid its hand in the twenties, so naturally it lost some tricks in the thirties.

Anti-clerical sentiments formed the excuse for a violent outbreak on 14 February 1831, when a Mass for the duc de Berry, assassinated ten years earlier, was held at the Church of Saint-Germain-l'Auxerrois, with white flags and fleurs-de-lis, a congregation of devout legitimists, and rows of aristocratic carriages with armorials waiting outside. It is difficult to believe that a crowd of rioters also found themselves there by accident, or that they unintentionally

The Constitutional Monarchy

allowed the legitimists to depart without more than an ugly scene before beginning the real attack. A detachment of National Guard which now arrived escorted the priests away through the mob, which was left to pull down and destroy images, crucifixes, and all the destructible furnishings of the church. Some of the rioters then made their way to the Archbishop's palace, next to Notre Dame, where a fine thirteenth-century building and a great library offered the prospect of even more enjoyable destruction. Books are always a temptation: they burn so well. The task was broken off when night fell, but was resumed the next day till the whole building had been demolished. In true revolutionary tradition mock religious rites were performed in the ruins. Similar scenes were witnessed in other towns, the authorities remaining neutral. Then, as rapidly as it had flared up, the agitation died down. The episode is a curious one. It is difficult to believe in the spontaneity of the outburst, but who organized it, and how did it spread through France? How far was there a deep-rooted and extensive anti-clericalism among the urban population, and how far was it artificially incited, the work of a mere handful stirred up by bourgeois anti-clericals? If we knew more about the provincial movements it might be possible at least to attempt to answer these questions.

Even the legitimists contributed to the prevailing disorder after 1830, with one feeble attempt to reverse the decision of July. The duchesse de Berry, mother of the legitimist heir, the young comte de Chambord, was the heroine of this romantic adventure. She travelled in disguise across France from Marseille, finding, like Bonnie Prince Charlie in similar circumstances, much profession of loyalty but little willingness to take up arms, until she reached the old centre of royalist resistance, the Vendée. There, a small rising was easily crushed. The duchess escaped and went into hiding but was captured later in the year. It then gradually became impossible for her to hide the fact that she was pregnant. Obviously this could not be a second *enfant du miracle*, and she had in the end to confess to the awful truth, that she was re-married to a minor Italian count. This ended the political significance of the romantic duchess. As a royalist supporter said, a mistake might have been forgiven the duchesse de Berry, a marriage excluded her from the royal family. This pathetic episode was the sum total of the Counter-revolution after 1830: things had certainly changed since 1789.

The last outbreak of violence linked with the July Revolution came in 1832, when the funeral of General Lamarque, a former Napoleonic general and a popular member of the Chamber of Deputies, was used by republicans and Bonapartists – to whom legitimists joined themselves – as the excuse for an attempted insurrection in Paris. The army and the National Guard, both now well under government control, suppressed it at the cost of some 800 killed and wounded. After this it was clear that the revolutionary movement was over; indeed this miserable affair looks forward to the street affrays of the Third Republic rather than back to the great *journées* of 1789 and 1792.

The new régime might not have survived its growing pains if it had had to rely on its first government. Its leading figure, in so far as there was one, was the banker Lafitte, but his conduct of affairs was so notoriously incompetent that he had to resign. Since France could not yet afford the weak government that Louis-Philippe really preferred, power fell into the hands of the most forceful of the existing ministers. This was Casimir-Périer, who declared that his policy was to combine order with liberty; but there is no doubt that the emphasis was on the former. France, he said, must be governed. In the elections of July 1831, Casimir-Périer made it clear that his government had no intention of being neutral. The prefects were instructed to use all their influence to secure the return of suitable candidates, though everyone was so new and untried that they found it difficult to know who was suitable. However, the great majority in the new chamber was conservative and prepared to accept a strong hand so long as there seemed any danger of reaction or further revolution.

The Constitutional Monarchy

Of the two bankers who had been patrons, and perhaps financiers, of the liberal movement under Charles X, Lafitte inclined to the left, whereas Périer, who regarded 1830 as not a change of system but only of person, was a leader of the 'resistance' to any liberal concessions. Naturally, whereas Lafitte has left the reputation of a weak minister, Périer was able to justify his reputation as a strong man. The new President of the Council also found his task of pacifying France facilitated by the ending of the economic slump. Louis-Philippe, however, whose position was now becoming securer, was not altogether happy with a strong minister who kept him out of cabinet discussions, and it was perhaps rather a relief to him when the cholera epidemic, failing to observe the strict class discrimination of the Périer régime, carried off his prime minister in May 1832.

Although the struggle to put curbs on the revolution had now in effect been won, the republican secret societies were still agitating and there was a good deal of repressed popular discontent. The government determined to take the offensive. The popular associations were attacked by direct prohibitions, by extending penalties from the organizers to all members, and by transferring trials arising out of breaches of the laws against political associations to courts without juries. The debate on these proposals suggested that the prime motive behind the new law was the fear of political revolution. The insecurity of the régime was still such that all opposition seemed dangerous. Resistance, declared Guizot, is turned by the opposition leaders into revolution. Thiers described the opposition as an illegal government, prepared to use the associations to overthrow the legal government. And in fact the Society of the Rights of Man was planning an armed rising, and a secret committee was formed to organize it. But in the event the government itself was responsible for provoking the armed outbreak.

Lyon was once again the scene of the major disturbances. In February 1834 the silk merchants again reduced their rate of payment to the weavers. A ten-day strike failed and the silk weavers returned to work. The city was peaceful when the government arrested six leaders of the strike, and anticipating the opposition that this action was bound to arouse, sent 10,000 troops to occupy the strategic positions and chief buildings of Lyon. Sporadic rioting broke out, and as so often, the authorities only offered a weak resistance until the insurrection had thoroughly developed. This is often attributed to callous calculation; it seems more likely to have been due to a natural slowness to react, and perhaps to mere stupidity. The rising, having been allowed to develop, was then ruthlessly crushed. A merciless struggle went on for four days. The royal troops gradually forced their way back into the town, while the forts on the outskirts bombarded the rebel-held quarters.

At the news of the revolt of Lyon troubles also broke out in many other towns, but only in Paris was there an attempt at actual insurrection. There, in the quarter of the Marais, some desperate republicans and their followers erected barricades. But Paris had a large garrison, and a National Guard which feared social revolution and the revolt of the workers more than anything else. They descended on the tiny nucleus of revolution, crushed it without difficulty, and proceeded to engage in a little private massacre in the rue Transnonain. Daumier made one of his most pathetically effective cartoons of it. The government might defend the actions of its supporters on the plea that it was just that those who had appealed to force should perish by force. Another view might be that what had happened in Paris was an attempt to exploit the genuine economic grievances of the workers by a small faction of political republicans. And yet a third view is that the republicans had played into the hands of the authorities, who were not sorry to have the chance of damning the workers of Lyon as revolutionary republicans for their attempt to defend their standard of living, and the republicans of Paris as social revolutionaries because of their connexions with the workers' movement.

After the failure of this pathetic attempt at a revolution,

out of 3,000 prisoners rather over 100 were selected for trial – a moderate measure of repression compared with the sequel to social struggles later in the century, when class hatred had become much more intense. And after the danger, or supposed danger, was over, public sympathies began to veer on to the side of the accused, whose trial was thoroughly mismanaged. Twenty-eight of them escaped from prison; and apart from a number of sentences to deportation or imprisonment, most of the prisoners were only condemned to periods of police supervision. On the whole, in spite of the massacre of the rue Transnonain, the republicans had discredited themselves by the events of 1834 and the government had behaved with comparative moderation.

An attempted assassination of Louis-Philippe in July 1835, by a bomb explosion which killed several National Guards, other persons round the king, and spectators, strengthened the hand of the government further, for the assassin, a Corsican named Fieschi, had been assisted by two members of the Society for the Rights of Man. Steps were taken after this to check the incitements to violence in the republican press. The Charter of 1830 had abolished censorship, but this did not mean that the government was powerless in its relations with journalists. Political journals had still to deposit a substantial sum as caution money. Conviction on such charges as offering an affront to the king or holding the government up to contempt might bring a fine of 1,000 francs, accompanied by a term of imprisonment for the editor. On the other hand, though juries were chosen only from the wealthy class which possessed the right of franchise, they had a regrettable tendency to acquit journalists charged with press offences. Louis-Philippe and his government continued to be showered with insults, and portrayed in venomous caricature by Daumier, Grandville, and other less brilliant but equally bitter cartoonists.

Casimir-Périer, from whom Louis-Philippe had been relieved by the hand of fate, was succeeded by a 'doctrinaire' ministry, including the able conservative peer

Broglie, Thiers, and Guizot, with a 'non-political' general, Marshal Soult, as nominal head. This was still much too strong a government for a king who wanted to hold the reins himself. A palace intrigue eliminated Broglie in April 1834, but after nearly a year of confusion he returned in March 1835, making the condition, like Casimir-Périer, that the cabinet should not meet in the presence of the king. But Broglie's authoritarian style was as little to the liking of the Parliament as of the king, and in February 1836 he lost his majority again. Louis-Philippe had now to split Thiers and Guizot, which he did by inviting Thiers to form a ministry. It lasted only six months; the king broke with Thiers over foreign policy, and then called on Molé, a peer who had served Bonaparte and the Bourbons in turn, and was equally willing to serve the house of Orleans. He was an official and a capable one, not a statesman; but it was an official that Louis-Philippe wanted, for, as he put it in rather unkingly language, '*c'est moi qui mène le fiacre.*' The series of events that began in July 1830 may be said to have been completed now, with all political or social opposition to the new monarchy driven underground, and Louis-Philippe himself the real head of his own government.

4. LOUIS-PHILIPPE

THE one and only Orleanist king came to the throne at the age of fifty-seven. He was already sixteen in 1789 and had been educated in the sentimental philanthropy of the *ancien régime* by Mme de Genlis. His presence in the armies of the Revolution provided Orleanist propagandists with the material for a military reputation, which somehow never stuck. An *émigré* in 1793, as the son of Philippe Égalité and an officer of the revolutionary army, he could hardly seek refuge among the allies. Wanderings in neutral countries, such as Switzerland, Scandinavia, the United States, and disagreements with Great Britain, occupied the next twenty years, leaving him a man of neither Revolution nor

The Constitutional Monarchy

Counter-revolution, a suitable king for a régime of the *juste milieu*; leaving him also with a love of wealth and power which were concealed beneath habits of bourgeois modesty. What he lacked was style. Louis-Philippe had neither the decadent grace of the eighteenth century nor the romantic panache of the nineteenth. He was gossiping, fussy, undignified, and with his pear-shaped face a gift to caricaturists. Above all, he was already ageing when he came to the throne. The skill and determination he showed in 1830–1 too soon turned into smug complacency and self-satisfied intrigue.

Yet Louis-Philippe had a good deal over which he might well feel self-satisfied. He had a model queen in Marie-Amélie of the Sicilian Bourbons, and five sons – Joinville, Orléans, Nemours, Aumale, Montpensier – handsome, distinguished, able in their different fields, and damned for ever by the wit who called them a family of brilliant second lieutenants. Within ten years he had established himself so firmly on the throne that his dynasty seemed secure. Legitimism had ceased to be a political force; republicanism was discredited among all proper-minded people and reduced to an underground intrigue; and that Bonapartism was not to be taken seriously had been shown when it could not even make a bid for power in 1830, as well as by the Strasbourg fiasco of Louis Napoleon in 1836, of which more later.

Hopes of a Napoleonic restoration apparently ended with the death of the young duc de Reichstadt, son and heir of the Emperor, *l'Aiglon* of romantic legend, in 1832. So innocuous did the Bonapartist legend seem, that the régime even tried to exploit it. Thiers filled in the gaps in his political activity with the composition of his *History of the Consulate and the Empire*. In 1833 Napoleon I was put back on the Vendôme column, though in civil attire. And in 1840 Joinville was sent to fetch the Emperor's remains from St Helena for reburial in the Invalides. The second fiasco of Louis Napoleon, this time in the form of a day excursion to Boulogne in 1840, showed once more that Bonapartism was not a force in France. Orleanist politics could pursue their placid if erratic course undisturbed by any fear of rapids ahead.

The absence of any effective nucleus of opposition was perhaps one reason for the weakness of Louis-Philippe's governments. The other was his own aversion from ministers with policies of their own. Molé was obviously no more than a stop-gap. With all the great figures in parliament ranged against him, his tenure of office was uncertain. In 1839 he appealed to the electorate, and in spite of all that official pressure could do, lost some thirty seats. The king had to look for a successor. He was in the dilemma of George III: weak ministers could not control parliament, and strong ministers pursued their own policies. Soult reappeared transiently, then Thiers, but once again foreign policy was the apple of discord. Since 1832 Louis-Philippe had been the effective manager of French foreign policy. He prided himself on his knowledge of Europe and his success in coping with its problems, not without some justification. He had kept the peace, brought about a *rapprochement* between France and the other great powers, played his part in solving the Belgian problem satisfactorily, and maintained French prestige.

Unfortunately he had given one hostage to fortune by encouraging Mehemet Ali's revolt against the authority of the Sultan. French opinion, tending to divide the world between friends of France and others, enthusiastically supported the Pasha of Egypt. But the success of Mehemet Ali, when war with Turkey broke out again in 1839, alarmed the other great powers, which in July 1840 issued an ultimatum calling on him to cease hostilities or face military intervention. French opinion was indignant. Thiers was all for war in defence of the French protégé, though it would be without an ally and against the four other great powers. France had a good deal at stake. With officers, teachers, business men, and loans, she was the dominating influence in the Egypt of Mehemet Ali, and stood to gain or lose a major position in the Near East according as Mehemet

The Constitutional Monarchy

Ali succeeded or failed. Thiers was the minister for a foreign policy that recalled the ambitions of Napoleon. On the other hand, the British government saw French influence in the Ottoman Empire as a menace to vital British interests. To British representatives Thiers replied that France would never tolerate the use of force by the other European powers against Mehemet Ali. This has been regarded as a policy of bluff, though it was one that might have led to war. But when British and Turkish troops intervened in Syria, and the local population turned against the occupying Egyptian forces, Thiers realized that he had over-estimated the strength of Mehemet Ali and accepted the situation. Having done so, he still wanted to save his face by making the threatening and now meaningless gesture of inserting a bellicose statement in the speech from the throne in October. This was too much for Louis-Philippe, who had been watching with increasing alarm Thiers' policy of going to the brink of war before he withdrew. He now exercised his influence in the Chamber to overthrow Thiers.

The game of general post that the king had been playing with his governments since 1832 was resumed with the appointment of Guizot as Minister of Foreign Affairs and Soult as nominal President of the Council. Contrary to all expectation, however, the new ministry was to last, with minor changes, to the final catastrophe. Guizot was perhaps the most intelligent and high-minded minister ever to preside over the ruin of a political system. A Protestant, with all the austerity of a French Huguenot, he accepted the politics of wealth and influence; a distinguished historian with profound critical powers, who envisaged behind changing circumstances the movement of great historical forces and the evolution and conflict of classes, he behaved as if he thought his own régime could somehow escape from historical fatality; a doctrinaire who had asserted mildly liberal principles under the Restoration, he never moved beyond the narrowest interpretation of them when he was in power.

Disdain for all opposition, and a certain noble serenity,

insulated him from the effects of the attacks that were continually made on him, but he gave the impression of rather more deviousness than seems compatible with his elevated character. He was undoubtedly a man of remarkable intellectual calibre, but one must not exaggerate the political skill that was shown by his long tenure of power; Guizot was free from the weakness which had undermined previous ministers – the intrigues of the king – for Louis-Philippe had found a minister who was indispensable to him. As for the support of parliament and the country, that was guaranteed by the electoral system. Each constituency had its college, many as small as 150 voters, and easily managed by the administration. The whole conduct of the elections was in the hands of the prefects, sub-prefects, and *maires*, one of whose chief functions was to secure the return of the official candidate. They practised every form of chicanery that was possible before the Second Empire turned the system of official candidatures into a fine art, though perhaps only fully in the election of 1846. Not that it mattered much: the propertied class was satisfied so long as its own wealth and social position were safeguarded. It was entirely content with a profoundly conservative régime that proposed no changes at home, and only such adventures abroad as were likely to involve no new taxes.

True, a new French Empire was founded under the constitutional monarchy, but this was the result more of the force of inertia than of considered policy. The Orleanist monarchy saw no profit or prestige in colonies, and if the forward movement begun under the Bourbon Restoration did not cease, this was due rather to the officials than to the ministers. After the first step had been taken with the attack on Algiers more determination was needed to stop the slow forward movement than to continue it. From the three initial conquests of Algiers, Oran, and Bône, French occupation was gradually extended until, in 1839, the Arab chief Abd-el-Kader abandoned his treaty and took to arms in the endeavour to check its progress. Bugeaud, promoted

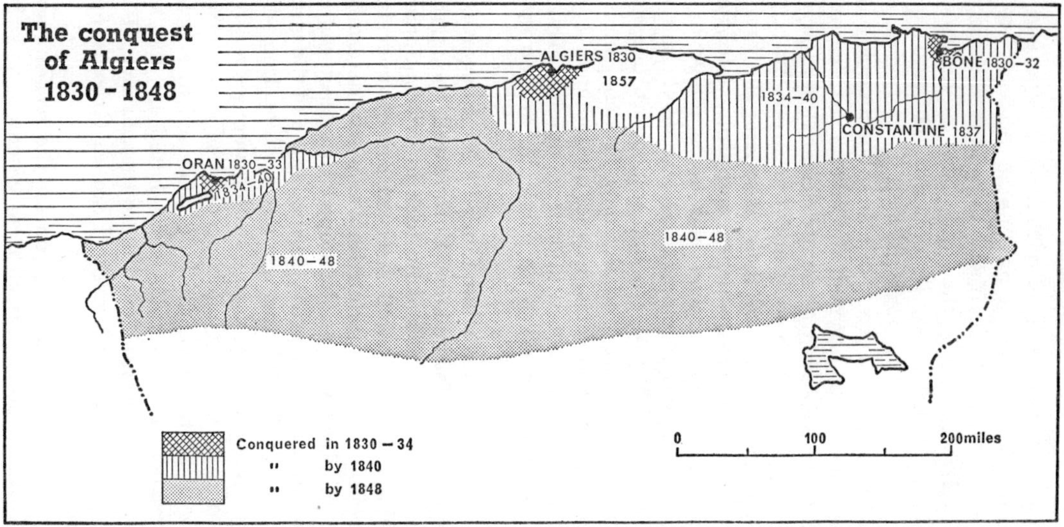
The conquest
of Algiers
1830 - 1848
ALGIERS 1830
1857
BÔNE 1830-32
1834-40
CONSTANTINE 1837
ORAN 1830-33
1834-40
1840-48
1840-48
Conquered in 1830 - 34
" by 1840
" by 1848
0
100
200miles

corporal on the battle-field of Austerlitz, who had already had much experience of fighting in Algiers, was put in charge by Guizot. He dealt with the scattered threat of Arab warfare by lightening the equipment of his troops and organizing them in mobile columns. He had under his command Cavaignac, Changarnier, Lamoricière, and the king's son Aumale, a group of able subordinates, but it took an army of some 88,000 men and several years campaigning before Abd-el-Kader was finally defeated and captured in 1847. The war was bloody and barbarous on both sides. The Algerians massacred their prisoners; the French destroyed crops, orchards, villages, and asphyxiated 600 men, women, and children, who had taken refuge in a cave. Behind the fighting, colonization was slowly but steadily proceeding. By 1847 Algeria had 109,000 Europeans, about half of them French, and the new French Empire, with its promises and problems, was solidly founded. It was the achievement of the constitutional monarchy, even though Louis-Philippe had taken no particular interest in it himself.

Foreign policy was what Louis-Philippe regarded as his special expertise, for he knew Europe well, though he knew it as an exile. Yet he had no luck in international affairs after the initial and well-deserved success over Belgium. The trouble was that, while he was wisely determined not to get involved in war, he hoped to collect some useful trophies at a cheaper price. As the failure of the gamble on Mehemet Ali showed, this was not possible. Louis-Philippe always felt something of an outsider among the sovereigns of Europe. If Victor Hugo's account of a conversation of 1844 is to be believed, the king confessed to a belief that both France and its ruler were hated by the kings of Europe, and he himself even more than France. 'I tell you frankly, they hate me because I am an Orleans, and they hate me for myself.'

This was perhaps the reason for the *rapprochement* with Great Britain, though to call it an entente is to stretch the meaning of the term. Superficially friendly relations were

The Constitutional Monarchy

patched up after the failure of Mehemet Ali and the dismissal of Thiers. Queen Victoria paid a state visit to Louis-Philippe in 1843, when she seems to have been mostly impressed with the muddle and lack of dignity of the French Court. The French king repaid the visit the following year.

Essentially the so-called Franco-British entente was no more than an expression of the personal liking and mutual trust of the French and English ministers, Guizot and Aberdeen. It was not even proof against a trivial dispute in a Pacific island, which arose out of the rivalry of French and English missionaries in Tahiti, and the not altogether incomprehensible habit of the local ruler of accepting the protectorate of whichever power had last sent a gun-boat there. An ambitious English missionary named Pritchard, who believed that the flag followed the Bible, attempted to interfere with this amicable arrangement and got himself expelled by the French in 1844. This produced much British indignation, for these were the days of *civis Britannus sum*. Under pressure from the Foreign Office, the French government expressed its regret, which aroused corresponding French wrath. In 1847, the French protectorate was recognized, which restored the situation as it had been before the Pritchard affair, but rumblings of discontent continued. As for the shadowy entente, that vanished when Palmerston returned to the Foreign Office in 1846.

Anglo-French rivalry had been particularly evident in the affairs of Spain, where marriage with the young queen Isabella was a political triumph which either the house of Coburg or that of Orleans might aspire to. Since either could have been happy with her, it was decided, in September 1843, that by a mutual renunciation neither should enjoy the prize. But Guizot, who was being out-manoeuvred by Palmerston, had to take counter-measures. He arranged a double marriage of the duc de Montpensier, son of Louis-Philippe, with the sister of Isabella, while the queen of Spain herself was to marry her cousin. Thus it was assumed that in due course there would be an Orleanist heir to the

A History of Modern France

Spanish throne. However, there must have been a miscalculation somewhere, for Isabella had a son and the whole intrigue came to nothing.

The lack of a glorious foreign policy, along with a supposed revival of Bonapartist sentiment, have been accounted main factors in the failure of the Orleanist monarchy. It will be more convenient to discuss the part played, or not played, by the 'Napoleonic legend', and the attempts of Louis Napoleon Bonaparte, at Strasbourg in 1836 and Boulogne in 1840, to exploit it, at a later stage. As for the lack of a glorious foreign policy, the belief that this was a cause of the revolution in 1848 may go back to a phrase of Lamartine, in 1839, which has had only too much success, – *'La France est une nation qui s'ennuie'*; but there is no reason to suppose that the poet was complaining of the absence of military glory. Like so many young literary men a royalist under the Restoration, Lamartine had become a liberal by 1830, and under the Orleanist monarchy was converted to the principle of universal suffrage, in reaction against the narrow and selfish plutocracy that ruled France. There was a cleavage growing up in France, not so much between the two nations of Disraeli's *Sybil*, for, unlike Great Britain, France had not yet come anywhere near that stage of industrial development, but between the mind and heart and ideals of France and its political and social structure. Genius was bored, as it normally is, with the rule of vested interests. Louis-Philippe had nothing to offer to a romantic generation.

5. AN AGE OF IDEALISM

The politics and economics of the July Monarchy were perhaps no more sordid than such things usually are: if they seemed so it was because this was a generation of unexampled idealism, of romantic and not always rational hopes or despairs, and of a widely diffused religiosity which was now spilling over the bounds of the Catholic revival,

The Constitutional Monarchy

producing a crop of new cults in England and America, and in France becoming closely linked with schemes for social regeneration.

In the history of art and literature there is no dividing line at 1830. Theocracy, of course, became a memory then; the romantic writers who had been royalists, like Hugo and Lamartine, now moved over to liberalism; and the humanitarian themes of the Enlightenment were resumed, though with a more emotional tone infused into them by the revival of religious feeling, the new sense of history, and the cult of the people. Politically, romanticism may be said to have migrated to the opposition in 1830, though a simple formula like this can hardly do justice to such a complex movement, with such diverse sources.

The strongest influence over the nascent romantic movement had been that of Rousseau, who set the tradition of romantic melancholy, self-enquiry, reverie, which was continued by Bernardin de Saint-Pierre and Chateaubriand. Lamartine, in the *Méditations* of 1820, brought the Rousseauist spirit of soul-searching, sorrow for lost love, search for religious consolation, into poetry There was something deeper and more classic in the pessimism of Alfred de Vigny; and the lyrical spirit was to be carried on in the sentimental, easy, and attractive poems of Alfred de Musset, in the prose of Théophile Gautier, who inspired the ballet *Giselle* (1841), which remains the perfect expression of a certain romantic feeling, and in the charm of the rustic Berrichon romances of George Sand.

But this muted note was not the characteristic or the dominant one in French romanticism. More exotic influences were also at work. Normally, in the history of art and literature, inspiration has come from France and spread to the rest of Europe; but the French spirit has been too self-contained and insular, and the French too unwilling to read foreign languages, for much to be accepted back in return. The Emigration and the Empire temporarily changed this situation. Mme de Staël's *De l'Allemagne* in 1810 introduced France to *Sturm und Drang*. Shakespeare was adapted for the

A History of Modern France

French stage in the late twenties by Alfred de Vigny. Gérard de Nerval translated Faust in 1828. One cannot pretend that the romantic drama which flowered in France under these influences was quite up to the level of Shakespeare or Goethe. It was closer to, and more directly influenced by, the historical novels of Sir Walter Scott, which had a great vogue in France under the Restoration, and inspired in 1826 the austere *Cinq-Mars* of de Vigny, in 1829 the *Chronique de Charles IX* of Mérimée, and, going back to the Middle Ages, that astonishing, ridiculous, and wonderful source-book of romantic clichés, *Notre-Dame de Paris* by Victor Hugo, in 1831.

The historical movement was also evident in painting. Delacroix painted scenes from recent and ancient history – the *Massacre of Scio* (1824) or the *Death of Sardanapalus* (1829) – with brilliant colour and drama. Géricault, as in his most famous painting, the *Raft of the Medusa* (1819), drew scenes of violent action and death. With Daumier romantic art became the expression of the social conscience and abandoned the Middle Ages.

Romantic medievalism had its most disastrous effects in architecture. The destruction of famous medieval buildings, including Cluny, mother house of the Benedictine Order and greatest abbey of medieval France, aroused the indignation of both romantic and religious medievalists. Led by Montalembert and Victor Hugo, a press campaign produced a Commission on National Monuments, with Prosper Mérimée as its secretary. The chief living authority on medieval architecture, Viollet-le-Duc, was put in charge of the work of preservation. Alas, the most complete neglect would have been more salutary. A new Vandal invasion could not have done worse, for that would merely have pulled down whereas Viollet-le-Duc also rebuilt. Moreover he did not work alone but had his emulators. Abadie raged through the West, restoring: at Angoulême he dealt with the deficiencies of the cathedral by taking down everything that was not text-book thirteenth-century style – this was most of the cathedral – and rebuilding it as he thought it

The Constitutional Monarchy

ought to have been built if the medieval architects had read the right text-books.

In literature and art the more ridiculous aspects of romantic medievalism, which was never married very happily to French traditions, can easily be overstressed. In contemporary life it was linked with an awakening of the social conscience. For all its enlightenment and humanitarianism, the eighteenth century never really faced the problem of poverty; perhaps it believed, with the Church, that the poor we shall always have with us. Particularly after the July Revolution, however, the humanitarian tradition of the Enlightenment combined with a new, and largely Rousseauist, religious influence, to make the amelioration of the condition of the poor the central object of social thought. 'Religion', wrote Saint-Simon in his *Nouveau Christianisme*, 'should direct society towards the great end of the most rapid amelioration possible of the lot of the poorest class.' The goodness of the people became a romantic doctrine, and the people was now no longer the idealized peasantry and honest craftsmen of the Rousseauist illusion, still surviving in the rustic idylls of George Sand, but the ragged and starving populace of Paris. They appeared in medieval guise in Hugo's *Notre-Dame*, and in a more contemporary costume in Eugène Sue's serial, *Les Mystères de Paris*. The fellowship of poet and pauper was exemplified by de Vigny, himself from a family of lesser nobility ruined by the Revolution, in his play *Chatterton* (1835), in which also can be detected the first shots in the war that was now beginning between the artist or man of letters and bourgeois society.

Though there was much idealistic republicanism, the battle was against a social order based almost exclusively upon distinctions of wealth, rather than against the monarchy as such. True, Louis-Philippe was for many the symbol of this social order, but the prosaic nature of the Orleanist monarchy has been exaggerated. The sons of Louis-Philippe were, in their various ways, a surprisingly intelligent and cultured group of men. The heir to the throne, the duc d'Orléans, had genuine literary interests;

his duchess, the adorable Hélène, was an admirer and patron of Victor Hugo. It was through her influence that Hugo became one of the exceptional men of literary genius in France to be admitted to the Académie Française before he was moribund, if at all, and it was through the duchess that he became a peer of France. He never forgot his debt to the house of Orleans or wrote ill of Louis-Philippe.

The cartoonists were less sparing of the king. The editor of *Charivari* fought a running battle with the censorship, and if a great cartoonist like Daumier experienced short prison sentences, it did not prevent him from creating a gallery of sub-human figures out of the Orleanist officials, judges, lawyers, and financiers. The character who symbolized the whole régime was taken from an inferior play about an amoral adventurer named Robert Macaire, who was built up by the great actor of the period, Frédéric Lemaître, into a monster of cynical rascality, and portrayed by Daumier as an out-at-elbows ruffian. He became the type of a society on the make, with no conscience, no pity, no standards of conduct. On a higher literary level we have the long series of novels that make up Balzac's *Comédie humaine*, which exhibits a society dominated by money, a world of men of property like the Forsytes without their principles. Oddly enough, Balzac himself, with his grandiose ideas, frantic struggle for fortune, financial adventures, bankruptcies, passionate love affairs, and craving for luxury, was a man of his age almost to exaggeration, and like so many of his own characters, and for the same reason, he was a believer in authority and the social function of religion.

The wealth of the rich might have seemed less blatant if it had not been for the equally unconcealed misery of the masses, particularly in Paris. The population of France grew from some 29 millions in 1815 to nearly 36 millions in 1851, and since the countryside already supported as many as it could under existing conditions, the bulk of the increase took refuge in the towns, particularly Paris. There was as yet no industrial development in France equal to providing them with work. Paris in 1848 had nearly 65,000 industrial

The Constitutional Monarchy

undertakings, of which only 7,000 employed more than 10 workers. It is probable that the standard of living of the urban populace had deteriorated drastically since the eighteenth century. The government, dominated by laissez-faire ideas, as well as by class interests, made no attempt to improve conditions.

In the third and fourth decades of the century many writers, a class in which the social conscience seems to have been more lively than in others, were acutely aware of the conjunction of extreme wealth with dire poverty. They were passing over from humanitarian sympathy to aggressive criticism of the social order and positive proposals for a new and better one. Thus Lamennais, under the Restoration a leading Catholic apologist and offered a Cardinal's hat which he wisely declined, found after 1830 that there was no room for his liberal ideas inside the Church. His *Paroles d'un croyant* marked the breach with Rome and he then moved on from religious heterodoxy to political liberalism. The people was the new Messiah, and Lamennais wrote passionately of its sufferings in *Le Livre du peuple* of 1841: 'They have said you were a flock and that they were your shepherds; you, the beasts; they, the men. Theirs, therefore, your fleece, your milk, your flesh. Pasture under their crook and multiply, to warm their limbs, quench their thirst, and satisfy their hunger.'

Lamennais himself did not offer any remedy for social injustice other than liberal democracy, though he was one of the founders of Catholic social reform. But this was a period of intense and original social speculation, in which socialist ideals first burgeoned. The greatest name to be mentioned in this connexion is that of the comte de Saint-Simon, of *ancien régime* nobility, who had fought in the war of American Independence and became an ardent revolutionary in 1789. His enthusiasm was not lessened when he made a fortune by speculating in nationalized property. An extravagant way of life under the Directory ruined him and he turned to plans for social regeneration. Among his collaborators were the young historian Augustin Thierry and the founder of positive philosophy, Auguste Comte. These fell away, but when Saint-Simon died in 1825, he left behind him a small band of disciples, including Hippolyte Carnot, future minister of the Second Republic, Michel Chevalier, the economist and later adviser of Napoleon III, and the Péreire brothers, the financiers of the Second Empire. The leadership of the group, which was rapidly developing into a Saint-Simonian Church, was taken over by the 'père' Enfantin, who turned it into one of the many nineteenth-century religions of love, and whose practical exercises in that direction brought him into conflict with the law. The real importance of the ideas of Saint-Simon was only to appear under the Second Empire.

Another social theorist whose writings pre-date 1830 was Fourier, in whom, as in the whole movement of which he is not the least eccentric representative, the influence of Rousseau is marked. The evils of civilization and the inability of government to remedy them are traced to property; the emphasis has now shifted from politics to economics. The social compact is seen as guaranteeing the rich the enjoyment of their wealth and impunity for their crimes. Fourier's solution was based – and this again indicated a new century – on new psychological principles, in which the passions were more important than the reason. He saw human nature as based on the *papillonne* or principle of variety, and to cater for this each man should take many jobs, not merely in his life but in each day. Fourier's new society was to be organized in Phalanges – self-contained communities which were to produce, on a principle of co-property, all that they consumed. The practical significance of these ideas was slight. Fourier, like nearly all the socialist or utopian writers of the period, was not as mad as he sounds, but he was planning for a pre-industrial world.

Among others, Buchez, the co-editor of the forty-volume *Histoire parlementaire de la révolution française*, combined Christianity and cooperation in the name of science. Pierre Leroux, a former Saint-Simonian, developed the idea of a religion of humanity. Cabet, who was influenced by

The Constitutional Monarchy

Owenite ideas from England as well as by a Rousseauist faith in the goodness of human nature, described a Utopian community in his *Voyage en Icarie*, and subsequently tried to realize it in America. Louis Blanc, a journalist, produced the idea with the most immediate appeal. His *Organisation du travail*, in 1839, was a simple but effective assertion of the 'right to work', and proposed to put it into practice by state intervention on the labour market. The most influential of all these socialist writers in the long run, as well as the most striking personality, was the working printer Proudhon, who became the *bête-noire* of the bourgeois by his work *Qu'est-ce que la propriété?* (1840), in which he gave the answer to his own question – '*C'est le vol*'. But his great influence on the French labour and socialist movements came later in the century.

The social thought of the period is a remarkable mixture of sense and nonsense, of a realistic appreciation of social evils combined with the proposal of sometimes fantastically utopian solutions. The element of escapism that is to be detected in this literature is also to be seen in the novels of adventure that proliferated at the time, exploiting the new medium of newspaper serials. Alexandre Dumas ransacked history for picturesque periods; Eugène Sue found mysteries in Paris; Mérimée and Balzac combined romanesque themes with realistic detail. Béranger played a part, by his popular lyrics, in turning the propaganda of the First Empire into a Napoleonic legend.

Yet even in the hey-day of the Romantic movement there were signs that it would not last. Stendhal's *Le Rouge et le Noir* and *La Chartreuse de Parme* are packed with romantic detail, but the spirit of their author was closer to that of the eighteenth century. Gautier's *Mademoiselle de Maupin* belongs to the same perverse genre as *Les Liaisons dangereuses*. In 1838 a young actress, Rachel, played Racine in a way that swept the trivialities of romantic drama off the boards. And already, while the romantic wave seemed to be engulfing everything, signs of a new attitude were appearing. Théophile Gautier, whom Lanson has described as the pivot of French literature in the nineteenth century, proclaimed the new gospel of 'art for art's sake' as early as a preface of 1832. Gérard de Nerval looked back to the *illuminés* of the eighteenth century and forward to the symbolists. That literature was not unaffected by the current preoccupation with the social problem can be seen in the novels of Hugo, Balzac, Sue, George Sand; and the first attempt at a scientific treatment of it brought the beginning of sociological thought, particularly in the work of Auguste Comte. He began as a teacher of mathematics and a disciple of Saint-Simon, but soon broke away and devoted the remainder of his life to developing the school of Positivism, which by an equal misconception of the nature of science and of religion, offered a new secular religion of science to those who had lost their traditional faith but could not manage without an inspired teacher and at least one form of certainty. More distinguished thinkers, like Renan and Taine, experienced strongly the influence of Comte's positivism, which has continued to exercise a spell over the French mind.

However wild or *a priori* much of the social thinking of the first half of the nineteenth century in France was, at least men were speculating about the problems of society. But between this thought and the policies of government there was an almost impassable gulf. The men who ruled France were not economically minded, and their electorate, as has been said, was largely one of landed proprietors. Hence the ruling élite was not likely to be interested in industrial development; and the comparative backwardness of French social conditions and economic development, for which the social structure of the *ancien régime* and the diversions of the Revolution and the Empire were in part responsible, continued under the so-called bourgeois monarchy.

A glance at some figures will easily substantiate this statement. The horse power at the service of French industry in 1832 was under 1,000; by 1848 it had multiplied by nearly seven times, but in Great Britain six times as

The Constitutional Monarchy

much horse power had already been employed in the twenties. In 1790 French production of coal was about one-twentieth of that of Great Britain. Its production increased by about three times under the July Monarchy, but it was still not sufficient to satisfy even the modest needs of France. The amount of iron ore mined more than doubled; but behind a high protective tariff the price of iron was far higher than in Great Britain and production far lower. Modern methods were only gradually introduced in smelting. The last charcoal furnace in France ceased production in the course of the First World War.

More progress was made in transport but adequate capital for its development was lacking. There was a historical reason for this. The provision of highways and bridges in France had always been the prerogative of the public service of the Ponts et Chaussées, and it was traditional for the state to finance them. Under the July Monarchy the nation demanded improved means of transport and the government was in fact prepared to go a long way towards meeting this demand. It could only do so, however, by government expenditure; and as fast as the announcement of a programme of public works aroused support, the finance necessary to pay for them aroused opposition. Moreover, since the wealthy class which formed the narrow electorate also included those who contracted for the works, suspicions of corruption, which were often too well founded, were naturally aroused. Some progress, of course, was made. A law of 1836 on the construction and upkeep of local roads was of considerable benefit to the rural population; and the length of canals in use doubled under the July Monarchy.

Railways were developed very slowly and with a good deal of discouragement from above. When a line was projected from Paris to Saint-Germain, Thiers declared it might be worth constructing as an amusement for the Parisians; and the scientist Arago warned against the menace to human health involved in travelling by rail. Private capital was unwilling to risk itself in the construction of railways; while the Charter blocked the spending of public money on them. In 1842 a compromise was reached by which the state should buy the land, and plan and lay out the lines, while private capital supplied the actual rails and rolling-stock. There followed, from 1844 to 1846, the first French railway mania. It was of short duration and was followed by a collapse of railway shares and a financial crisis. Too many of the new lines, indeed, had been constructed to serve the interests of local politicians rather than economic demand. In 1848 many of the little local lines were bankrupt, and France had 1,921 kilometres of railways, compared with 3,424 in Prussia and 6,349 in Great Britain.

The first half of the nineteenth century in Great Britain has been described as the period of the race between population and industrialization. In France, while population was increasing only slowly, the level of production was rising even more slowly. Inevitably the standard of living fell and the material for a social revolution piled up, at least in the large towns. A bad harvest or a slump in business would produce a critical situation. Economic factors do not make revolutions by themselves, however, and to understand how the Orleanist régime met its fate we must turn back to politics.

For all the apparent strength of the Guizot administration, it was attacked with increasing vehemence from both left and right – this should not have surprised a régime which claimed to represent the *juste milieu*. The attack from the right took the form of a challenge to its educational policy. The quarrel was bound to become acute with the progress of both religious and state systems of schools. The achievement of the Restoration in education has seldom been adequately appreciated. A decree of 1816 laid it down that there should be a school in every commune and that education should be free for the children of parents who could not afford to pay. This represented an ideal rather than a fact, but by 1820 out of 44,000 communes there were schools in 24,000, a great advance on the previous situation.

The Constitutional Monarchy

The last government of Charles X issued an abortive law reorganizing the teaching service. Guizot, in 1833, repeated the effort in a law which has been called the first charter of primary education in France. Each commune, or group of neighbouring communes, was to have a primary school, and each department, or group of departments, a training college for elementary school-teachers, the *école normale primaire*. Between 1830 and 1848 the number of *écoles normales* grew from 12 to 47. Secondary schools were obligatory in the chief towns of each department, and in all towns with more than 6,000 inhabitants. These schools were either conducted by lay *instituteurs*, teachers who had to have a certificate from a training college, or by brothers of a religious order who were exempted from the requirement. This privilege of the religious schools of course ensured that the state schools would gradually come to be educationally superior. At the same time, by putting the teachers under rigid local and central control, the law of Guizot ensured that they could only escape from the control of the Church by falling under that of the state.

The importance of the rôle of the teachers in inculcating law and order and a proper respect for the powers that be was recognized from the beginning, recognized that is in principle, but not in material recompense. Guizot's circular to the teachers in 1833 was engagingly frank on this point. 'A profound sentiment of the importance of his work must sustain and animate the teacher,' he wrote; 'the austere pleasure of having served mankind and contributed to the public weal must be the worthy payment which his conscience alone gives him. It is his glory to use himself up in sacrifices and to expect his reward only from God.' This was true to the facts, if tactless; but a class of underpaid teachers, with at least more instruction than the petty local tyrants of Church and State who rendered them fully conscious of their social and financial inferiority, was not in fact likely to provide a cement of society.

Of course the more schools there were, the more intense became the competition between Church and State for the control of them. The July Monarchy had started off, as we have seen, to the accompaniment of a violent anti-clerical reaction against the clericalism of the Restoration. The affiliations of the Church, moreover, were naturally with the divine-right monarchy and therefore with the legitimists. By 1841, when the new Archbishop of Paris, Mgr Affre, paid an official visit to the king, relations between Church and State seemed much ameliorated; but a strong faction in the Church, led by the clerical journalist Louis Veuillot and the *Univers*, persistently agitated against what was called the 'University monopoly' of education. The parties of the left retaliated by reviving the Jesuit bogey. In 1843 Michelet and Edgar Quinet published jointly the courses they had given at the Collège de France under the title *Des iésuites*; but the clerical campaign, organized by the Catholic writer Montalembert, was the more effective.

The government offered a new law on education in 1844, making various concessions. Quinet's lectures were suppressed. Guizot brought himself to declare, in 1846, that children belonged to the family before the State, and that the State did not claim the exclusive right of education: religion also had its rights. Unfortunately clerical ambitions had grown with the success of the clerical propaganda, and it turned out that the new educational law proposed by the government, because it provided definitions where there had previously been laxity, threatened to make the situation of clerical education worse instead of better. Moreover the anti-Jesuit campaign had unexpected success. Montalembert and the party of 'liberty of education' were dissatisfied. Legitimism, which was also practically invariably ardently Catholic, remained unreconciled to the rule of Louis-Philippe. Religious opinion was in no state of mind to support the régime in an emergency, if one occurred.

On the other side, the left, so badly defeated in the early thirties, had been continuing its apparently hopeless opposition in the press and at the polls. The *National*, edited by Armand Marrast, denounced the corruption of the political system unceasingly, though it only called for

The Constitutional Monarchy

moderate and peaceful reforms. Those for whom it was too moderate, inspired by the eloquent young lawyer, Ledru-Rollin, the rising hope of the more advanced reformers, founded, in 1843, the *Réforme*, as an organ of more democratic opinion. The radicals were now rallying their forces for the first time since the disaster of 1834, and in the demand for universal suffrage they had found a principle on which to unite.

Though Ledru-Rollin, surprisingly, given such a narrow franchise, secured election to the Chamber of Deputies, the parliamentary opposition as a whole had really more quarrel with the personnel than with the system of government. In 1845 Odilon Barrot and Thiers, tired of seeing another minister instead of themselves in office for the unexampled space of nearly five years, joined forces on a programme of electoral and parliamentary reform. It seemed the only way to shift Guizot, and it gave them the opportunity to join in the cry, always popular in France, of corruption.

In 1846 Guizot appealed confidently to a satisfied electorate, which hardly needed the nips and nudgings of the prefects to be gathered safely into the fold. The governmental machine could congratulate itself on a notable triumph when, after the elections, the address from the throne was accepted by a vote of 248 to 84. The majority was indeed almost too large for its own good. There were too many 'progressive conservatives', like de Tocqueville, in its ranks – enough in fact to elect an opposition candidate as vice-president of the chamber. The awkward subject of parliamentary reform and the extension of the franchise reappeared, though the government produced the – to it – decisive argument that if the country – that is the existing privileged class of electors – had wanted the franchise to be extended, it would have shown this in the election. Guizot revealed behind the demand for the extension of the franchise the terrifying shadow of universal suffrage, and made the classic pronouncement, *'Il n'y aura pas de jour pour le suffrage universel.'*

The cry of corruption was still the most effective weapon that the opposition had, and though there is no reason to suppose that the Guizot régime was any more corrupt than those which preceded or followed it, circumstances enabled this cry to be exploited effectively at what was to be a critical time. A criminal trial in 1847 brought out in evidence the correspondence of a former Minister of War, which revealed large payments, for the purpose of securing industrial concessions, to the then Minister of Public Works, Teste, now President of the Appeal Court and a peer of France. Teste was prosecuted and attempted suicide. Both of the former ministers were condemned to civic degradation and three years in prison.

This was followed by the affair of the duc de Praslin, who battered his wife to death for love of an English governess. Brought to trial before the peers, he succeeded in committing suicide with arsenic. Together these cases were taken as a revelation of the manner of life of the governing class, which itself had its confidence sapped by such apparent justification for the continual denunciations of corruption to which it was subjected.

Meanwhile the parliamentary opposition, seeing how hopeless the situation was in the Chamber, determined to carry the campaign to the country. In July 1847 it organized the first of a series of political banquets, at which leading orators denounced the government, made much play with corruption, and called for parliamentary reform. Thiers, who abstained from the banquets, was himself conducting an unrestrained campaign of speeches in the Chamber against the foreign policy of Guizot. The minister and the king, confident in their parliamentary majority and forgetting how little it really represented in the country, did not weaken before the verbal attacks from all sides. In January 1848 they prohibited further banquets, and the opposition, now becoming a little alarmed at its own boldness, but unwilling to lose face by yielding too obviously, made a private arrangement with the authorities. Its supporters were to assemble for the banquet, but to accept

The Constitutional Monarchy

a police order to disperse peaceably, and the case would then be tried in the courts. This was very reasonable for it was really only a squabble between different factions in the small governing class. Banqueteers do not come from the ranks of the disinherited, and the opposition only wished to exert sufficient pressure to put themselves and their friends in, and Guizot and his friends out.

But while the parliamentary leaders were preparing to retreat, their followers were pressing forward. The two journals, the *National* and the *Réforme*, were the centres of a more determined agitation. They called on the people of Paris to take up the struggle that the deputies had abandoned. This was to introduce a factor into the situation which on all sides had been curiously ignored. It is a striking comment on the class structure of France that the governing class, engaged in its political rivalries, does not appear to have thought that the condition of the people was anything that needed to be taken into consideration.

A bad harvest in 1846 and potato blight had affected most of Western Europe. An industrial crisis also brought widespread unemployment. The slump had perhaps touched bottom in 1847 and the curve of economic activity was beginning to rise again, but those who were suffering from it, with little attempt at relief from public or private charity, could hardly be expected to appreciate this fact. Again, as in 1787-9, and to a lesser extent in 1830, a political agitation coincided with an economic crisis, and those who had started the agitation found that it led them much farther than they ever intended or expected. As in 1830, the basic fact was the refusal of the king to be parted from his minister until it was too late, and in his fall the minister dragged the king down with him.

In place of the abandoned banquet of 22 February 1848 there was a popular procession of protest through the streets. The government felt the need for a counter-demonstration, and though the king had not reviewed the National Guard since 1840, it was summoned to his defence. Unwillingly it assembled on the morrow at the *mairies* of the different *arrondissements*, but as its members made their way to their appointed places they called out '*Vive la Réforme!*', presented a petition at the Palais Bourbon, where the Chamber of Deputies sat, sang the Marseillaise, prevented the troops of the line from controlling the crowds, and shouted '*À bas Guizot!*' Unwillingly Louis-Philippe, after a fatal delay, through the veils of aged self-satisfaction and obstinacy appreciated that something unusual was happening, and asked for the resignation of his minister.

Now it was seen that there had in fact been some point in his clinging to office, for the whole system disintegrated when the man who had been the key-stone of the arch fell. Indignation among those who had staked their whole political future on the survival of the régime, was followed by a *sauve-qui-peut*. The politicians began to look for an alternative, and in the streets the crowds were getting out of hand. The king appointed Molé to succeed Guizot, and Bugeaud, who had mastered Paris in 1831 and 1834, to the command of the army. The dismissal of Guizot took some of the edge off the crowds ranging up and down the boulevards, and it still seemed that the situation might be saved. But then, late on the evening of 23 February, occurred the incident which turned a riot into a revolution. Victor Hugo gives a vivid description of the episode. He writes, 'The crowds which I had seen start cheerfully singing down the boulevards, at first went on their way peacefully and without resistance. The regiment, the artillery, the cuirassiers opened their ranks everywhere for their passage. But on the boulevard des Capucines a body of troops, both infantry and cavalry, was massed on the two pavements and across the road, guarding the Ministry of Foreign Affairs and its unpopular minister, M. Guizot. Before this impassable obstacle, the head of the popular column tried to stop and turn aside; but the irresistible pressure of the huge crowd weighed on the front ranks. At this moment a shot rang out, from which side is not known. Panic followed and then a volley. Eighty dead or wounded remained on the spot. A universal cry of horror and fury arose: Vengeance! The

The Constitutional Monarchy

bodies of the victims were loaded on a cart lit with torches. The cortège moved back amidst curses at a funeral pace. And in a few hours Paris was covered with barricades.'

On 24 February the king replaced Molé with Thiers, ordered Bugeaud to withdraw his troops, and spent the day in political negotiations. Paris was now in the hands of the mob, which had captured the Hôtel de Ville and advanced on the Tuileries. After the disaster of the previous day there seems to have been no serious thought of an appeal to the army, though it was still loyal and had its links with the dynasty. The sons of Louis-Philippe were closely associated with the army. The duc d'Aumale had fought in Algeria, where he was now governor-general; the duc d'Orléans was popular in military circles because of the interest he had always taken in the army. Nevertheless, outside Paris, and once the riots had triumphed there, not a shot was fired in defence of the dynasty.

On the afternoon of 24 February, collapsing in senile despair, Louis-Philippe abdicated in favour of his grandson, the little comte de Paris. It was the end of a régime that had been so lacking in principle that it could only be known by the name of the month of its founding, as the July Monarchy.

III

THE SECOND REPUBLIC AND THE SECOND EMPIRE

1: 1848: FROM THE FEBRUARY DAYS TO THE JUNE DAYS

1848 IN FRANCE was a revolution by accident. If the revolution had not happened then, it may be said, as of other revolutions, that it would have happened at some other time, whenever the 'conjuncture' – the term in current French historical jargon that has replaced the 'psychological moment' – was appropriate. But of course, if it had occurred later or earlier it would have occurred in different circumstances and would have been a different revolution. The revolution was not the fore-ordained result of the emergence of new social forces that could not be contained in the old institutions, for none of adequate importance had yet arisen; it was rather the accidental though highly probable result of the inherent weakness of government in France. Since 1789 no régime had possessed the conditions necessary for stability. A series of political upheavals had fragmented conservative forces, the unity of which was the prerequisite of political stability, by introducing ideological cleavages which cut across economic ties and destroyed the cohesion of the forces of property and order. Simplifying the situation, we may say that in 1848 the propertied classes were split between the old *noblesse*, legitimists, and clericals, for whom an Orleanist king was worse than no king at all; those men of property and officials who liked to think themselves liberal, who were inclined towards anti-clericalism and reasonably satisfied with Louis-Philippe; and a rising class of educated and professional men, of varied economic standing, with republican sympathies. As for the mass of rural small proprietors, because of the memory of 1789 the peasants were still labelled in the public mind as potential revolutionaries: the events of June 1848 were to show how mistaken was this opinion, but in February there was no way in which their weight could be cast into the scales against change.

Indeed, hardly any element in French society outside Paris could materially influence events in the crisis of February. This was a second inheritance from the Revolution and Napoleon: authority had been concentrated so thoroughly in the ministries at Paris that whoever held Paris held France. And Paris, of course, was the most difficult part of France to hold. Under the Orleanist monarchy it was a witch's cauldron fermenting with dangerous ideological ingredients.

The collapse of divine right left a void, which the revolutionaries of 1789 attempted unsuccessfully to fill. Their principles were too self-contradictory, and too difficult to reconcile with hard political and social facts, to provide the ideological basis for a new society. The new ruling classes that emerged from Revolution and Empire had used democratic and egalitarian ideas to justify their attack on the older privileged classes, but with no intention of allowing the same principles to be turned against themselves. France, throughout the nineteenth century, was an oligarchy of wealth, especially landed wealth, and office; but unlike the British governing classes in the same period, the French *élite* was insecure, not only because its internal divisions went much deeper, but also because it did not believe in itself. It had no reason to: it had neither inherited an old tradition of government nor had it evolved any Burkian or Benthamite philosophy to provide a moral basis for its new powers and privileges. Too often its self-justification took the form of a cynical assertion of material interests. At the same time it lacked the crude virtues of a get-rich-quick society. Sunk in a stubborn and unimaginative defence of its vested interests, it lacked the enterprise necessary even for its own economic progress. With only a little harshness, we might say that the French ruling class, heir of the great Revolution, was devoid of social conscience, devoted – inevitably – to its own property rights, and indifferent – not quite so inevitably – to the conditions of life, or death, of the populace beneath it. Because the ruling classes were weak they feared to make concessions in advance, but were quick to appeal to force when a threat had materialized. The Orleanist monarchy has been unfairly blamed for its failure to alleviate the misery caused by the economic crisis of the forties: this is to be attributed to the forces of society rather than to the fault of the government.

There was no reason to fear any threat to the social order from conditions in the countryside or in the provincial towns, apart from Lyon. Paris was another matter. The population of the capital was both growing and changing in character. The centralization of the life of France in Paris played its part in promoting the drift of population there, even from comparatively distant provinces and before the railway era. Beginning as a seasonal immigration, it turned into a permanent transfer. Under the Orleanist monarchy the population of Paris, within what were to be the increased limits of 1860, grew from roughly 860,000 to 1,250,000. There had been little industrial development to give work to these extra arms, and little increased agricultural production to provide food for the mouths. There is no coincidence in the fact that two countries which escaped serious trouble in 1848 were the only two in which industrialization had made substantial progress – Great Britain (but not Ireland) and Belgium. In France the population, already before 1789 rather more than the country could support without a declining standard of living, had continued to grow, though at a slower rate, with no substantial industrialization to assist in its absorption.

How a political quarrel between the Ins and the Outs unintentionally set fire to this inflammable social situation has already been indicated. Perhaps it would not have done so if there had not already been 1789 to provide such a

A History of Modern France

model. So de Tocqueville thought. In the presence of the revolutionary mob which invaded the Assembly, he could not persuade himself, he said, that there was a real danger of bloodshed, despite the muskets and bayonets and sabres. *'Nos Français,'* he wrote, *'surtout à Paris, mêlent volontiers les souvenirs de la littérature et du théâtre à leurs manifestations les plus sérieuses.'* It seemed to him, he added, that they were playing at the French Revolution rather than continuing it. The revolution of 1848, Marx said, could find nothing better to do than to parody that of 1789-95. Nevertheless the fighting in February was real enough to destroy a monarchy; the days of June 1848 were to see a bitterer social war than ever the first Revolution knew; and an empire was to emerge from the republic in four years instead of fourteen.

Once the régime of Louis-Philippe and Guizot had collapsed in Paris, its hollowness was shown by the rapidity with which its adherents joined in a general *sauve qui peut* and proclaimed their allegiance, along with legitimists, republicans, clericals, anti-clericals, liberals, socialists, and all, to the revolutionary government. In its opening days this was a revolution of fraternity and universal love. The hero of Flaubert's *L'Éducation sentimentale,* after the February Days revisiting the fair friend whom he had left on his previous visit in a somewhat disgruntled frame of mind, found that the revolution had restored harmony. 'Now that all was peaceful and there was no cause for fear, she kissed him and declared herself for the Republic – as Monseigneur the Archbishop of Paris had already done, and as, with a marvellous alacrity, the Magistrature, the Council of State, the Institute, the Marshals of France, Changarnier, M. de Falloux, all the Bonapartists, all the Legitimists, and a considerable number of Orleanists, were to do.'

The government to which France entrusted its fate, of course provisionally, on the morrow of the February revolution, was as accidental a product as the revolution itself. The Chamber of Deputies, which was an

The Second Republic and the Second Empire

Orleanist chamber, was watching with hearts full of sentiment the lovely Duchess of Orleans, mother of Louis-Philippe's grandson in favour of whom he had abdicated, and listening to emotional appeals on their behalf – 'The crown of July', declared Odilon Barrot, 'rests on the head of a child and a woman' – when the *blouses* and the National Guards burst into the hall with shouts of '*À bas la Chambre*', '*Plus de députés*'. The courage of the members and the hopes of the dynasty vanished together: only a republican government would pacify the mob. Out of the tumult the names of seven leading republican figures – Lamartine, Ledru-Rollin, Marrast, Arago, Crémieux, Marie, Garnier-Pagès – emerged. At the Hôtel de Ville a left-wing demonstration had put forward the socialists Flocon and Louis Blanc, and a solitary, symbolic (of nothing in particular) worker, Albert. These names were added, and thus did France receive its new government.

The first act of the Provisional Government was to proclaim the right of universal suffrage, swelling the electorate overnight from a quarter of a million to nine millions, and laying the foundations for the subsequent Bonapartist dictatorship. Next, it abolished slavery on all French territory, thus freeing about half a million slaves, a belated reform, introduced without any preparation or precautions, which brought immediate economic disaster to the slave colonies.

A more pressing problem was that of unemployment in France, and principally Paris. The general European slump had reached bottom in 1847 and conditions were slowly improving; but in France the uncertainty produced in the business world by the Revolution prohibited any recovery and in 1848 the economic crisis was intensified. Shops were closed, craftsmen without work, men dismissed from the few factories; credit was lacking, private charity quite inadequate, and government assistance totally absent. To the starving horde of unemployed, or to those who were vocal amongst them, one idea had filtered down. How the economic position had changed in the past half century is shown by the shape of this idea. They no longer, as between 1789 and 1794, called for a maximum on prices; the demand now was for work, embodied in Louis Blanc's formula, *le droit au travail*. It is evidence that the labouring masses in the towns now thought of themselves primarily as producers rather than as consumers.

In a revolutionary situation something had to be done to satisfy their demands or those of their spokesmen. It was not too difficult to find an innocuous solution. Louis Blanc and Albert, political innocents compared with the politicians, were put at the head of a Parliament of Industry which met at the Luxembourg and was allowed to talk its way through the crisis. Louis Blanc's plan for National Workshops, which involved the state in providing credits for industry, was rejected. To the Minister of Public Works, Marie, and many others, it seemed a revolutionary proposal, alien to the spirit of brotherhood that had prevailed in February. If the name National Workshops was adopted, it was only as a sop to the followers of Louis Blanc; in fact all the Workshops, or Ateliers, ever amounted to was a system of registering the Paris unemployed for the payment of a wretched dole. By June 1848 some 120,000 were in receipt of this pittance and the lists had been closed to exclude perhaps 50,000 more. To give the impression that something was being done, a young engineer named Thomas was entrusted with the task of organizing the so-called Workshops. In spite of opposition, he managed to set about 12,000 men to work levelling a small hill on the site of what was later the boulevard Montparnasse. The prevailing attitude of mind among the wealthy classes, though intensely protectionist in relation to foreign trade, was sternly non-interventionist in respect of internal economic activity. When the government of Louis-Philippe had proposed to meet the economic crisis of 1847 by a programme of public works, a legislative body of proprietors naturally rejected the proposal. The Provisional Government, in so far as it ever even contemplated the same programme, met with the same resistance.

The Second Republic and the Second Empire

Orthodox economics also insisted, and more successfully than in 1789, that the National Debt was sacred. To maintain public credit, interest continued to be paid scrupulously on state loans, the budgetary gap being filled by imposing an extra tax of 45 centimes, which fell mainly on the peasantry. This was the most misconceived of all the Provisional Government's measures. Whereas the National Assembly of 1789 had, intentionally or unintentionally, lightened the burdens of the peasantry, the revolution of 1848 actually increased them. Here is at least one factor which helps to explain the changed attitude of the peasants to revolution.

The mutual fear and suspicion of the middle classes and the populace in Paris, which had been violently intensified, though not created, by the economic crisis, came into the open very early in the Revolution. On 16 March the better-off members of the National Guard, distinguished by their uniform and fur caps, staged a rather futile demonstration which is known as the manifestation of the *bonnets à poil*. There followed on the next day an imposing and far larger counter-demonstration by masses of Paris workers. The situation was tense but Ledru-Rollin, known as the most sympathetic to the people among the middle-class republican leaders, acquired considerable, though not lasting, prestige by pacifying the demonstrators. Though the great body of conservative republicans did not trust him and detested his ideas of moderate social reform, it was evident that he could not be dispensed with while the danger from below existed; so he had to be tolerated.

In the key position of Minister of the Interior, Ledru-Rollin had the responsibility for organizing the election of a Constituent Assembly. Universal suffrage represented a leap in the dark, and the more they thought about the implications of this sudden and unprepared granting of their democratic demands, the darker the outlook seemed to the democratic factions; for the great mass of the new electors were illiterate peasants, likely to follow the lead of their clergy, local landowners, and notables. The only hope the left-wing politicians could see lay in a postponement of the elections, to give them time to indoctrinate the peasants and teach them who their real friends were. Hence a series of petitions flowed in from the clubs of Paris in favour of postponing the elections, which was also one of the demands of the demonstrators of 17 March. In more general terms it may be said that the democrats of 1848 were faced with the constant dilemma of democracy: can the sovereign people, if it so wishes, be allowed to abdicate, has it the right to repudiate democracy? Suppose it chooses to follow a conservative, or even a reactionary policy, instead of a progressive and reforming one, is this permissible? The members of the great Committee of Public Safety had been faced with the same question and their answer was the Terror. Ledru-Rollin and the republicans of 1848 did not contemplate this solution. They would doubtless have been less despised by historians if they had been more bloody-minded. Unfortunately they were idealists who believed in their own principles.

Within the limits which seemed legitimate to him, Ledru-Rollin did what he could towards the winning of the elections. The essential first step was the replacement of the Orleanist administrative machine. All the prefects, and all but twelve of the sub-prefects, were dismissed, and revolutionary commissaires appointed in their place. By mid-April tried republicans were at the head of practically every department. The Provisional Government instructed them not to imitate the usurping governments of the past in corrupting the electors. Ledru-Rollin, rather more frankly, addressed them with the rhetorical question 'What are your powers?' and replied, 'They are unlimited. ... The elections are your great task.' By this he meant that the duty of the commissaires was to enlighten the electors and purge the administration of non-republican officials who might exercise a dangerous influence.

The discredited and disorganized Orleanist machine could not resist Ledru-Rollin. On the other hand the clerical party, with an anti-Orleanist record behind it, was

The Second Republic and the Second Empire

not afraid to engage in open political agitation under the leadership of Montalembert's central Committee for Electoral Liberty. It was supported energetically by most of the bishops. Few leaders of the Church were as far-seeing as the bishop of Viviers, later Cardinal Guibert, who wrote, 'I am convinced that we are doing an imprudent thing, and that the few votes in favour of religious liberty we may be able to send to the Chamber are not worth the sacrifice of the fine position we have won by our isolation from political power since 1830.'

Faced with the clerical threat, the Minister of Education, Hippolyte Carnot, called on the village school-teachers to counteract the clergy by spreading the republican faith. This was the beginning of the ideological struggle between the *curé* and the *instituteur*, but the struggle was as yet a very uneven one. The Church was still far stronger than the State in the rural communes, and the republicans were not unaware of this fact. Possibly they fixed on Easter Sunday for the elections in the hope of keeping the faithful away from the elections. If so, it was a gross miscalculation. Mass was celebrated at an early hour in the morning, and the villagers marched to vote with the priest at the head of the procession, sometimes in harmony, sometimes in undignified rivalry, with a republican *maire*.

Apart from propaganda, a game at which the local notabilities and priest could usually defeat Ledru-Rollin's commissaires, the elections were notably free. The failure of the more advanced republicans supported by Ledru-Rollin is evidence of that: Ministers of the Interior did not normally lose elections in nineteenth-century France. There was a poll of 84 per cent and the vote of the peasantry ensured that the Constituent Assembly should be in a majority conservative and traditionalist in its complexion. Four-fifths of the deputies were men of the district which elected them; four-fifths were also over 40; nearly 700 out of nearly 900 were men of substance paying a tax of over 500 francs a year. Half the deputies were monarchists, divided into some 300 Orleanists and 150 Legitimists.

About 350 were committed to support the clerical campaign for freedom of education. There was a mere sprinkling of red republicans, and still fewer socialists. The conservative nature of the Assembly was demonstrated by the voting on two proposals. Only 82 members supported a motion recognizing the right to work; and only 110 out of 900 were in favour of that most revolutionary of all measures, a graduated income tax. Of course, even a vote of one in eight for such a measure would have been inconceivable in the great French Revolution. Ledru-Rollin's attempt to secure an advanced republican Assembly had thus decisively failed. His influence in the government naturally declined, and he would probably have been pushed out of it by the new Assembly if it had not been for the support of Lamartine, who thereby sacrificed much of his own prestige.

It was an Assembly interested in political, but opposed to all economic, change. From the beginning it exhibited the besetting sin of the Second Republic, an obsession with political dogma. This appeared in the Assembly's insistence on turning the Provisional Government into an Executive Commission, appointed by the Assembly, which had the duty of deliberating on policy, while a separate body of Ministers had the duty of carrying it out. This division was introduced for the purpose of maintaining the sacred principle of the separation of powers.

The left-wing leaders of Paris, frustrated by the elections, carried on an increasingly bitter agitation in the press and the popular clubs. Their violent speeches, invocations to social revolution, songs like

Chapeau bas devant ma casquette,
À genoux devant l'ouvrier,

did not lessen the alarm of the middle and upper classes. Since one thing that all France definitely wanted was not to be involved in a revolutionary war, with characteristic ineptitude the club leaders decided to use a petition for assistance to the Polish revolution as the excuse for an

The Second Republic and the Second Empire

attempt to overthrow the National Assembly by a mob demonstration after the established model. This attempted 'push' on 15 May, under the revolutionary leaders, Barbès and Blanqui, who hated one another even more than they hated their opponents, was easily put down by the regular troops and the National Guard. Its only result was that practically all the left-wing agitators disappeared from the political scene, either in flight abroad or into prison. Hence they cannot be held responsible for the great popular rising of June.

The revolt of the June Days is one of the most mysterious episodes of its kind. It is not easy to find another popular movement, especially of such magnitude, in which not a single leader, even of the second or third rank, can be identified. The psychological preparation for the June Days is not difficult to see, and it can be granted that there was plenty of inflammable material in Paris. The hope of salvation, with which the unemployed and starving masses had poured out of their garrets and cellars in February, had given place to disillusionment when under a republic economic conditions became worse instead of better. Class hatred in Paris reached perhaps its highest point, before the Commune, in 1848. De Tocqueville, returning to the capital after the elections, found the aspect of Paris terrible and sinister. 'I saw society split in two: those who possessed nothing united in a common greed; those who possessed something in a common fear. No bonds, no sympathies existed between these two great classes, everywhere was the idea of an inevitable and approaching struggle.'

It is a classic fact of revolutions in a predominantly agrarian economy that the late spring or early summer is the point of greatest danger, when the previous year's harvest is exhausted and the new one has not yet come in. Semi-starvation was the lot of the masses of unemployed in Paris. The dole handed out by the so-called National Workshops was only a slight alleviation of their misery, and even so, many of the unemployed were excluded from it and the National Assembly was determined to get rid of it as rapidly as possible. For the chairman of the Labour Committee of the Assembly, the comte de Falloux – a devoted son of the Church and proud aristocrat, whose grandfather, a cattle-merchant, had been ennobled by Louis XVIII in 1823 – the National Workshops were 'a permanent and organized strike', 'an active centre of dangerous agitation'. To the suggestion that if they were dissolved there might be resistance, he replied, 'Have you not the National Guard? ... Take what measures you choose, we guarantee they will not meet with serious resistance; and if we do encounter it, let us not be afraid to use force, force without the shedding of blood but that moral force which belongs to the law.'

As a result partly of de Falloux's pressure, on 22 June it was decreed that all unmarried workers in the National Workshops should join the army, and the remainder go to the provinces, under penalty of losing their payments. This seems to have been the spark which set off the rising in Paris, though how or why is far from clear. It is alleged that those who were enrolled in the National Workshops did not in fact participate in the June Days to any great extent, but there is no doubt that it was, as it seemed to contemporaries like de Tocqueville, a workers' movement, a revolt of the helots, a servile war. The numbers involved in the actual fighting must not be exaggerated; they were probably not more than 20,000, one in ten or less of the workers of Paris. Their first step was to erect barricades, which cut off the poorer quarters of Paris. These were necessary because with the black powder then used it was difficult to fire from other than a standing position. Held by desperate men, with flanking fire from windows, in the narrow, winding streets of old Paris, the barricades could only be taken when cannon had been set up against them, which was a slow and dangerous process. Then, when a barricade had been rendered untenable, its defenders could move back, breaking through the party walls of the houses, to another line of defence prepared in advance.

The unresisted opening stages of the revolt were possible

The Second Republic and the Second Empire

because of the absence of troops, which was due not to calculation but to the difficulty of provisioning them in Paris and to the lack of barracks; but once the regular troops were brought into action the result was a foregone conclusion. The general entrusted with putting down the revolt, Cavaignac, a staunch republican but also intensely conservative, moved in infantry and artillery steadily for the kill. The army was reinforced by detachments of National Guard, volunteers from the provinces, where the hatred of Paris had reached fever pitch. Even at the time of the election of the Constituent Assembly de Tocqueville had been struck with the spirit of fraternity which sprang up between all owners of property, rich or poor, in his rural department of the Manche, and the universal hatred and terror which they experienced at the thought of the 'anarchists' of Paris.

In six days of bitter street fighting the rebel quarters were conquered street by street. How many of the insurgents were killed in the struggle or shot out of hand when captured cannot be estimated. The prisoners, thousands of whom were to be sent as forced immigrants to Algeria, were piled into improvised dungeons such as Flaubert describes: 'Nine hundred men were there, crowded together in filth, pell-mell, black with powder and clotted blood, shivering in fever and shouting in frenzy. Those who died were left to lie with the others. Now and then, at the sudden noise of a gun, they thought they were all on the point of being shot, and then flung themselves against the walls, afterwards falling back into their former places. They were so stupefied with suffering that they seemed to be living in a nightmare, a funeral hallucination. The lamp hanging from the arch looked like a patch of blood; and little green and yellow flames flew about, produced by the effluvium of the vaults. Because of a fear of epidemics a commission of enquiry had been appointed. On the first steps its president flung himself back, appalled by the odour of excrement and corpses. When the prisoners approached a ventilator, the National Guards on sentry duty stuck their bayonets, haphazard, into the crowd, to prevent them from loosening the bars.

'The National Guards were in general pitiless. Those who had not been in the fighting wanted to distinguish themselves now, but all was really the reaction of fear. They were avenging themselves at once for the journals, the clubs, the mobs, the doctrines, for everything that had provoked them beyond measure in the last three months; and despite their victory, equality (as if for the punishment of its defenders and mockery of its enemies) was triumphantly revealed – an equality of brute beasts on the same level of blood-stained depravity; for the fanaticism of vested interests was on a level with the madness of the needy, the aristocracy exhibited the fury of the basest mob, and the cotton night-cap was no less hideous than the *bonnet rouge*. The public mind became disordered as after a great natural catastrophe, and men of intelligence were idiots for the rest of their lives.'

Victor Hugo said that in the June Days civilization defended itself with the methods of barbarism. They were a turning-point in many respects. The army, like the peasants of which its ranks were so largely composed, passed from one side of the barricades to the other in June 1848. The Grande Peur of 1789, Valmy and Jemappes, the four sergeants of La Rochelle, and a host of other memories identified the peasant with social disorder and the army with revolution. Almost at a blow the myth – for it had become a myth by 1848 – was ended: the peasant became the embodiment of social conservatism and the army the bulwark of order.

2. THE TRIUMPH OF LOUIS NAPOLEON

AFTER the June Days the Army held power in France and the Assembly survived under its protection. 'This poor Assembly', wrote Victor Hugo, 'is a true soldier's girl, in love with a trooper.' The trooper was Cavaignac, whose principles excluded military dictatorship. He took the place

The Second Republic and the Second Empire

of the discredited Executive Commission and appointed a moderate republican ministry to hold office while the Assembly completed its constitutional proposals. It did this by November. The Constitution it made was much more influenced by theory than any of the preceding Constitutions since 1789. The change in social ideals in the course of sixty years can be seen in its preamble, which – significantly enough – took the place of the former declaration of rights. The individualism of 1789, with its emphasis on rights, now had to share its claims with a recognition of duties and a new emphasis on fraternity. This may not have meant much in the France of the June Days, but even lip-service was a sign of a changing climate of opinion. Politically there had been rather less change in republican ideals. There was still the old attempt to reconcile the principles of separation of powers and sovereignty of the people. All power comes from the people, but this power must be divided: the conclusion was the election of a single chamber and a unique head of the government, both by universal suffrage and both directly responsible to the people, the one entrusted with total legislative authority and the other with all executive power.

The crucial decision as it turned out later, and indeed as it appeared at the time, was the embodiment of the executive power in the person of a President elected directly by the whole nation. The election of the President by direct universal suffrage was supported by the right and the moderates, and opposed by Ledru-Rollin and the red republicans. The fear of the tyranny of a Convention still haunted moderate opinion: de Tocqueville warned against the danger of turning the President into a mere agent of the Legislative Body. Grévy, the author of a famous amendment, admitted the danger, but saw a more dangerous precedent in the career of Napoleon I. 'Are you sure', he asked the Assembly, 'that there will never be found an ambitious man, anxious to perpetuate his power, and if he is a man who had been able to make himself popular, if he is a victorious general, surrounded with the prestige of that military glory which the French cannot resist, if he is the offspring of one of the families which have reigned over France, and if he has never expressly renounced what he calls his rights [there could hardly have been a more obvious reference to Louis Napoleon], if commerce is languishing, if the people are in misery ... will you guarantee that this ambitious man will not succeed in overthrowing the republic?' The answer was given by Lamartine: If you want to do so, he said, confuse the legislative and executive powers, add the judicial and call your system by its true title – the Terror. He admitted that there were names which attracted the crowd as a mirage draws the flocks to it; but concluded, in a phrase from which his reputation has never recovered, *'Il faut laisser quelque chose à la Providence.'* The Grévy amendment was defeated by 643 to 158 votes and the Second Republic had committed a delayed suicide.

The Presidential election followed in December 1848. Among the candidates Cavaignac was the standard-bearer of the conservative republic and Ledru-Rollin of the red republicans; Raspail and a sprinkling of other candidates represented the left-wing; and there was a name of destiny – Louis Napoleon Bonaparte.

It is time to say something of Bonapartism as a political movement in France, now that at last it was on the point of becoming one. It may seem paradoxical, yet it is probably true, that the Napoleonic Legend, while essential to the existence of the Second Empire, played only a secondary part in its creation. About the origin of the Legend there need be little dispute; it was the deliberate creation of Napoleon I, by his official propaganda while he was Emperor, and in the imaginative picture he tried to draw while he was in exile of himself and his aims. To the legend of the pacifier who suppressed the internecine strife that had been tearing France apart, the protector of religion who had brought persecution to an end, the saviour who rescued society from the Jacobins and the Terror, the administrator who gave France efficient government and restored its financial and economic prosperity, the great general and

The Second Republic and the Second Empire

military hero who had made Europe into a French Empire, was added an even more mendacious picture of the great champion of liberal ideals, of freedom for the oppressed nationalities of Europe, and of peace. In 1815 the facts were a little too close for all this to have very much effect, and by 1830 the Napoleonic legend was no more than a romantic survival of no political significance. It seemed so little dangerous that the Orleanist régime did not hesitate to exploit Bonapartist sentiment for the purpose of acquiring a little badly needed popularity.

The two adventures of Louis Bonaparte, at Strasbourg in 1836 and Boulogne in 1840, confirmed the belief that Bonapartism, if it was not a spent fire, was one that was too damp ever to burst into flames again. The Emperor's nephew, it is true, had shown rather more skill with the pen than with the sword. He had produced, in 1832, a volume of *Rêveries politiques* – possibly not the best title to advertise its author as a man of action. More effective for the creation of a public image of the pretender – even if only an *image d'Épinal* like the popular cut-outs of Napoleon and his soldiers – were an artillery manual and a booklet on the extinction of pauperism. Louis Napoleon Bonaparte's most important production was *Des idées napoléoniennes* in 1839. This should have been taken more seriously than it was. As with later dictators, if it had been possible to believe that Louis Napoleon meant what he said, the subsequent history of France would have come as less of a surprise to contemporaries.

After the Boulogne adventure, Louis Bonaparte's light was extinguished for the next six years by not very rigorous imprisonment in the fortress at Ham, where he was provided with the modest amenities of life including a mistress, and from which he walked out disguised as a builder's labourer in 1846. In February 1848, therefore, he was again a potential saviour at the disposal of France, only hardly anyone as yet seemed to think of him in that capacity. He made a fleeting appearance in Paris soon after the revolution but found the political climate uncongenial and returned to London, where by enrolling as a special constable against the Chartists he did something to bury the memory of the carbonarist and conspirator and build up a picture of himself as the defender of law and order. So slight was the Bonapartist sentiment in France on the morrow of the revolution, that a Bonapartist paper could only survive from 25 February to 3 March, and the tiny group of devotees of Louis Napoleon could make no impression on public opinion.

By June there was evidently a change in this respect. Possibly the apparently imminent collapse of the social order had already started the swing to a potential saviour of society. Supplementary elections then returned Louis Napoleon for Paris and four other departments, with practically no organization or propaganda to support his candidature. This should have been an omen, but a miscalculated letter that he sent from London to the President of the Assembly aroused feeling in the Assembly against him. Wisely he appreciated that the time was not yet ripe and resigned. Further elections, in September, saw him returned in five constituencies and at the head of the Paris list. Despite this, the republicans of the Assembly for the most part remained unimpressed by the Bonapartist danger. When he rose in the Assembly, the insignificant appearance of the bearer of such a great name, and a halting speech in a German accent, convinced them that they were right. But though it would still be an exaggeration to speak of a Bonapartist party, supporters were gathering and conducting a more active propaganda, by journals and by the production of prints, medals, brooches, and knick-knacks of various kinds with Napoleonic inscriptions or associations.

As the presidential election came nearer the obscure Bonapartists who had been backing what had seemed for so long a forlorn hope found themselves joined by more prominent figures. Ambitious Orleanist politicians like Thiers and Odilon Barrot, disappointed in their expectation of office by the revolution they had done so much to provoke, hoped to use Louis Napoleon to return to power.

The Second Republic and the Second Empire

Barrot called him 'our excellent young man', and Thiers, who advised him to shave his moustache, said he was 'a cretin whom we will manage'. De Tocqueville, with a mixture of shrewdness and misjudgement, described him as 'an enigmatic, sombre, insignificant numskull'. Whatever their views of him personally, many former Orleanists, unfettered by attachment to political principles but with a keen eye on the main chance, prepared to jump on the Bonapartist band-wagon. More idealistic motives inspired Victor Hugo, who also kept a sentimental attachment to the memory of the Emperor his father had served. From the time of the *Ode à la colonne* his poems had done as much as any writings, except those of Béranger, to keep the Napoleonic memory alive. In 1848 he saw himself as the prophet and adviser of a liberal Bonaparte; and Louis Napoleon was not indifferent to the prestige that the support of France's greatest poet could give. After the election the poet was a guest at the first dinner given by the new President at the Élysée. The offer of the Madrid embassy tempted Hugo, with his memories of imperial Spain, but it was not what he had hoped for. In youth he had declared, '*Je veux être Chateaubriand ou rien*', and Chateaubriand had been Foreign Minister. Though disappointed, he continued to support the President until the 2 December added political to personal disillusionment.

The beautiful Miss Howard, with whom Louis Bonaparte had lived since 1846, came over in the autumn of 1848 to add her fortune to the others that were being invested in his future, and after the election to be for a time official mistress in the Prince President's little court. Spiritual support was added to secular. The clerical party, headed by Montalembert and Falloux, was legitimist in principle but prepared to do a deal with Louis Bonaparte in the interest of clerical control of education. Because Louis Napoleon had the support of the great banker Fould, it has been supposed that the financiers and also the industrialists were among his backers; but in fact they were more firmly Orleanist than the politicians, and suspicious of both the

A History of Modern France

ideas and the associates of Louis Bonaparte. On the other hand his connexion with the Saint-Simonians brought him the support of that sect and its adherents, such as the Péreire brothers. While the republicans remained aloof, some socialists saw hope in Bonapartism.

The two great journals of the February revolution opposed the Bonapartist candidature, the *Réforme* supporting Ledru-Rollin and the *National* Cavaignac. Louis Bonaparte had on his side Girardin's *Presse*, because of its editor's enmity to Cavaignac, the *Constitutionnel* under the influence of Thiers, Victor Hugo's *Événement*, and a number of provincial journals. But though the Bonapartists spent as much as they could on propaganda in the press, they only had the support of a minority of papers.

It is possible to believe that even if he had had none of this support Louis Bonaparte might still have been elected President. The populace in the large towns had no reason to vote for the victor of the June Days and the repressive and reactionary régime with which he was identified. The peasants of the countryside, who formed the great mass of the voters, were under the influence of a panic fear of red terror and confiscation of property spread by the men of order; they needed a saviour of society and who could fill that rôle better than a Napoleon. 'The idea of authority is attached to that name', wrote Barante, 'and it is authority that they want.' The idealism behind Ledru-Rollin, the social conservatism and official influence behind Cavaignac, were powerless against this wave of emotion. Ledru-Rollin secured 370,119 votes, Cavaignac 1,448,107, and Louis Napoleon 5,434,226; on the extreme left Raspail had a pitiable 36,920. Lamartine's star had long since set: in all France he could only gather 17,910 votes.

The first act of the new President was to take the oath of loyalty to the Republic and swear to defend the Constitution. If he had any mental reservations he kept them to himself; he was always good at keeping his own counsel. He appointed a conservative Orleanist ministry under Odilon Barrot, which reflected the political complexion of the

The Second Republic and the Second Empire

Assembly, left the government to them, and devoted his time to tours through France. This enabled him to exhibit his real brilliance as a propagandist, and at the same time to leave the onus of repressing the forces of the left on the Assembly. The red republicans had reacted to their defeat by drawing closer together in a nation-wide organization under the name of the Solidarité Républicaine, with central and local committees and a staunch Jacobin, Delescluze, as its secretary. The task of repression was begun with the outlawing of this society in January 1849.

The Constituent Assembly had no real justification for its continued existence now that the Constitution had been made and put into effect, but it hung on as long as it could, in a moribund condition. Finally it had to dissolve and in May 1849 elections were held for a Legislative Assembly. The conservative forces of all kinds, sometimes called the 'party of order' though they were too divided to constitute a real party, organized themselves for the election through a committee in the rue de Poitiers. It included legitimists, Orleanists, Bonapartists, Catholics, and even moderate republicans. The prefects, who had replaced Ledru-Rollin's commissaires, now returned to their customary rôle and played a large part in the elections. Of course, the supporters of order obtained a large majority of 500 out of 750 members. The conservative republicans of the *National*-Cavaignac school were reduced to a small group of 70; the men of February – Lamartine, Dupont de l'Eure, Garnier-Pagès, Marie, Marrast, Carnot, and others – were rejected by the country. What was unexpected and alarming to the forces of order was the comparative success of the red republicans, with 180 seats. Ledru-Rollin came second on the Paris list. The explanation, of course, lay in abstentions from voting, especially of many of the peasantry. The total vote in the country had sunk to 40 per cent of those entitled to vote, and of these one-third had voted for the reds. Evidently the left was still far from defeated. But what the conservative forces could not achieve in the elections, the left-wing politicians in Paris managed to do in a single day.

Undeterred by the lessons of 1848 they staged a futile attempt at revolution on 13 June 1849. Whereas in 1848 the cry had been Poland, now it was Rome. There was at least this justification for the demonstration: that a French force under Oudinot was about to overthrow the Roman Republic and reinstate the authority of Pius IX, which it did shortly after. The attempted insurrection in Paris and a number of provincial towns obtained no popular support. Ledru-Rollin and most of the left-wing deputies fled abroad, others were imprisoned; and the government and the Assembly had a fair excuse for passing more severe repressive legislation.

As well as an energetic suppression of the reds by police measures, the conservatives now began to feel that a more positive inculcation of the principles of social order was needed. The 'panic of property' which followed the June Days had weakened the anti-clericalism of many of the propertied classes and of their leaders such as Thiers. The merit of clerical education as a means of instilling the principles of social discipline and the sacredness of property into the minds of the lower orders was now more adequately appreciated. It found expression in an educational law proposed by Falloux in June 1849 and finally voted in March 1850. Meanwhile, in January 1850, had been voted the so-called 'little law' on education. This attributed the appointment and dismissal of primary teachers to the prefects, a right which they kept until 1944. The *loi Falloux* itself gave members of religious orders the right of opening schools without requiring any further qualification, and introduced councils with strong clerical elements to control the University.

On a general policy of weakening the left, the President and the Assembly were able to cooperate. But Louis Napoleon soon showed the Barrots and the Thiers that he was not the puppet President they thought they had elected. In October 1849, though it still had a majority in the Assembly, he dismissed the Odilon Barrot ministry and issued a message justifying his action to the country. 'To

The Second Republic and the Second Empire

strengthen the Republic menaced on all sides by anarchy,' he began, turning against themselves the chief weapon of the parliamentary factions, 'to maintain externally the name of France at the height of her renown, men are needed animated by a patriotic devotion, proof against everything, who understand the need for an undivided and strong rule and for a clearly formulated policy, who will not compromise authority by irresolution, and who will be as deeply conscious of my responsibility as of their own.' For his new ministry, therefore, he chose new men from outside parliament; and to show that it was to be a presidential and not a parliamentary government, he appointed no president of the council. He himself was to be its head.

President and Assembly, however, were still capable of receiving a shock from the country. In March 1850 by-elections were held to replace the 30 deputies condemned after the events of 13 June 1849. In the face of intense repression the democratic republicans rallied their forces once again. Despite all the efforts of the administration the left won 20 seats out of the 30, and in Paris the three left-wing candidates were returned with large majorities. In a subsequent election to fill a vacancy at Paris, the novelist Eugène Sue, now a name of terror to the respectable classes who had read his newspaper serials with avidity, was returned.

The panic of the Assembly revived: in spite of all the measures of repression, universal suffrage was still, it appeared, dangerous. In May 1850, therefore, a law was introduced to deprive of the franchise all who had suffered any condemnation by the courts – given the repressive legislation this would eliminate most of the militants of the left – and all who had not three years residential qualification in the same canton. The effect was to exclude about 3 million out of $9\frac{1}{2}$ million voters. Supported by Thiers with an unmeasured denunciation of the 'vile multitude', the law was passed in May 1850 by a majority of 433 to 241. It gave the President the opportunity to present himself once more as the defender of the rights of the people, and his demand for the abrogation of the law, in November 1850, was only rejected by 355 to 348.

Louis Napoleon had by now attracted to himself the support of a substantial group in the Assembly. By his propaganda tours, and the fact that his star was obviously still rising, he obtained an increasing backing in the country. He particularly worked on the army, and in January 1851 felt strong enough to dismiss the republican general Changarnier, who commanded the forces, both regular and National Guard, in Paris. Despite its earlier suspicions, the world of business, fearing a renewal of disorder when the President's mandate came to an end in 1852, and dissatisfied at the rather slow recovery from the slump, was now beginning to see its best hope in the continuance of Louis Napoleon at the head of the state.

Unfortunately this was not possible, or so it seemed. The constitution did not permit the re-election of the President. To overcome this obstacle the administration organized a campaign of petitions for its revision. So energetic and so successful were the prefects, that nearly all the *conseils généraux* in France supported the plea for revision. The Assembly yielded to this pressure by appointing a commission to examine the question, which concluded against the proposal. A vote in July 1851 was by 446 to 278 in favour of revision, but this was not the constitutionally necessary two-thirds majority. There was a renewed flood of petitions, but now Louis Napoleon and his little group of intimates had decided to settle the matter in an extra-parliamentary way.

The support of the army was ensured by bringing over from Algeria Saint-Arnaud and other colonial generals, with no civilian prejudices in favour of republics or parliamentary methods. The Bonapartist inner circle was now fairly complete. Louis Napoleon's half-brother Morny, a gambler of genius, was the chief organizer of the *coup d'état*. De Maupas, a *préfet à poigne*, was brought from Toulouse to become Prefect of Police. Persigny, who had shared Louis Bonaparte's defeats before 1848, rightly

The Second Republic and the Second Empire

joined in his coming triumph. After several postponements the *coup* was finally fixed for 2 December, the anniversary of Austerlitz.

On the night of 1-2 December the conspirators moved into action. Troops under an Algerian general occupied the Imprimerie Nationale, the Palais Bourbon, newspaper offices, printing works, and the main strategic points in Paris. In the *mairies* of the *arrondissements* the drums were broken, the bell-towers of the churches were guarded. The Parisians woke in the morning to find placards announcing the dissolution of the Assembly, the restoration of universal suffrage, new elections, and a state of siege in Paris and the neighbouring departments. In an *Appel au peuple* the President accused the Assembly of conspiracy – a nice touch – and fomenting disorder. A proclamation to the army declared, 'Soldiers! it is your mission to save the country.' Sixteen members of the Assembly and some 80 other known opponents were seized by troops in their homes. Some 300 deputies, excluded from their chamber, met in the *mairie* of the X^e *arrondissement* to protest, and were duly arrested in their turn.

On the morning of 2 December the saviour of society, accompanied by his generals, rode out from the Élysée. In a city occupied by 50,000 troops there was little danger, but also, to his disappointment, little enthusiasm. There were even some slight hostile demonstrations, but the day passed with no sign of resistance. On 3 December, however, Victor Hugo and a few republicans formed a Committee to organize opposition. A barricade was erected in the faubourg Saint-Antoine and on it a deputy, Dr Baudin, was killed. His name was not forgotten. The danger was slight for the masses were on the side of the dictator. When Flaubert's hero asked a worker if they were not going to fight, he received the answer, 'We're not fools enough to get ourselves killed for the bourgeois! Let them settle it themselves!' They did in their way. On 4 December more barricades appeared, manned by a few hundred republicans who had not forgotten 1848. The generals were determined to have done with this nonsense: 30,000 troops, with artillery, musket, and bayonet, were let loose against the resistance, which was crushed in a few hours. Only a few hundred were killed, either in the fighting or shot when taken prisoner. The most dramatic episode occurred on the boulevard Poissonière, where the soldiers, in a state of natural excitement, fired several volleys into a large crowd of passive onlookers. It was not a very glorious beginning for the Second Empire.

3. A BOURGEOIS EMPIRE

IT was difficult to make a *coup d'état* without breaking some heads as well as an oath, and so Louis Napoleon had found, doubtless to his regret for he was a humane man. If he could have obtained the power and glory by honourable and peaceful methods he would certainly have preferred them. In addition he had to begin with repression, not so much because the feeble resistance in Paris and a few minor movements in the provinces needed repressing, as because unless there were some repression there would hardly have seemed any reason for a *coup d'état*. Altogether 26,884 arrests were effected throughout France. Of those arrested, 9,000 were transported to Algeria and 239 to Cayenne, 1,500 expelled from France, and 3,000 given forced residence away from their homes. Soon after, a commission of revision freed 3,500 of those sentenced, and by 1859, when an amnesty was offered to all the remainder except Ledru-Rollin, the number still penalized was only 1,800. The Second Empire might have been astonished at its own moderation and one would have expected it easily to live down the slight splashes of blood that accompanied its birth-pangs. Somehow it did not, and even the Emperor never quite put them out of his mind.

One of the first steps of Louis Napoleon was to confiscate the extensive property which Louis-Philippe, with almost excessive paternal affection, had collected for his large

The Second Republic and the Second Empire

family as well as for himself. It was used to make grants to societies for mutual aid, for constructing workers' dwellings, and so on; but it looked a little too much like bribery with stolen property, even for a number of Louis' supporters. His enemies called it, *'le premier vol de l'aigle'*.

Such comments showed a bad spirit. It was desirable that the country should envisage recent events in the proper light; so by a decree of 17 February 1852, largely the work of Rouher, the press was brought under a more severe control than it had known since the First Empire. No journal dealing with political or social questions was to be issued without the permission of the government; the caution money was heavily increased; the list of press offences was enlarged and penalties strengthened; those accused of press offences were to be tried without a jury; after three warnings by the Minister of the Interior to Paris journals, or by a prefect to provincial ones, a journal could be suspended by administrative action and in the last resort suppressed.

The general clauses of a new constitution did not need long discussion, for Louis Napoleon regarded himself as invested with the constituent power by the plebiscite that had confirmed his seizure of power. The President was to have, as before, the nomination of all officials, from top to bottom, as well as of the Senate, the Conseil d'État, the High Court of Justice, and the Ministers. There was to be a Legislative Body, elected by universal suffrage in single-member constituencies, in which the prefects and sub-prefects, experts at electoral management, the majority of whom had passed over from the service of Louis-Philippe to that of Louis Napoleon, could make certain – by all the traditional devices – that only the official candidate had much chance of succeeding. The result of the elections that were held in March 1852 was a foregone conclusion. Four legitimists, one independent, and three republicans (who refused to sit) were elected; the remaining 253 members were official candidates, chosen by the administration to uphold the Bonapartist cause in the constituencies. The labourers were not considered unworthy of their hire: in the

A History of Modern France

same month the salaries of the prefects were doubled. 'The dictatorship with which the people has entrusted me ceases today', declared Louis Napoleon in an official pronouncement on 30 March. It was only to cease, in the humiliation of Sedan, eighteen years later.

The possibility of failure seemed far removed at the outset. The new régime was lucky in the stars under which it was born, for the lean years in European economy were at an end and the new government was able to take advantage of a rising tide of economic activity. Shares rose rapidly in value on the Paris market. The Bank of France reduced its interest rate to 3 per cent. A triumphal tour of a regenerated France in the autumn of 1852 by Louis Napoleon was followed by the proclamation of the Empire and a plebiscite in which 7,800,000 voted yes and 250,000 no.

Even allowing for two million abstentions this was a decisive endorsement of France's new ruler. Yet what kind of man he was very few knew. Aged forty-four in 1852, he was still almost completely an unknown quantity to the country that had entrusted its destinies to him. The son of Josephine's daughter Hortense Beauharnais, and Napoleon's brother Louis, the un-Napoleonic appearance of Napoleon III, as he chose to be known, and the adventures of Hortense subsequent to his birth, had led to doubt being cast on his paternity, though almost certainly without justification. He was brought up by his mother, after she and Louis had separated, among the flotsam and jetsam of the Empire in exile. It was the drifting, raffish life, in Germany, Italy, England, Switzerland, of a cosmopolitan adventurer. Queen Victoria, when she met the new Emperor, remarked that unlike Louis-Philippe, who was 'thoroughly French', Louis Napoleon was 'as *unlike* a Frenchman as possible', and much more German than French in character. She was a shrewd judge and meant it as praise.

The first political action of the young Louis Napoleon was in Italian, not French, politics. He joined an abortive Carbonari rising in 1831 and had to fly the pursuing Austrians in disguise. Possibly the tutorship of Philippe le

The Second Republic and the Second Empire

Bas, son of the Robespierrist, had aroused his youthful idealism. His first political declaration – the *Rêveries politiques* of 1832 – proposed the regeneration of France by a peculiar combination of Napoleon II and the Republic. Only after the death of the duc de Reichstadt was it possible for Louis Napoleon to put forward the Bonapartist claim on his own behalf.

It is difficult to know at what stage he began to feel he was a man of destiny. Queen Victoria, when she met Napoleon III in 1855, was impressed by his genuine belief that all he had done and did was only in fulfilment of his destiny. But if a superstitious belief in his fate deceived him, it need not deceive us or lead us to underestimate his real abilities. Chance had not dealt Louis Napoleon many cards apart from his name. He was no orator and wisely chose to listen rather than speak, unlike Louis-Philippe, whose garrulity was a legend. The charm which he could exercise over other men, and even more over women, owed little to advantages of appearance. Greville describes him as 'a short thickish vulgar-looking man'. Practically all the Bonapartes, of course, were rather vulgar. In addition, Louis Napoleon had no taste in literature or art. It would be an interesting question whether the official art of the Second Empire was, or was not, more boring, pretentious, and vapid than that of the First. That there was no originality in Louis Napoleon does not perhaps matter, for originality is not normally conducive to political success. On the other hand, like the first Napoleon he had a great capacity for picking up other men's ideas; his mind was immensely receptive. It can hardly be denied that between his election in 1848 and the *coup d'état* in 1851 he played his cards with great shrewdness and beat the politicians at their own game. He had more natural generosity and humanity – when his ambitions did not get in the way – than most dictators; and his sympathy for the lot of the French working-man went beyond the mere requirements of the cult of popularity. If we say that in the last resort he had no moral scruples, this is to refer to his single-minded devotion to the quest of power, in which he gave those who observed him the impression, if not of the frantic possession of a Hitler, at least of a quieter, but equally unswerving kind of somnambulism. Louis Napoleon's taciturnity gave the illusion of depths that were not there. It is difficult to dislike him; but equally difficult to respect him.

Napoleon III never became more than an adventurer, even when he was on a throne; and for all his triumphs he never seems to have enjoyed them. Perhaps he was already prematurely old when success came. Perhaps he had trained himself to sacrifice everything else, including happiness, to success in his chosen objectives. Only in some such way can his marriage be explained. Evidently the new Emperor would have to marry if he was to perpetuate his dynasty. Negotiations for one or two minor royalties had proved abortive when, unfortunately, Louis Napoleon's roving eye was caught by a Spanish beauty in transit through Paris. She was of noble birth, twenty-six years old, and a notorious virgin. It was a challenge and he attempted his usual gambit of seduction, which totally failed. Even fairly mature Spanish grandees were not easily seduced, especially if there was the prospect of something better. In January 1853 it materialized in the form of marriage. 'She has played her game with him so well,' wrote the British ambassador, 'that he can get her in no other way but marriage.' But though she was beautiful, an admirable model for a fashionable painter like Winterhalter, with all the dignity that Napoleon III himself sometimes lacked, and in the end exhibited courage and greater force of character than the Emperor, Eugénie was a bad choice in almost every other respect. She was not very intelligent, but very religious, or at least clerical in a Spanish way. Her influence, and that of her friends, over the policy of the Second Empire was almost invariably unfortunate. There were personal difficulties too. Her mother, it turned out, did not live up to her daughter's standards: she collected debts and lovers. Eugénie, on the other hand, proved to be one of nature's virgins, incapable of responding to the Emperor's sensu-

The Second Republic and the Second Empire

ality, and he periodically resorted to Miss Howard, now created comtesse de Beauregard, and subsequently to many others. After the birth of the Prince Imperial in 1856, which nearly cost the Empress her life, marital relations ceased.

However, the succession was secured, so far as the life of one heir could do so, and the element of loyalty to a dynasty, though a very new one, could begin to play a rôle in politics. Bonapartism was more than mere attachment to a name. An opponent might say that it was a synthetic substitute for real political principles, a combination of inconsistent and irreconcilable objectives, of value only as propaganda. But among the supporters of Napoleon III there was one group, with which he himself had considerable sympathy, which – so far as its ideas went – could supply the Second Empire with a policy and some sort of working philosophy behind it. These were the Saint-Simonians, now more or less recovered from the père Enfantin's aberrations. Saint-Simon as the John the Baptist of Positivism may be left where he belongs, in the classes on moral philosophy of the *écoles normales*. 'It seems', writes one *normalien*, 'that his best title to fame is in having transmitted from Condorcet to Comte the idea of a positive policy founded on social science.' A better claim may be found in the implications of his well-known parable. Suppose, Saint-Simon says, France were to lose suddenly its fifty leading scientists of all kinds, artists, architects, engineers, doctors, bankers, merchants, ironmasters, industrialists in every branch, masons, carpenters, and workers in every craft – it would immediately sink in the scale of civilization and become inferior to all those countries of which it is now the equal. On the other hand, suppose it kept all its leading men of science, arts and crafts, commerce and industry, but lost the whole royal family, all the ministers and counsellors of state, the prefects, judges, archbishops, bishops, and all other ecclesiastical dignitaries, and in addition the ten thousand wealthiest landed proprietors living solely on the income from their property – the loss would undoubtedly grieve the French, being a humane people, but it would not materially affect their prosperity or their position in the world. In other words, Saint-Simon was asserting the primacy of the productive classes in society, of economic over political ends. It was also a protest against the dominance of the conservative propertied classes which was established by the Revolution.

Saint-Simon died in 1825, but his disciples continued and systematized his ideas of economic progress. The problem before France, as they saw it, was stated by Michel Chevalier in *Des intérêts matériels en France* in 1838. The new ruling class, he says, has won political power only in alliance with the people. If it is not to be overthrown in its turn it will have to meet the material demands of the people. This can be done only by means of the development of credit, communications, and education. The events of 1848 went a long way towards justifying this analysis, but they also showed that the position of the propertied classes was stronger than he supposed and that they had no intention of adopting Chevalier's remedy, or any other, except that of crude repression. They viewed the Saint-Simonian idea of the expenditure of large sums by the State to counter economic depression with horror. The Saint-Simonians themselves were not unaware of the strength of the opposition to their ideas and looked to strong government as the only means of economic and social reform. It was natural, therefore, that they should have welcomed the coming to power of Louis Napoleon, who himself had been attracted by the novelty and promise of Saint-Simonian ideas. They provided him with an economic programme, and with some of the personnel to put it into practice. The expansion of credit, railways, industry, trade, even the rebuilding of Paris, for which there had been a Saint-Simonian plan in 1832 – in fact, practically all the major economic developments, and therefore nearly all the real and lasting achievements of the Second Empire – derive from the inspiration of Saint-Simon and his followers. Though on a smaller scale and in a more restricted field, Saint-Simon might almost be called the Bentham of nineteenth-century France.

The Second Republic and the Second Empire

The key to economic progress in France lay in the growth of credit, as the Saint-Simonians correctly saw. It is sometimes assumed that the Second Empire was promoted, in their own interests, by the financiers. The truth is rather, on the contrary, that the financiers were promoted by the Second Empire. The affiliations of most high finance were with the old order of Orleanism or with the conservative republic. The only names that stand out on the side of Louis Napoleon are those of the Péreire brothers and Achille Fould. Existing banks and orthodox financiers catered mainly for the wealthy and conservative *rentiers*, interested principally in government loans. For the growth of industry new banks were needed. The Comptoir d'Escompte, founded in 1848 and developed with the encouragement of the Emperor, was primarily a commercial bank. Later it developed considerable colonial and Far Eastern interests. The Crédit Foncier, founded in 1852, was given a monopoly of mortgage finance, and its moderate terms facilitated the extensive rebuilding of the towns of France during the Second Empire. The Crédit Agricole dealt in farm mortgages and other agricultural finance; it ran into difficulties later, but this was after 1870. Private banks were also developed, the most famous being the Crédit Mobilier of the Péreire brothers, Saint-Simonians, who plunged heavily in French and foreign railways, a French steamship line, and government loans. Later, in 1863, the Crédit Lyonnais was set up; conducted with the traditional caution of the Lyonnais businessmen, it has flourished to the present day.

A wave of economic expansion followed the establishment of the Empire. It was concentrated particularly on the development of railways. After a slow beginning, the companies were rationalized by being reduced to six, and the pace of construction was so accelerated that by 1859 France had nearly three times as great a length of line as in 1851. By 1870 France had almost as extensive a network of lines in operation as Germany or Great Britain. Railway development stimulated, of course, the production of coal and iron. The consumption of coal was trebled, and the use of horse power in industry quintupled, between 1851 and 1870. The average price of steel was practically halved. The greatest of the iron-works, at Le Creusot, was bought by the Schneider brothers in 1836 when its annual production was 5,000 tons; in 1847 it was 18,000, and the increased pace of growth under the Second Empire is shown by the rise from 35,000 tons in 1855 to 133,000 in 1867. In the same period the foreign commerce of France practically trebled.

Meanwhile the growth of the French population had slackened, so that the increased wealth of the country was not swallowed up by the excess of mouths. Moreover the shift from the country to the town continued. The proportion of urban population grew from 24 per cent to 31 per cent, and this probably represented a rise in the average standard of life in the countryside, for it was the landless labourers and the poorest element there which declined most. The growth of railways, which played their part in facilitating the movement from the country, also broke down some of the traditional rural isolation.

The share of the state in providing the actual finance for this general economic development should not be exaggerated. Up to 1860 the public works programme was financed mainly by private investment. Budgetary expenses for this purpose were indeed smaller than they had been under Louis Philippe; whence those developments in which for one reason or another the private investor was not interested – roads, canals, ports – languished. The same was true of agriculture. The peasants, whose votes had established the Second Empire, were those who profited least from it. They were suspicious of all new methods; the legal structure of France protected the small proprietor in his jealous independence of any interference, and the subdivision of the land prohibited any general or coordinated schemes of improvement.

The programme of public works which Louis Napoleon inaugurated was in his mind a continuation of the policy of

The Second Republic and the Second Empire

the First Empire. He himself wrote of Napoleon I, 'The public works, which the Emperor put into operation on such a large scale, were not only one of the principal causes of domestic prosperity, they even promoted great social progress.' While these motives were certainly present to the mind of Napoleon III, the propaganda value of public works was also not absent, particularly if they could be effected in full view of the public. The improvement of Paris, in continuation of the work of Napoleon I, was therefore among the first projects to be taken in hand after the *coup d'état*.

The need to render Paris, like all the other great urban agglomerations of Europe, habitable, was patent enough; but it would be a mistake to attribute the improvements solely to the pressure of hard facts. Reforms, in Paris as in London, did not come about by the automatic pressure of circumstances; they were the conscious achievement of the disciples of a Saint-Simon and a Bentham, and in France the result of deliberate government policy. It was not confined to the capital: at Lyon, the prefect Vaisse effected an almost equally dramatic transformation.

The first attempt of Napoleon III, after the *coup d'état*, to promote a policy of public works was frustrated by the conservative financial ideas of the officials in charge, but in 1853 one of the most energetic of the prefects was brought to Paris. This was the Alsatian Protestant, Haussmann, who had hitched his administrative wagon to the rising star of Louis Napoleon as early as the presidential election of 1848. As a godson of Prince Eugène, Haussmann had almost an hereditary claim to be regarded as a Bonapartist. Forceful and cunning, ambitious, unprincipled, formidable in bulk and character, he was the ideal agent for the Second Empire in a grade a little lower than the highest. He was to be Prefect of the Seine from 1853 to 1870. Such a man did not shrink from unorthodox, but up to a point justified, financial methods. The theory behind them was simply that the new values created by the reconstruction of the older sectors of Paris would themselves pay for the work that had to be undertaken.

A History of Modern France

The scope of Haussmann's demolition and reconstruction is amazing. He gave Paris eighty-five miles of new streets with wide carriage-ways and pavements shaded with trees. Private enterprise lined them with houses and shops, to a height and with a façade prescribed by the authorities, and in a style that represented Haussmann's idea of architectural beauty, for the Prefect of the Seine had the born philistine's conviction of his own impeccable artistic taste. Viollet-le-Duc, apart from the injury he did to Notre-Dame, was kept out of the rebuilding of Paris by Haussmann, who was neither romantic nor medieval. His passion, like that of Napoleon I, was for vistas. The place de l'Étoile looks very fine from the air: it is a pity that it is not normally seen from that angle. Napoleon III, indeed, reproached Haussmann that in his love of straight lines he neglected the needs of traffic. The new railway stations, for example, were left without adequate approaches.

The best things in the re-planning of Paris were due to the influence of Napoleon III. His memories of London inspired the creation of many squares and other open places. The Bois de Boulogne, which had been a rather dull royal forest, cut across by long straight avenues for the hunters, was given by the Emperor to the city. At the instigation of Morny a race-course was created at Longchamps; it rapidly became a fashionable social resort, the profits on which largely paid for the transformation of the uninteresting *bois* into a landscaped park. A similar treatment was accorded to the Bois de Vincennes on the east of Paris. Napoleon III was also responsible for the construction of the Halles, the great central market, as a functional structure of metal and glass.

Apart from the long straight roads he drove through Paris, and the vistas they afforded, Haussmann's greatest achievement was in the drainage of the city. The sewers of Paris before him are luridly described by Victor Hugo in *Les Misérables*. By the end of the Second Empire the visit, especially of the great sewer which Haussmann liked to call his Cloaca Maxima, was a tourist attraction. A further

The Second Republic and the Second Empire

virtue of the sewers was that they had been built without tearing anything else down, for much of old Paris and many fine and historic buildings were sacrificed to make it a Second Empire city. A sentimental regret for what was lost, and even an aesthetic distaste for what replaced it, would neither, perhaps, be justified if a fine modern city with improved living conditions had been built. But the tradition of urbanism, the Florence of the Medici, the Paris of Louis XV, the Nancy of king Stanislaus, had now come down to the boulevard Malesherbes and the place de l'Opéra. Behind the state-prescribed façades of Haussmann's streets the builders could put up what they liked, and often new and more imposing slums replaced the older and more picturesque ones. Running water was only supplied at the option of the owner of a building, who often decided that it was an unnecessary luxury, since it involved the payment of a water rate. The function of the grand new sewers must not be mistaken: they were to remove the rain-water from the streets and prevent flooding. Sanitary, or rather insanitary, refuse still had to be carted away by an army of men at night in the traditional fashion, or sunk in cess pits, or deposited illegally in streets and gardens. Another, equally unpleasant, aspect of the city was the large area taken up by decaying bodies. Haussmann is not to be blamed for this; his plans for a great municipal cemetery outside Paris were successfully resisted by those who were determined that when they could do no more mischief there alive, they should leave their dead bodies to pollute the air and drinking water of the city.

The attention that was paid to Paris was not given to its surroundings. The Wall of the Farmers General (on the line of the present outer ring of boulevards), with its sixty gates, was now no longer the effective limit of occupation. A shift of population was taking place to the large area between this wall and the fortifications of the Orleanist Monarchy. Railway works and factories attracted a suburban population; and many of those who continued to work in Paris were drawn outwards by the cheapness of living in what was becoming a huge, poverty-stricken, higgledy-piggledy encampment of shacks. However, in the great enterprise of Haussmann good and bad were mixed up together, and his achievement suited his day and generation. Contemporaries who began by opposing and went on to mock his efforts, came to admire the results.

The crown of them all was to be the new Paris Opera, built by Charles Garnier, inspired by the eighteenth-century Bordeaux Opera, and calculated for the gratification of a society even richer and more luxurious than the eighteenth-century mercantile aristocracy of Bordeaux, as well as for a less chaste artistic taste than that of the age of Louis XV. Within and without it was loaded with decoration in all the styles known to history. A separate carriageway led into a private entrance to the imperial box, for Napoleon remembered the attempt by Orsini and the murder of the duc de Berry. A huge entrance hall and elaborate stairs, for the arrival and reception of foreign or French notabilities; a foyer for the circulation of the fashionable throng; an auditorium surrounded by boxes to preserve the privacy of wealth and rank or facilitate amorous intrigue; a stage as deep as the auditorium, on which the most grandiose spectacles could be presented – such was the Paris Opera, a worthy setting for the luxury and splendour of Second Empire society, where Napoleon III and his Empress might shine amidst the wealthiest *nouveaux riches* and the most beautiful courtesans of Paris. This was a dream picture: in 1871 the Opera was still unfinished. It was completed, with the constitutional laws of the Third Republic, in 1875.

The Second Empire was the real bourgeois monarchy, an age of plutocrats without the culture or taste of an eighteenth-century Farmer General, of fashionable priests without the religious feeling of a Lamennais or a Lacordaire, of well-disciplined academics without the intellectual distinction of the Orleanist scholars, of glittering *demimondaines* whose possession was one of the chief forms of ostentatious expenditure and signs of worldly success. The

The Second Republic and the Second Empire

fashionable painters and writers were even more insignificant than usual in modern times. Apart from Daumier's cartoons, Millet's paintings exhibiting the dignity of labour, and Courbet's bourgeois-shocking realism, the only painters of real distinction were the rebels of the Salon des Refusés in 1863 who, rejected by official art, founded the great impressionist school of the Third Republic. The most lasting artistic creations that belong properly to the Second Empire are the comedies of Labiche and the operettas of Offenbach. What was on a higher level represented either a survival of the romanticism of the early century, or a direct or implied protest against the new society and its standards. Victor Hugo, fulminating in exile from the Channel Isles, launched *Les Châtiments* against 'Napoléon le Petit'. The cult of realism that is associated with the Third Republic developed in fact under the Second Empire, which recognized its enmity when the publications of *Madame Bovary* and the *Fleurs du Mal* were prosecuted in 1857.

If we want to see the spirit of the Second Empire at its best and most triumphant, we must look at the Exhibition of 1855, organized in imitation of the Great Exhibition of 1851 in London, but representing none the less a genuine aspiration after economic progress and pride in the beginnings of achievement.

4. L'EMPIRE C'EST LA PAIX

An age of materialism and money-making was opening, selfish and – especially after the June Days – hag-ridden with class hatred, but all classes were striving, with varying success, for the same thing – a higher standard of living. The desire for adventures, either domestic or foreign, if it ever existed, was over. Nationalist historians have represented a nineteenth-century France constantly harking back to the military glories of the First Empire. Nothing could be more misleading. There were many grievances against the July Monarchy, but its lack of bellicose ardour was not one of the causes of the 1848 Revolution. If the left-wing republicans and socialists aroused the opposition of the nation under the Second Republic, it was not least because of the fear that they might involve France in war with Europe. Louis Napoleon had judged the desires of the country rightly when he proclaimed, *l'Empire, c'est la Paix*.

They had not changed by 1853, when the Russian occupation of Moldavia and Wallachia led to a Russo-Turkish War. France was involved because she claimed to be the protector of Roman Catholic interests in the Near East, and a quarrel over the custody of the Holy Places had been the occasion, if not the cause, of the Russo-Turkish war. The French Emperor was indignant at the Russian aggression and at what seemed to him a humiliation for France; but though clerical support might have been expected, the country as a whole entered the Crimean War not only without enthusiasm, but with patent reluctance. However, confused as were the events leading up to the outbreak of war in March 1854, the responsibility of Napoleon III for them was comparatively slight. Nor can he be held personally responsible for the incompetence with which the war was conducted, particularly by his British ally.

The news of the fall of Sebastopol in September 1855, after much disappointment and disillusionment, was greeted in France with an outburst of rejoicing. It was assumed to mean peace, and if it had not meant peace, opposition to the continuance of the war would have been widespread. The Peace Congress was held at Paris in the spring of 1856. It was a triumph for Napoleon III, though what France gained by the war it is difficult to say.

If the Crimean War was the result of accident, the same can hardly be said of the next war that the Second Empire was involved in. The legend of Napoleon I as the liberator of Italy, the early association of Louis Napoleon with the Italian Carbonari, and his genuine nationalist ideals, given his obstinate, fatalistic habit of clinging to the ends he had once set himself, made it certain that the Emperor would endeavour to do something for Italy. Cavour was fully

172

The Second Republic and the Second Empire

aware of this and played on Napoleon III in all the ways he knew. The insane attempt by the Italian revolutionary, Orsini, to assassinate Napoleon III and Eugénie as they arrived at the Opera, which killed eight people and injured many more, was just the thing to appeal to the over-clever mind of an ex-conspirator as an opportunity to turn it to precisely the opposite ends from those that any reasonable calculation could have anticipated. Orsini, of course, had to be executed, but first he had to play the rôle, which his appearance and the Emperor cast him for, of the romantic patriot. Through his would-be assassin, Louis Napoleon was able to proclaim indirectly his allegiance to the ideal of Italian liberation.

The next step was the secret conference with Cavour, in July 1858, at Plombières, where, in the absence of his ministers, the Emperor reached a verbal agreement envisaging war against Austria. The Italian war, which was now planned, shows even more clearly than any of the other wars of the Second Empire, that they are not to be attributed to pressure from below, or to the French desire for glory, so beloved of historians, or to a supposed need to cement the Emperor's authority. They were the necessary result of his foreign policy, which he kept largely in his own hands, partly through belief in his star, and partly because he never fully trusted any of his ministers. This was why, says Émile Ollivier, 'he adopted the custom of dealing directly with the ambassadors on important occasions, to the exclusion of his ministers.' The meeting at Plombières was followed by a year of declarations which seemed to make war inevitable, yet which, under the pressure of French and European opinion, stopped short of actually provoking it. There is a possibility, indeed, that Napoleon was playing an insidious game of bluff, which would be characteristic of him, and hoping in the end to achieve something without war. His last-minute agreement to a European congress to discuss the future of Italy, though he pretended to those who wanted war that it was not intended seriously, casts some doubt on the sincerity of his bellicose gestures. The cunning of Cavour and the folly of the Austrians robbed him of the choice and in April 1859 war began.

Despite these equivocations, the Italian War was essentially the Emperor's own. The ministers were opposed to it; the clergy and those who followed their lead, the peasantry and most of the better-off classes, were against it. Only the enemies of the Emperor, the republicans and their clientele in the towns, viewed it with favour. The Emperor had seemed to be working for war by all the methods he could, with little regard for scruple, or even for French interests, as if he were infatuated. It was the even greater folly of the Vienna government and the Austrian ultimatum that gave him the chance to bring France into the war on a temporary wave of anti-Austrian sentiment. Whatever the feelings of the peasants who furnished the mass of the troops, their departure for the war brought cheering crowds into the streets of the cities; and when the Emperor himself, leaving Paris from the Gare de Lyon, had to pass through the workers' quarter of Saint-Antoine, there were scenes of great enthusiasm.

Perhaps as a Bonaparte, Napoleon III was expected to be, and may – though this is more doubtful – have expected himself to be, a military genius. Really, considering his total lack of military experience, the fact that he did not get his armies into a complete mess, indeed into rather less of a muddle than professional generals had done in the Crimean War, or than the Austrian generals did with the troops opposed to him, is very much to his credit. The Austrians, who had advanced into Piedmontese territory, were defeated first at Magenta, which saved Milan, and then at Solferino, after which the French and Piedmontese were on the point of invading Venetia.

It is unlikely that this luck would have lasted, and there were other considerations which called for serious reflection. Things were not turning out quite as Napoleon III had expected. Revolutions in the smaller Italian states were throwing them into the arms of Piedmont. The revolt of

The Second Republic and the Second Empire

the papal province of Romagna increased the opposition of the French clericals to the war. Prussia was mobilizing on the Rhine. The Austrian forces were now in a stronger position, resting on the famous fortresses of the Quadrilateral. Solferino had brought enough glory and bloodshed for both the Emperor and his people. As after the fall of Sebastopol, only now even more so, there was a general cry for peace. All this might easily have been anticipated, but it apparently took Louis Napoleon by surprise. He reacted quickly by opening negotiations with Francis Joseph, and less than three weeks after the battle an armistice was concluded at Villafranca.

By its terms, Lombardy was to be ceded to France, for her to transfer to the Kingdom of Sardinia; but Austria was to keep Venetia, and in the Italian states which had revolted their former rulers were to be restored. Since he had failed to unite all Northern Italy to Piedmont, Napoleon could not claim the cession of Savoy and Nice to France, which had been part of the agreement with Cavour. The fact that the other Italian states were united to the Kingdom of Sardinia in the course of 1860, and that France could consequently annex Savoy and Nice, was a purely adventitious gain, but it meant that at the last minute the Emperor's luck had held. Though some clerical and right-wing support was alienated, and the Foreign Minister, Walewski, whose sympathies were with the papal cause, had to resign, republican and left-wing opinion – which presented a much more serious opposition – became more favourable to the Empire. The real miscalculation of the Italian war lay in its effect on the European situation, but this was only gradually to be revealed.

Napoleon III was much more interested in asserting the rôle of France among the Great Powers than in developing imperial ambitions outside Europe. In the colonial, as in every other field, it is difficult to trace a consistent policy through the aberrations of the Second Empire. The Emperor began with a prejudice against Algeria, which he called *'un boulet attaché aux pieds de la France'*. His romanticism, or his national ideas, or perhaps even his idealism, brought about a drastic reversal of policy in 1863, when, in a public letter to the Governor General, he condemned the confiscation of native land for the colonists. 'Today', he declared, 'we must convince the Arabs that we have not come into Algeria to oppress and despoil them, but to bring them the advantages of civilization. ... Algeria is not a colony properly speaking, but an *Arab kingdom*. ... I am just as much the Emperor of the Arabs as of the French.' One result of this new orientation of French policy was a drastic diminution in colonization, and attempts to introduce large-scale capitalist enterprise which failed. The government of Algeria continued to be in military hands until 1870, when a parliamentary enquiry condemned the system and the government restored the authority of the prefects.

Senegal, considered of secondary importance, had the good fortune to be governed from 1854 to 1865, with a brief gap, by one of the wisest colonial administrators France has had. This was Faidherbe, an engineer captain in 1854, who established a system of indirect rule and extended French authority inland. When he retired, he had wrested large populations from the overlordship of the Moors and sketched out the plan of an extensive and prosperous colony. He established the pattern of pacification, organization, and assimilation which was to be continued with remarkable success for many years. In 1857 the port of Dakar was founded. Attempts to develop the native agriculture of Senegal were markedly successful. A cadre of able colonial administrators was built up. Altogether, in Africa under the Second Empire we can see the beginning of the modern problems of colonial government, and tentative answers, emerging sometimes through the influence of the Emperor, and sometimes in spite of him.

In the Far East French missionaries and merchants led the way, to be followed by small expeditionary forces. An Anglo-French punitive force in 1860 occupied Pekin, burnt the Summer Palace, and looted everything it could lay its hands on, to show the superiority of European civilization.

The Second Republic and the Second Empire

A French force annexed Cochin-China in 1862 and a French protectorate was established over Cambodia.

Nearer home, Turkish massacres of Christians in Syria led to a French expedition there in 1860, which afforded the occasion for international recognition of France's traditional interests in the Levant. Finally, it was in 1859 that Ferdinand de Lesseps began the construction of the Suez Canal, in spite of English opposition. The most ambitious of the overseas projects of Napoleon III was to be in Mexico, but this must be dealt with later, at the moment when the reckoning was sent in.

This colonial expansion was carried on without any suggestion of rivalry or conflict with Great Britain. This is all the more remarkable because French opinion, throughout the Second Empire, was even more than normally Anglophobe. At the Congress of Paris it was remarked that an uninformed observer might have thought the Russians the allies and the British the recent enemy. Yet Napoleon III was determined not to make the mistake of his uncle and allow himself to be drawn into hostilities with Great Britain. This determination, in the light of his European ambitions, was undoubtedly wise, and perhaps all the more so because it ran counter to the dominant trend of French opinion, while in England anti-French feeling was so strong that coastal fortifications were constructed and corps of volunteers enlisted for defence against France.

After the Italian war, the Emperor began seriously to reflect that perhaps after all the Empire ought to mean peace. Fear of further wars was beginning to weaken confidence inside France. He had by now thoroughly stirred up Europe and shattered the status quo. This may have been one reason for the negotiation of the Cobden Free Trade treaty with Great Britain. It was intended as a gesture of reassurance. In a letter published in January 1860, Napoleon announced that peace would be used to develop national wealth and improve the conditions of the agricultural population and the workers. At the same time he had a genuine belief in the benefits to be derived from the adoption of free trade principles. Chevalier had persuaded him to accept the plan for a commercial treaty with England before Cobden met the Emperor. It had not been a difficult task, for Napoleon III had a genuine interest in the well-being of the populace of France, and believed that a reduction in the traditionally high French tariff wall would promote it.

He kept his plans secret from those ministers who were not likely to agree with them. Walewski, who was out of sympathy both with the Italian and the commercial policy, was removed from the Foreign Ministry in December 1859. In January 1860 Napoleon published a letter to his Minister of State, Fould, in which he announced measures for the improvement of French agriculture and industry with the aid of government loans, in preparation for the commercial treaty. Because the Legislative Body, weak as it was, would not abandon protective duties quietly, the Emperor resorted to a reduction by executive action. Cobden and Chevalier negotiated the Anglo-French free trade treaty, which was signed in January 1860. The French industrialists, fanatical protectionists, reacted with combined panic and fury. Petitions were got up; manufacturers descended on Paris to protest – those from Rouen even chartered a special train – but all to no avail. By the terms of the treaty France agreed to bring absolute prohibitions of import to an end, and to reduce her tariff to a maximum of 30 per cent within two years and 25 per cent in five years. Great Britain practically abolished all customs dues on imports from France, except for those on wines and spirits. In actual fact the French government went further than it had promised in reducing customs rates.

Commercial treaties followed with other states. In matters of trade the Second Empire was the only liberal régime France has ever known. It did not seem to harm French prosperity. The small iron works, still dependent on wood, the iron mines of the North, rapidly being worked out, were hurried to their end by foreign competition, but British competition brought down the price of iron and so stimu-

The Second Republic and the Second Empire

lated the growth of railways and the introduction of machinery.

On the other hand, the hopes of a period of international peace to be promoted by the adoption of a free trade policy were hardly fulfilled. In the sixties the Second Empire was entering on a period of misfortunes and mistakes. Though he had his long-term objectives, the actual policy of the Emperor had always developed as a series of lucky improvisations. Now his luck was changing, or perhaps we might say that the unpaid debts resulting from earlier gambles were coming in for payment. He was less equal to them than formerly, because a disease of the kidneys and bladder was increasingly weakening him and sapping his capacity for decision.

In the fifties Louis Napoleon had built up the prestige and influence of France in European councils with considerable success. What this meant was that France was returning to the position among the Great Powers that her population, wealth, and military potential justified. It is also fair to say that for a number of different reasons the competition inside Europe was not formidable at this time, while the Emperor sedulously avoided any serious dispute with Great Britain. But in the sixties the situation began to change, partly as a result of Napoleon III's own actions. His semi-romantic, early nineteenth-century ideas of foreign policy were no longer appropriate in the harsher climate of blood and iron that was sweeping over Europe; and also it must be admitted that, in the age of Cavour and Bismarck, Louis Napoleon was out of his class.

There was another, and perhaps more fundamental, cause of the failure of French foreign policy in the sixties. France could now only maintain her prestige and keep up her relative position among the Great Powers of Europe by preparing for, and facing the possibility of, eventual war. But by 1860 the French nation had fought in ten years two more wars than it wanted. The Emperor himself had his fill of war and moreover was well-informed of the strongly pacific trend of public opinion. This was perhaps the decisive factor, which needs to be emphasized. Napoleon III never forgot that he had been brought to power by the masses of the people. His authority had not been created by, nor did it depend on, the army. There was no great party machine, as in modern fascist and communist dictatorships, to hold the people down. His was a personal and plebiscitary dictatorship, and what the people had given the people might take away. The Emperor was therefore almost pathologically conscious of his dependence on public opinion, and lacking the machinery – apart from a press of which the known subservience was the measure of its lack of influence – or the modern techniques for manufacturing opinion, he had often, indeed too often for the well-being of the country, to follow it. The problem was to discover what the public, in so far as a public existed, was thinking. Here the Second Empire had to fall back on the method of earlier régimes, by relying on a continuous flow of reports on the state of opinion from its own administrative agents.

Dependence for information on those who have a vested interest in representing the situation in the most favourable light, for naturally they do not wish to cast discredit on their own services or their efforts to influence opinion, can prove very dangerous, and leave a government – as it left Louis-Philippe and Guizot – in sublime ignorance of their own isolation from the country. The stronger the government, the greater the danger of this. The governments of the Second Empire were weak, though the régime was not equally weak. The prefects and other officials would doubtless generally have been anxious to provide the answers that their superiors wanted if they had known what these were, but often they did not; and particularly in his later years the Emperor was genuinely trying to discover what public opinion demanded, in order to satisfy it. Sometimes, it is true, he initiated policies under the impression that they would win popular favour, and then found it difficult to liquidate them when this proved a miscalculation. But he was no longer prepared, as he had been when he assumed

The Second Republic and the Second Empire

responsibility for the Italian War and the Treaty of Commerce, to swim against the tide.

When Poland revolted against Russian rule in 1863 the Emperor followed opinion faithfully in first alienating Alexander II and sacrificing what was almost a Russian alliance by protesting against the suppression of the Poles, and then exhibiting his weakness by doing nothing to follow up the protest, beyond proposing a congress. Great Britain, suspecting French ambition to recreate a Polish client state in Eastern Europe, refused to support this proposal. The next year, when Prussia and Austria seized the duchies of Schleswig and Holstein, it was Great Britain that proposed the congress, and Napoleon III, in a futile hope of extracting compensation from Prussia on the Rhine, who refused his support. Neither France, nor Great Britain, of course, was prepared to fire a shot in support of the smaller nations of Europe; in these circumstances their notes and diplomatic manoeuvres could not be anything but useless gestures.

In 1866 came the Austro-Prussian War, in preparation for which Bismarck had played Napoleon III like a cynical animal trainer with a greedy but rather stupid beast, enticing him into the desired position with the proffer of a choice morsel – of not clearly specified territory on the Rhine – but all the time intending to snatch it away at the last moment. Louis Napoleon, of course, was not foolish enough to count on Bismarck's gratitude for the reward of his neutrality. He believed that Austria was the stronger of the two Germanic powers, and with his old pro-Italian and anti-Austrian obsession, gladly saw Italy join in on the side of Prussia to redress the balance and wrench Venetia from the Austrian Empire. His miscalculation was basically due to the fact that the Austrian Empire was still for him what it had been for Napoleon I, the real enemy in Europe. Prussia, on the other hand, was seen as the weak state defeated at Jena and a natural ally of France. French opinion also, as Bismarck had assured himself through his informants in France in advance of the war, was determined that France should keep out of it. Louis Napoleon even contemplated an alliance with Prussia and Italy against Austria; and when Thiers in a brilliant speech warned France against a policy that was setting up a united Germany and Italy as dangerous rivals to France, Napoleon went out of his way to repudiate this view and proclaim his belief in the primary interest of France in smashing the Vienna settlement of 1815. After the rapid Prussian victory, the foreign minister, Drouyn de Lhuys, and the Empress were for immediate war, and this was the moment when France might have resorted to war with the best chance. Unfortunately, although French sentiments were now anti-Prussian, the habit of sitting on the side-lines and cheering or booing without intervening in a dangerous game had gone on too long to be changed overnight. France was still profoundly pacific and Napoleon had done nothing to prepare French opinion for the necessity of resisting Prussian aggression. At the critical moment he was ill, and his strongest minister, Rouher, was opposed to armed intervention. All the Emperor could fall back on was the notorious 'policy of *pourboires*' – territorial compensation to be extracted by weakness from strength – the left bank of the Rhine, Belgium, Luxembourg. What Great Britain, the German states, and the states involved in the proposed bargain, when it became known – and Bismarck saw to it that it did – thought of these proposals need not be said.

Meanwhile the French garrison, kept in Rome under pressure from the French Catholics but withdrawn in December 1866, had been brought back in October 1867. A small French force assisted the papal troops in repelling Garibaldi at Mentana. This completed the antagonization of Italy. Between 1863 and 1867 Louis Napoleon succeeded in alienating practically every state of any importance in Europe.

Outside Europe earlier colonial successes had led up to a much more ambitious scheme to undo what Napoleon III might well consider the mistake that Napoleon I had made in selling Louisiana. As always, a series of accidents seemed

The Second Republic and the Second Empire

to mark the path of Napoleon III to the end which, when he had attained it, could be seen to have been in his mind all the time. A moderately reforming and anti-clerical government in Mexico under President Juarez having repudiated the foreign loans incurred by its predecessor, in 1862 a debt-collecting Anglo-Franco-Spanish expedition was sent to Mexico. When the other two contingents withdrew, a French force remained at Vera Cruz to experience a defeat at the hands of Juarez' men. This, of course, had to be avenged for the sake of French honour and imperial dignity. Reinforcements were therefore sent out, which captured Mexico City and organized an Assembly of Notables. This offered the throne of Mexico to a Habsburg prince, Maximilian, put forward by Napoleon III. The Civil War meanwhile prevented the United States from opposing the breach of the Monroe Doctrine.

A mixture of motives inspired this attempt to establish a client state of France in the Americas. To the expected extension of national power and prestige was added the hope of economic gain – perhaps a persistence of the legend of the wealth of the Indies. Morny had a more personal hope of gain in the form of a commission of 30 per cent on the repayments to a great Swiss creditor of Mexico. There was strong Catholic support for a plan which promised to overthrow the anti-clerical Juarez government; at Rome the French campaign was proclaimed a crusade. The French expedition proved a much bigger military commitment than had been expected; in the mid-sixties nearly 40,000 of the best French troops were tied up on the wrong side of the Atlantic, when the balance of Europe was being changed. The situation was not improved by the fact that the French general, Bazaine, quarrelled with the other leaders of the imperial forces, married a young Mexican girl, and may have had ambitions of setting up as a ruler on his own. Guerrilla warfare dragged on with a continued drain of men and money – the adventure rapidly becoming intensely unpopular in France – until the end of the American Civil War announced the end of the French intervention in

Mexico. In 1867 the French troops were withdrawn, while Maximilian remained to be shot by the Mexicans, and his Empress went mad. It was a tragic end to a squalid and foolish adventure. Worse was to follow, but before tracing the foreign policy of Napoleon III through to the final catastrophe, it is necessary to say something of the concurrent decline of his authority at home.

5. TOWARDS THE LIBERAL EMPIRE

LITTLE has been said so far of the politics of the Second Empire. But the impression should not be given that apart from its foreign and colonial adventures, the only thing that really counted in its history was economics. The politics of a dictatorship, like that of an absolute monarchy, normally consists of mere court intrigue. If this is increasingly less true of the Second Empire, that is because it was rather a weak and half-hearted dictatorship. The simple preservation of parliamentary forms is not particularly significant; nor can we learn much from the elections, at least in the earlier years. Dictatorships, since they cannot tolerate opposition, normally suppress it by force, as the Second Empire did in the beginning. But Napoleon III also liked to pretend that it did not exist. This belief was made the easier by the fact that the majority of the nation undoubtedly supported him to the end. However, nothing less than a hundred per cent support is really satisfactory to a dictator. To secure the appearance of almost unanimous support the Second Empire relied on electoral management.

After 1852, the next elections were held in 1857. Opposition was still weak and the government was supported by just over 84 per cent of those voting (62 per cent of the electorate) as against 83 per cent in 1852. The prefects and their subordinates secured the election of the official candidates in all except thirteen constituencies; and of those who succeeded without the blessing of the Minister of the Interior eight were independents whose opposition to the

The Second Republic and the Second Empire

régime was very mild. The remaining five were republicans, four, including Jules Favre, Émile Ollivier, and Ernest Picard from Paris, and one from Lyon. The Party of Five, as it was known, counted for rather more than its minute size might suggest, because the eloquence of Ollivier and Favre, and the wit of Picard, made a striking contrast to the dull pomposities of most of the yes-men of the prefects. But the fact that these republicans had accepted a seat in the Legislative Body was already a long step in the direction of reconciliation with the régime. The Italian War, with which they sympathized, carried them still farther. By 1859 the Emperor felt his position so thoroughly consolidated that he offered an amnesty to all political exiles, with the solitary exception – and this is significant – not of any of the socialists but of the leader of the red republicans, Ledru-Rollin.

In 1860 the first step away from dictatorship and in the direction of a real parliamentary system was taken. Since the Empire was at the height of its success and under no necessity to make concessions, and the change was introduced against the advice of the ministers except Morny, it must be attributed to Napoleon III himself. His motives, as always, remain inscrutable. One possibility is that he may have found himself too much at the mercy of his ministers, having neither the expert knowledge nor the assiduity to examine and control all they said or did in his name. He now allowed the Legislative Body and the Senate to hold annual debates on the speech from the throne, in the presence of ministers who were to reply to them on behalf of the government. An official report of debates was also to be published.

In 1861 a further step was taken. The vote of the budget by sections, instead of *en bloc*, was conceded. Political life was reviving, and in 1863 for the first time the government went into the election faced by a real, if hopelessly divided, opposition. This only won 32 seats, 15 to the Catholic opposition and 17 to the left. The Empire still had rather over five million votes out of over seven millions, but the opposition obtained a vote of two millions, compared with under half that figure in 1852 and 1857. An ominous fact was that out of the twenty-two largest towns in France, eighteen had given a majority to the opposition candidates. Paris elected Thiers and eight republicans.

These elections had been managed by the devoted Persigny, who had followed the star of Louis Bonaparte from Strasbourg to the Tuileries. Minister of the Interior after the *coup d'état*, and subsequently Ambassador in London, he had returned to the Ministry of the Interior in 1860. It was characteristically inconsequent that Louis Napoleon should have put back into the key position this enthusiastic, authoritarian Bonapartist, just at the time when an attempt was being made to moderate authoritarianism. Persigny's ruthless application of the system of official candidatures in the election of 1863 could only have been justified by conspicuous and increased success. The absence of this was equivalent to failure, and the resentment that his methods aroused suggested that they were becoming anachronistic. So Persigny had to go, with a dukedom as a consolation prize.

The leading influence over the domestic policy of the Emperor for the next two years was to be that of Morny, the most brilliant, unscrupulous, and from a political point of view perhaps the ablest and wisest of the Emperor's collaborators. The duc de Morny had a special qualification for his rôle, since he was the Emperor's half-brother. He was the son of Hortense Beauharnais, Louis Napoleon's mother, by General de Flahaut, her lover, himself an illegitimate son of Talleyrand. This double illegitimacy was to add up to a great dignitary of the Second Empire, but already under Louis-Philippe Morny had won a fortune by speculation and a seat in the Orleanist Chamber of Deputies. He, more than anyone else, perhaps even more than Louis Napoleon himself, was the architect of the *coup d'état*. He quarrelled with the Emperor over the confiscation of Orleanist property, which may perhaps be set off against some of his own rather dubious financial transactions. In 1854 he became President of the Legislative Body, and he

The Second Republic and the Second Empire

believed all through that France must return to a qualified parliamentary régime, in which the position of Napoleon III would perhaps not be so very different from that of Louis-Philippe. Morny's charm, his capacity for managing men, his combination of bonhomie with the air of a *grand seigneur*, his dashing ways with women and with wealth, his shrewdness and essential sense of the possible, made him one of the chief assets of the Second Empire and an ideal agent for the transformation of the régime into what was to be called the Liberal Empire. Morny envisaged an imperial government freed from the incubus of the rigid authoritarians, the unimaginative conservatives; a parliamentary Empire, which should be led and managed by himself and in which the oratorical talent which he lacked should be supplied by some brilliant orator of the left, such as Émile Ollivier. Among a crowd of technicians, *fonctionnaires*, political managers, and general second-raters, he stands out as something like a statesman. If he had lived, his ability might increasingly have supplemented the failing powers of Napoleon III. His death, at the age of fifty-four, in 1865, was perhaps the single most disastrous event for the Second Empire in a period that was increasingly filled with disasters. It postponed the coming of the liberal Empire for five years, and meant that when it did come, it should be under much less favourable auspices.

The series of disasters in foreign and colonial policy bears witness to the strength rather than the weakness of the Second Empire. In all of them, it is true, public opinion was the accomplice of the Emperor, as it had been in December 1851; but a régime with less support could not have passed through them with such immunity, nor have been so little shaken by the growing opposition in France.

This opposition was now coming as much from the right as from the left. The relations of the Empire with the Catholics had changed markedly since 1852. At the time of the *coup d'état* a few bishops, like Sibour of Paris, saw ultimate dangers for the Church in too close an identification with the new régime. Lacordaire despaired, but most

Catholics welcomed it. Montalembert only hesitated for a few days; Veuillot was enthusiastic. Napoleon III paid part of the price for the support of the Church by increasing the financial contribution of the State to the Church, thus enabling clerical salaries and pensions to be raised. Legal recognition was accorded to congregations of women and a large loophole was left for congregations of men. Between 1852 and 1862, 982 new religious congregations were authorized. The Panthéon was restored to religious use.

Under state patronage the Church in France grew in size and vigour. Membership of religious orders increased from some 37,000 at the beginning of the Second Empire to nearly 190,000 by the end, mostly of course women but three times what it had been in 1789. This was not a mere numerical growth; religious zeal mounted as well as numbers. The episcopate was distinguished by scholars, administrators, politicians, theologians. The lower clergy, disciplined by their training in the seminaries and their total subjection to the bishops, showed none of the dangerous independence of the eighteenth century. The laity was kept in a state of religious zeal by a well-organized propaganda. Perpetual Adoration became general and the cult of the Virgin occupied an increasingly dominant position in religious worship. In 1854 the doctrine of the Immaculate Conception of the Virgin Mary, supported by the Jesuits and opposed by the Dominicans, was promulgated. Visions were seen and miracles happened. In 1858 the events occurred at Lourdes that were to make it the greatest holy place of modern Catholicism. In these circumstances where all the anti-clericals of the Third Republic were to come from seems a mystery.

Perhaps they might have been fewer if the liberal Catholics of the Second Empire had been more; but these were only a tiny minority. The organ of liberal Catholicism was *Le Correspondant* of Montalembert; and with such collaborators as Albert de Broglie, Dupanloup, Falloux, and Lacordaire, its intellectual distinction was guaranteed. On the other side were those for whom the *loi Falloux*, by which

The Second Republic and the Second Empire

clerical control of education had been greatly extended, was not enough. The law was attacked bitterly by the Intransigents, the leader of whom was the powerful Catholic journalist, Louis Veuillot. Born of peasant stock, trained as a lawyer's clerk, as editor of *L'Univers* he was the voice of the Church militant and spared neither opponents nor allies. Any concession was a crime; persecution was a sacred duty. Veuillot was one of the athletes of faith: to call any happening a miracle was for him to render it *ipso facto* worthy of faith. The liberal Catholics were worse than infidels or heretics.

At the opposite pole to Veuillot was Dupanloup, Bishop of Orleans, a politician, a frequenter of salons and academies, and as restless and fervid a controversialist as Veuillot himself. Dupanloup had most of the intellectuals of the Church behind him. Veuillot had – what was more important – Rome; and through him French Ultramontanism was identified with the religious views that prevailed at the Vatican under Pius IX. The publication of the Syllabus of Errors in 1864, if it might easily have been foreseen as the inevitable recognition of the need to condemn and ban all liberal ideas, came as a shock to the French liberal Catholics. It aroused the latent Gallicanism of the French Church. The opposition to Rome was led by the Archbishop of Paris, Mgr Darboy, appointed in 1863 and destined to die before a Communard firing squad in 1871. The conflict between liberal Catholics and Ultramontanes reached its peak in 1869–70 with the Council summoned at Rome to proclaim the dogma of papal infallibility. Dupanloup agitated in press and pamphlet; Darboy tried to bring in Napoleon III against the papalists; but it was no time for the tottering Emperor to assert himself. Veuillot sent back from Rome brilliant reports for *L'Univers*, demolishing the enemies of the Pope. It was doubtless significant of something that the most powerful voice among the French Catholics was now that of a successful journalist. The victory of the Ultramontanes was complete.

It was during the Second Empire that the cleavage between the majority of French intellectuals and the Church, which had begun under Louis XIV, was renewed. Even the political alliance of the Church with the State began to wear thin before the end of the Second Empire. The Italian War alienated the sympathies of many Catholics, who manifested their dissatisfaction in the elections of 1863. The Emperor, in turn displeased, not only removed the pro-clerical Walewski from Foreign Affairs but appointed Victor Duruy as Minister of Education, to defend the interests of the lay University against the clericals and struggle for the emancipation of education from religion. Duruy cautiously modified the educational system, increasing the number of State schools and reducing the fees, as first steps towards free and compulsory education. He also introduced changes into the traditional syllabus, including a more secular education for girls. In these years, also, anticlericalism was spreading and becoming more aggressive. Among the middle classes Freemasonry, now more or less purged of the misty illuminism of the eighteenth century, was one of the chief means by which it was expressed. And because of the alliance – however strained it had become – between the Church and the Second Empire, anti-clericalism was associated with republicanism.

The growing opposition, of both right and left, is much more interesting than the time-serving politicians and bureaucrats of the Empire. This should not lead us to exaggerate the size or strength of the oppositions. To the end there was no possibility that either could have obtained a majority in the country, still less have overthrown the régime. Their chief effect was in weakening its self-confidence, and in leading the Emperor, who was acutely conscious of changes in public opinion, to feel the need for concessions. Another factor in the situation was his own declining health, which both weakened his grasp and made him more conscious of the problem of the succession. As has been said, the death in 1865 of Morny, who might have been able to guide the régime into more liberal paths with the alliance of Émile Ollivier, delayed the changes which

The Second Republic and the Second Empire

Napoleon probably already had in mind; but in a letter of January 1867 he announced coming constitutional reforms. They may not seem to amount to very much – the chief were that the right of interpellating ministers in the Legislative Body was to be substituted for the debate on the address, that ministers were to speak in support of their legislative proposals, and that the control of the press was to be somewhat relaxed – but conservative resistance held up the new press law for a year.

Until 1868 the press had been kept by direct or indirect methods under effective governmental control. A paper could only be published with government permission and on depositing substantial caution money to meet the fines it might incur. For any article that the authorities disliked it could be warned, and after two warnings was liable to suspension. As well as banning the publication of hostile articles, the government also circulated favourable ones, which were reproduced throughout the country by journals which wished for official support. Most of them did, for it brought advantages in the form of access to information from government sources, such as in England *The Times* had, and also more direct forms of favour – the publication of official notices amounted to a disguised form of subsidy and outright payments were not unknown.

The press law of 1868 ended this administrative control of the press and allowed new journals to be established without preliminary authorization. It was much more dangerous for the régime than any of the constitutional reforms. Immediately there was a proliferation of new sheets, among them the notorious *Lanterne* of Henri Rochefort, which reached a sale of half a million by June 1868. After three months of calculated and brilliant, if irresponsible, insults against the whole Bonapartist establishment, it was suppressed by legal action. Another episode resulting from the relaxation of the press laws occurred in 1868, when the stalwart *quarante-huitard* Delescluze and another journalist started a fund in their papers to erect a monument to the deputy Baudin, who had been killed in the *coup d'état* of 1851. The government made the mistake of prosecuting them. The trial provided the opportunity for a young defence lawyer, just beginning his political career, to deliver a resounding denunciation of the crime of December and all who had been accomplices of it. Gambetta had made his appearance on the political scene.

Everything seemed to be conspiring against Napoleon III in the last, unhappy years of his rule. Economic progress, which had been the great idea, and up to a point the great achievement, of the régime, slackened. There was a severe crisis in the cotton industry in the sixties, attributable mainly to the effects of the American Civil War and to increased competition within France as a result of the development of rail transport. The silk industry suffered from a disease of the silk worm. In the vineyards the appearance of phylloxera in 1863, to become widespread after 1875, began to produce depression. The later sixties indeed belied some of the golden hopes which the economic development of the fifties had raised, though they did not undo the progress that had already been achieved.

The financial crisis was more dangerous for the régime. The Second Empire had been founded on credit, it flourished while the credit lasted, and began to break down when the springs of credit dried up. The steadily increasing threat of war undermined confidence increasingly in the eighteen-sixties. Monied men ceased to invest and left their money idle in the bank: this was known as the *grève du milliard* – the thousand million francs that went on strike. Those with capital to invest feared the adventurous disposition of the Emperor now that he had ceased to want adventures. With more reason they were alarmed by the deterioration in the international situation.

The great financial house which was most closely identified with the Second Empire was naturally the one which suffered most in this crisis. The Crédit Mobilier found in 1866 that its commitments had outrun its mobilizable resources. Its titles to property were still extensive, and given time and the cooperation of other financial houses it

The Second Republic and the Second Empire

could have weathered the storm. But the adventurous methods introduced by the Péreire brothers had alienated the world of orthodox finance, which cheerfully allowed them to sink. In the course of 1867 their shares fell from 1,982 francs to 140, and their credit to the point at which the legitimist, lawyer Berryer, in a law-suit arising out of the crisis, could describe the Crédit Mobilier as 'the greatest gambling house in the world'. The Rothschilds and the more traditional bankers now took their revenge for the earlier triumphs of the Péreires; and the Emperor – for all their services to his régime – could only make a weak and unsuccessful attempt to come to their rescue. As soon as they had safely gone under for the third time, the Crédit Mobilier was refloated by rival houses. But in ruining the Péreires and launching a campaign against 'Saint-Simonian finance' the orthodox bankers had delivered a deadly blow to the already tottering credit of the Second Empire. Perhaps this was not altogether unintentional. They had been suspicious of Louis Napoleon from the beginning, and now they were beginning to believe that a parliamentary government might be more conservative and a better guarantee of property and wealth than an Emperor. As so often, we see the prefigured shape of a coming régime appearing behind the increasingly blurred outlines of the existing one.

The government that had to cope with this critical situation was one from which the paladins of the Second Empire had disappeared, but the party hacks, the official spokesmen, and – at best – the administrators remained. The Empire had not been able to renew its cadres or its leaders. Fould, uncommitted rival of the Péreires from the beginning, was at the Ministry of Finances. Haussmann ruled Paris. In 1863 Baroche added Cultes to Justice, and Rouher became joint Minister of State with Billault, who had been the voice of the Empire in the Legislative Body. Before the session opened Billault had died, and the chief burden was to fall on the broad shoulders of Rouher.

The question which contemporaries and historians have

asked themselves is whether henceforth Rouher or the Emperor determined the policy of the declining Empire. Ollivier called the minister the vice-emperor; the wits declared that France had not a government but a 'Rouher-nement'; high officials and foreign diplomats looked to him for the best indication of the policy of the Emperor. He had been a notable servant of the Second Empire from the beginning. With a capacity for hard work and intrigue, a determination pushed to the point of obstinacy in pursuing a fixed line of action, and the rather crude cunning of an Auvergnat, Rouher rapidly made himself almost indispensable to an Emperor whose own powers were noticeably weakening. With the close collaboration of Fould and Baroche, he built up a subservient clientele in the Legislative Body. Yet he could never feel quite sure of his position: there were many rivals round the Emperor, and he could not afford to make a mistake or a concession. His position was essentially that of a political manager and an advocate rather than a statesman. He envisaged his task as one of defending a régime and implementing its policy, not of supplying the policy himself. Garde des Sceaux on the eve of the *coup d'état* of 2 December, Rouher had probably had a larger share in drawing up the Constitution of 1852 than anyone. He was thus committed to the Bonapartist idea from the outset, that is to a dictatorship which rested on universal suffrage – in other words to the official candidature and electoral management. By character, training, and conviction he was opposed to any liberal concessions. He could only hold his position and continue to function so long as the political system which needed him, and which he had done so much to create, lasted. The death of Morny left him free to pursue his own authoritarian tendencies, one sign of which was the appointment to the Ministry of the Interior of La Valette, who combined a heavy hand with a light head.

Yet the government of Rouher was essentially weak, as was shown when it was faced by the one really vital issue, that of rearmament. The series of military defeats inflicted

The Second Republic and the Second Empire

on the Austrian Empire, begun – by Napoleon III's own act – at Magenta, and culminating at Sadowa, had changed the balance of power in Europe. In face of the rise of Prussia and the isolation of France, only a rapid French rearmament could redress the situation. A commission, appointed after Sadowa in 1866, revealed the weakness of the army – the exemption, in practice, of the sons of the better-off classes from military service; the reliance mainly on professional soldiers and only such as were attracted by the meagre pay and not worried by the dullness of life in barracks; the slowness to adopt the new weapon, the *chassepot*, which only began to be introduced in 1866. But when, early in 1867, the commission produced proposals which would have made military service less easy to avoid and created an effective reserve, there was an almost universal outcry. Government supporters in the Legislative Body feared for their seats; opponents saw a stick with which to beat the government.

Finance was the other major obstacle to rearmament. The earlier wars, colonial expeditions, the Mexican adventure, had still to be paid for. A programme of public works was needed to check the growth of unemployment. The government could not face, at the same time, extensive borrowing to modernize the army. Eventually a few relics of the proposed reforms were passed in the Army Law of January 1868, amid demonstrations of protest from the republicans in the cities, and even these reforms were not put into practice effectively. Throughout the years of increasing international tension the republicans and monarchists opposed rearmament. Napoleon III, who saw the dangers of the international situation, had not the strength either to avoid, or prepare for, the coming clash; and Rouher seems to have been pinning his hopes on a policy of peace at almost any price.

Although Rouher was the main target for the attacks of the opposition and a sufficiently large if pachydermous one, almost as fierce a fire was concentrated on another apparently permanent feature of the Second Empire. This was the prefect of the Seine, Baron Haussmann. Like the Péreire brothers and Rouher, what particularly singled him out for attack was his close association with Napoleon III; and again the attack was launched with the aid of the Rothschilds, as well as with ammunition furnished by Fould from the Ministry of Finances. For Haussmann, to rebuild Paris, had relied on unorthodox methods of raising credit. As building costs increased, and with the slackening of economic activity, speculators who were willing to invest in the property values his new roads created became less easy to find, he was driven to more and more daring expedients to finance his operations. When all these were exhausted, in 1868 he had to come to the Legislative Body to ask for retrospective sanction for a loan amounting to about a quarter of the whole French budget. Fundamentally, the financial position of the rebuilding of Paris was probably sound, but it had been achieved by daring methods which even a parliament still largely composed of official candidates could hardly accept. Rouher, who, like Fould, had no love for Haussmann, practically disavowed him. A future minister of the Third Republic, Jules Ferry, made his mark on the political scene with a pamphlet entitled *Les Comptes fantastiques d'Haussmann*. The Emperor did not yet abandon the prefect who had served him so well, but the fate of Haussmann, and of more than Haussmann, was to turn on the elections of May 1869.

In this situation the wisest policy for Napoleon III might have been to attempt to raise his régime above the electoral battle. There was, after all, no serious possibility of a movement to overthrow the Empire. Legitimists, Orleanists, conservative Republicans, men of property, and peasants, the Empire was still what divided them least. Napoleon III could have afforded to leave the election in 1869 comparatively free; but Rouher could not. He flung everything he had into the struggle, though his own unpopularity was such that his support was the greatest handicap he could inflict on his own candidates. Paris, Lyon, and all the big cities produced crushing majorities against

Paris in the nineteenth century

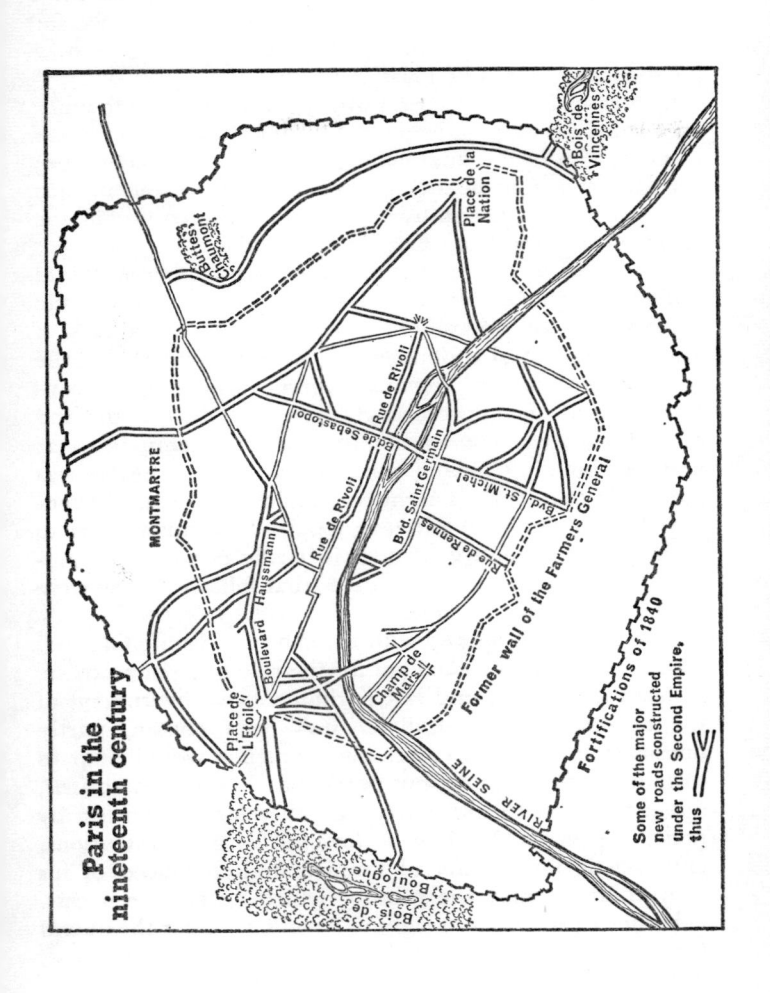

the government. The opposition won some 3,300,000 votes (a million and a half more than in 1863) to 4,400,000 for the official candidates, and it yet remained to be seen how far the latter would be loyal to Rouher.

The Emperor, ill and exhausted, was in no state to enter on a stern struggle in defence of his minister. Persigny was warning him of the unpopularity of Rouher and Baroche; his always inconvenient relative, Prince Napoleon, was intriguing; the Legislative Body was evidently on the point of escaping from Rouher's control.

Unwilling to resign in time, the 'vice-Emperor' found himself, when Napoleon at last decided to yield to the demands of the opposition, faced with the bitter task of announcing the abandonment of his own policy and the concession of the parliamentary liberties which he had consistently and uncompromisingly refused. This was the end of the Bonapartist constitution that had been set up in 1852; and the building having tumbled down in ruins, it was inevitable that its chief architect should go. The same evening Rouher tendered his resignation: Haussmann was to follow him in January 1870. It is hardly necessary to enumerate the constitutional changes that followed, they were to endure so short a while.

The year 1870 opened with the choice of Émile Ollivier, whom Morny had picked out for the rôle five years earlier, as head of the first and last parliamentary government of the Second Empire. Ollivier had been chosen, partly doubtless in the belief that his eloquence would help to sustain the new régime, but partly because he was an *isolé*, not committed to any party and therefore supported by none. He was a dazzling orator, full of good intentions, enthusiastic for the liberal Empire, and convinced of his own ability to play the rôle for which he had been cast. Whether this belief was right or wrong, whether the liberal Empire could have endured, or how it might have evolved, was never to be known.

The new constitution was put into formal shape in April 1870: it established government by a cabinet responsible to

The Second Republic and the Second Empire

parliament. Evidence of the new spirit that it was intended to introduce into the political life of France was a circular of the Minister of the Interior to the prefects: 'You will take care not to subordinate the administration to politics, and you will treat with equal impartiality worthy men (*les honnêtes gens*) of all parties.' The liberal reforms were submitted to a plebiscite on 8 May and approved by 7,358,000 votes against 1,572,000 with 1,894,000 abstentions. It was a triumph for the Empire: republicans and monarchists both recognized it as such. Napoleon III had obtained practically the same number of affirmative votes as in 1852, despite a long series of misfortunes. Although the towns were the centres of opposition, it is claimed that the attachment of the workers to Napoleon III remained lively to the end of the Empire. At any rate, when they did revolt it was only after the Empire had fallen. In the early summer of 1870, though the Empire was in process of evolution, there seemed not the slightest danger of revolution.

6. THE PRICE OF DICTATORSHIP

NEMESIS was to come in the shape of war, not unjustly, on an Empire that had denied its own promise that it was peace. The complicated international manoeuvres that led up to the Franco-Prussian War have been narrated many times and given various interpretations. The offer of the throne of Spain to a Hohenzollern prince, and its acceptance – after much hesitation – in June 1870, precipitated the crisis that had been threatening ever since Sadowa. French opinion was outraged, and the Foreign Minister, the duc de Gramont, a light-weight to have to deal with such a serious situation and an opponent such as Bismarck, declared that a Hohenzollern king in Madrid would be a *casus belli*. In spite of attempts, after the war, to suggest that Napoleon III had dragged an unwilling country into war, the evidence is strong that public opinion throughout France felt that the time had come to make a stand against

Prussian aggression. France had been out-manoeuvred by Prussia too many times in the recent past to be in a mood to accept one more humiliation. The Empress and the court at Saint-Cloud expressed the general sentiments of the nation when they called for a firm stand, and if necessary war. The popular demonstrations in Paris were described by republican politicians after 1870 as 'organized by the police'. There seems to be no justification for this view. Nor should they be dismissed as the mere outburst of a frivolous populace. They were the natural reaction to the history of the previous ten years. Émile Ollivier himself is alleged to have declared, 'Enough humiliation: it is no longer Rouher who controls the government of France.'

However, Ollivier was no fire-eater, and when the acceptance of the Spanish throne was withdrawn by the Hohenzollern prince, he rejoiced that peace had been saved. Napoleon III, who knew the real weakness of the French army, and had been striving by personal approaches to the other European courts to secure a Hohenzollern withdrawal, without which, he realized, he could not avoid war, also believed that peace was saved. He counted without the French need, after years of humiliation, for a victory, if only on paper; and one seemed at last within grasp. Let France demand something more secure than a mere withdrawal, something in the nature of guarantees: the Legislative Body would probably have overthrown Ollivier if he had not done this, and it reflected a widespread opinion, at least among the politically vocal classes. What the peasants thought, or if they thought, cannot be known. Equally, what Ollivier would have done in the face of this movement of opinion cannot be known, for the liberal Empire was too new to permit the normal processes of a parliamentary and cabinet government to operate.

The crucial decision was taken not in parliament or by the head of the government, but at the court of Saint-Cloud, and by a little, and in every sense irresponsible, group headed by the Empress, with the acquiescence of the Emperor. The only minister present was Gramont, who

The Second Republic and the Second Empire

telegraphed immediately after the meeting at Saint-Cloud to Benedetti, French ambassador at Berlin, instructing him to demand a personal guarantee of the withdrawal of the Hohenzollern candidature from the Prussian King, which, it was added, he could hardly refuse '*s'il n'est véritablement animé d'aucune arrière pensée*'. However much this may look like a deliberate attempt to snatch war from the jaws of peace, such an interpretation would be mistaken. The Empress and her entourage were still haunted by the insecurity of a dictatorial régime, which they felt to be more insecure than ever now that it had been launched on the experiment of liberalization. Only a striking diplomatic victory, they believed, could restore the tottering prestige of the Bonapartist cause. And the man over whom they expected to gain this victory was Bismarck.

The king of Prussia seems to have behaved with complete propriety, but of course refused Benedetti's demand for a declaration which would have been almost an admission of his own dishonesty. Bismarck, to whom the episode was reported, saw his opportunity and gave the press a short statement which read like a brusque rebuff from William I to Benedetti: there is no doubt that he knew what he was doing. This was the so-called Ems telegram. When it was published in France a wave of emotion swept through the country – the Empress, Gramont, Ollivier reflected the feeling that practically all the newspapers were proclaiming, and that was manifested on the boulevards of Paris and in the streets and squares of every town in France.

On the day after the interview at Ems, the Imperial Council met repeatedly, with the Empress present, and decided on mobilization. The Emperor was too incapacitated by illness to oppose the irresistible current of opinion, even if he wanted to; but when Ollivier reported to the Legislative Body, it was seen that the current was not quite as irresistible as it had seemed. Certainly it was resisted. The centre and the left envisaged the approaching war as an attempt to undo the concessions of the liberal Empire, which in part it was, and they had a spokesman in Thiers, who in private had already been one of the few in France to foresee defeat, and in public denounced a policy which involved shedding torrents of blood to avenge a few insulting words. Ollivier, whatever his earlier doubts, was now carried away by his own eloquence, and – in one of those phrases with which a man can damn his own reputation for ever – declared that he accepted the responsibility of war 'with a light heart'. On 19 July war was declared on Prussia.

The blunders of Napoleon III's foreign policy ensured that France should enter the war with no allies, but on the side of the government hardly anyone, except perhaps the Emperor himself, supposed that there was any need for them. '*À Berlin*' was the war-cry on the boulevards and the password of the army. There was a run on maps of Germany in the shops; it would have been unpatriotic, defeatist, and absurd to suggest that maps of France might be more useful. As recently as 1859 France had been patently the leading military power of Europe, and the revelation of defects in the French army had not affected public confidence. Yet from the beginning the French army was out-numbered, out-gunned, and out-manoeuvred. The mobilization was so muddled that the Prussians, unexpectedly even to themselves, were able to take the offensive at once. The French, nominally under the supreme command of the Emperor, who was suffering cruelly from his illness and could only sit his horse in agony, experienced a series of defeats – at Wissembourg, Fröschwiller, and Forbach – in the first week of August. Alsace was lost and Lorraine invaded. The Prussian generals made their share of mistakes, but they showed more capacity for coping with the new conditions of warfare created by the railway and intensive use of artillery than did the French, conditioned by thirty years of North African warfare to the cultivation of *élan* and the neglect of logistics.

The conduct of the campaign on the French side was rendered even more ineffective by the Emperor's continual hesitations, and the absence of any coherent plan of campaign. After the initial defeats he was coolly pushed out of

The Second Republic and the Second Empire

his nominal supreme command by the generals, who were as responsible for them as he was. In his place Bazaine became commander-in-chief. He had risen from the ranks, was known for his personal courage, and had lost the favour of the court after dubious conduct in the Mexican campaign. This was sufficient to make him the favoured candidate of the left, and public opinion practically forced him on Napoleon. But the Emperor, while he was in the field, could not avoid the ultimate responsibility for military decisions; and Bazaine was not the man to take any positive action on his own. He withdrew with a large army on Metz, where the Prussians cut him off by a victory at Gravelotte. Meanwhile, the Emperor, with Marshal MacMahon, was gathering a new army on the Marne at Châlons.

When the news of the defeats reached Paris, the Empress, left behind as regent, summoned the Legislative Body, which called for the dismissal of the ministers and generals whom it held responsible for the defeat, and the appointment of a new government chosen by the Assembly. Eugénie at least had the courage of her lack of judgement and did not yield to this. She appointed a Bonapartist ministry under General Cousin de Montauban, comte de Palikao, who took his title from a victory in China, in place of the defunct government of Ollivier. It was patent to everyone that only a military victory could save the Empire. Palikao's order to MacMahon to march to the relief of Bazaine, unjustifiable from a military point of view, was dictated by political considerations; failing this, he said, revolution would break out in Paris. In a forlorn hope, MacMahon and the Emperor led their army in the direction of Metz, where Bazaine remained in a state of inaction that was later to bring the charge of treachery on him. His motives were at least peculiar – but then he had always been what he looked, rather a peculiar individual. In their turn, MacMahon and Napoleon found themselves penned in at Sedan. Under the bombardment of the Prussian artillery a continuation of the struggle meant only futile slaughter of the encircled troops. On 1 September, beaten and broken, the

Emperor surrendered with 84,000 men, 2,700 officers, and 39 generals.

At Paris, recently so gay with optimism, opinion was reeling under the report of defeat after defeat. The news from Sedan brought revolutionary crowds out into the streets. Eugénie and the Prince Imperial fled to England. The Second Empire disappeared: it had become such a phantom that the mob was not even concerned to take revenge on its adherents. Napoleon III was perhaps never less hated or more pitied than in his fall. The Legislative Body, to anticipate a revolutionary movement from the extreme left, proclaimed a provisional Government of National Defence. It was headed by General Trochu, already military governor of Paris, and it included the leaders of the parliamentary opposition, but not Thiers. Far too shrewd to allow himself to be put in a position of responsibility for what he foresaw as inevitably a humiliating defeat, Thiers undertook instead a futile mission to the courts of Europe to plead for intervention.

The usual kind of vulgar libels were produced by the Parisian journalists against Eugénie, as formerly against Marie-Antoinette. Now it was *la femme Bonaparte, ses amants, ses orgies*. But there was surprisingly little anti-Bonapartist demonstration. Patriotic enthusiasm and a belief that, as in 1792, the republic would spell victory, excluded other emotions. Of course, the political machine of the Second Empire collapsed. The new Minister of the Interior, Gambetta, replaced all the prefects of the fallen régime. He began preparing for a national war. The size of the National Guard in Paris was doubled, and at the end of the month it contained 360,000 men. By this time Paris had been surrounded by German forces, which had pushed on beyond the city and occupied all France north and east of Orleans except for Paris. The Government of National Defence was now deprived of contact with the rest of the country and with its own delegation at Tours, whither Crémieux, a venerable survivor of '48, had been sent, on the ground that he was the oldest.

The Second Republic and the Second Empire

When it became evident that a more energetic leadership was needed, it was decided to dispatch Gambetta, on 7 October, across the German lines by balloon to Tours, where he assumed the functions of Minister of War along with those of the Interior. The son of an Italian immigrant and a Frenchwoman from Gascony, and born at Cahors, Gambetta was a southerner by birth and upbringing. His comparatively humble origins left their mark in his uncouth appearance and manners, which did not conceal his charm and ability or diminish his oratorical powers. In all these respects he reminded his contemporaries – and perhaps was not sorry that they should be reminded – of another great Frenchman in another time of troubles, Danton. An early career in the law led on to politics, and in 1869, at the age of thirty-one, Gambetta was elected to the Legislative Body as a member for Belleville, on the strength of the radical programme of political reform known as the Belleville programme. In the autumn of 1870, as heir of the *quarante-huitards* and of the Jacobins of '92, he believed that even in this crisis the republic could save France and hurl back the invader.

To second him at the improvised Ministry of War Gambetta chose the engineer Charles de Freycinet, as cool as Gambetta was excitable, but equally determined. In spite of the reluctance of the rural masses, who were now longing only for peace, the two civilians summoned from the soil of France huge new armies in a way that the generals could never have done; but to provide them with efficient officers was not possible, and to train and arm them time was needed. They had hardly begun to take the field before another military disaster occurred. Bazaine, passive in Metz, intriguing with Bismarck for the restoration of the Empire, perhaps hoping to march his troops back to suppress the republic in Paris, playing, as formerly in Mexico, an equivocal role, capitulated with 173,000 men. The only military objective left now – and it was a forlorn hope – was the relief of Paris. The army that Gambetta had formed on the Loire, under the command of a Bonapartist general with a reputation for ruthlessness, d'Aurelle de Paladines, won an initial victory at Coulmiers and on 7 November reoccupied Orleans. A full-scale sortie from Paris, attempting to join forces with the army of the Loire, was driven back, but already d'Aurelle de Paladines had decided that he could go no farther and had been dismissed by Gambetta. His army was now split by a German counter-attack into two forces, one led inadequately by Bourbaki, another general of the old school, pessimistic, passive, lacking like Bazaine in all the qualities of leadership; and the other with skill by Chanzy, one of the few French generals in the war who, if he was defeated, at least did not go into battle expecting it in advance. In the north-east Faidherbe was struggling ably to contain the German advance, with temporary success.

The sudden, unexpected, heroic resistance of republican France, after the imperial armies and generals had crumpled up so ignominiously, had taken the Prussian command by surprise; but when they recovered from the shock and deployed the forces freed by the capitulations at Sedan and Metz, the result was a foregone conclusion. By January 1871, Chanzy had been driven back fighting from Le Mans to Mayenne. Faidherbe was in retreat. Bourbaki, sent to the east to threaten German communications, led his army into internment in Switzerland. The delegation at Tours, no longer safe there, withdrew to Bordeaux.

Resistance was concentrated now in Paris, where, in numbers at least, there was a formidable force, well armed and gathered behind powerful fortifications. In numbers, indeed, the besieged were superior to the besiegers. Trained troops of course were lacking, though a Mobile Guard of reservists had some military value and a small volunteer body of *francs-tireurs* combined courage with lack of discipline. Practically the whole male able-bodied population of Paris was enrolled in the National Guard, to the number of some 350,000 men, whose duty it was to man the defences of the city. There they became simply a semi-armed rabble, demoralized by lack of military training or occupation of any kind, for the Prussians had no intention of taking Paris by storm when it could so much more easily be starved into surrender. The circle round Paris had been completed on 25 September and the beleaguered population, much larger than was estimated at first, in a fever of patriotism and hope awaited relief from without by the new armies of Gambetta, joining with a victorious sortie from within. It had little information of what was happening in the rest of France, for while balloons could carry letters out of Paris, they could not, because of the prevailing westerly winds, return.

Shortage of food rapidly made itself felt. The poorer suffered greatly, and the lower middle class, whose small shops and trades were ruined, perhaps most of all. On the other hand, luxury restaurants remained open with full menus, apart from vegetables and sea fish, throughout the siege, even if exotic dishes such as kangaroo or elephant, and humble ones like cat, had to appear on the list. As winter came on, cold was as great an enemy as hunger. The trees in the Champs-Elysées were cut down and a swarm descended on them to seize firewood, like the ragged army that daily prowled in the no man's land beyond the fortifications to bring back roots and greenstuff. The Seine began to ice over and soldiers were frozen at their posts. From cold and hunger the death rate mounted. The quest for food became a universal occupation. Edmond de Goncourt, walking in the dusk, hears a girl murmur – *Monsieur, voulez-vous monter chez moi . . . pour un morceau de pain.*'

Bismarck, impatient and seeing political dangers in delay, was pressing for a bombardment of Paris, believing that this would terrorize the inhabitants into surrender. The German generals resisted his pressure for some time, partly because the experiment had already been tried of bombarding Strasbourg, with marked lack of success. However, on 5 January, the weapon of terror was added by the bombardment of Paris. It lasted several hours each night for twenty-three nights. About 12,000 shells fell on the city, killing or wounding some 400 persons, helping to found the modern German tradition of war, but having little effect on the spirit of resistance in Paris.

A History of Modern France

The extremists of the left, who had emerged from hiding or prison with the fall of the Empire, were now the leaders of republican patriotism. 'The Frenchmen of 1870 are the sons of those Gauls for whom battles were holidays,' declared Delescluze. Blanqui entitled the journal he founded *La Patrie en danger* and proclaimed the determination of the people to fight to the death and to save Paris at all costs. Believing as they did in the necessary victory of republican forces, defeat naturally was equated with treachery. When the Parisian offensive of 27 October was beaten back three days later, and at the same time arrived the news of the capitulation of Metz, the left-wing leaders called out the mob, invaded the Hôtel de Ville, and began to organize a revolutionary government. Loyal battalions were fetched up and brought the situation under control. There was a similar reaction to a final *sortie en masse* on 19 January, which failed with heavy loss. It has been regarded as an attempt by Trochu to demonstrate to the Parisians the hopelessness of the situation and so prepare the way for capitulation, but as he put himself at the head of the troops this may not be altogether fair to him. The defeat led to another march on the Hôtel de Ville, which was dispersed by the Mobile Guard. The transformation of the patriotic struggle against the invaders into a social struggle inside France was beginning. Elsewhere – in Lyon, Marseille, Toulouse – revolutionary communes had already been set up, but had been brought under control by Gambetta's prefects.

The propertied classes, who had most to lose from the continuance of the war, had long been ready to abandon the struggle. Thiers had all along believed in negotiating with the enemy, under the impression that the price of peace would be cheaper the sooner it was concluded. After the failure of the left-wing rising of 22 January the government in Paris felt safe in accepting the inevitable armistice. By its terms Paris was to capitulate and there was to be a three weeks' suspension of hostilities to allow for the election of an assembly which could negotiate a peace.

The war was over. It was the defeat of an army in which

The Second Republic and the Second Empire

were reflected all the defects of the state and society created by the Revolution and Napoleon. The army, like successive French régimes, was possessed by the blind belief in itself of an all-powerful bureaucracy, and by a corresponding inability to make adjustments to cope with the unexpected. The result was total collapse in the face of a crisis. The army also reflected the inherent social conflicts in France. The older aristocratic families had given up their traditional military role rather than serve a state which had abandoned the legitimate monarchy. The bourgeoisie saw no attractions in such an underpaid and despised profession as the army; it was able to avoid the selective service, if its sons drew an unlucky number, by the system of paying for a substitute. The officers of the army were largely drawn from the ranks and their position was the reward of bravery and brawn rather than brains. The higher command went by court favour. What the officer corps lacked in tradition and social background was not made good by the system of military education, for this was as conservative and inappropriate to a post-seventeenth-century world as all other education. When the Minister of War, Leboeuf, said that the army was ready, he spoke truth by its own standards. In fact, sunk in an inspissated conservatism, the French army, a true mirror in this respect of French society, was quite unprepared to meet the challenge of a new age. It was still, for all effective purposes, an *ancien régime* army, with all its defects and lacking only some of its virtues. 'French troops', writes Mr Michael Howard, 'straggled, looted and drank as European armies had for four hundred years past.' It had to meet a German army which in comparison was an organized and disciplined military machine. The successes of the German gunners showed, Mr Howard says, that a new age of applied technology in war had begun; the disasters that befell the French cavalry showed that an old age had ended. 'The German victories, as was universally recognized, had been won by superior organization, superior military education, and, in the initial stages of the war at least, superior manpower.'

The new armies of France, called out of the earth by the genius of Gambetta and organized by Freycinet, represented an even newer response to the problem of modern war, but in 1870 a brilliant improvisation that could not succeed. Gambetta, his policy of national defence having failed, resigned. Although he was elected by nine departments, the result of the elections was overwhelmingly against him. He recognized defeat and withdrew from France.

The electoral decree was issued on 24 January and the election held on 8 February. To bring to an end the electoral management of the Second Empire, *scrutin de liste* was introduced in place of single-member constituencies. The new prefects had not the influence to make the election, and in any case had been instructed not to do so. The vote was largely a plebiscite for peace and against the dictatorship of Gambetta. Many electors were prisoners or in the new armies; over 40 departments were occupied by the enemy. The population, which could only look for guidance to its local notables and clergy, returned conservative lists everywhere save in Paris and some other large towns, in parts of the east, and in a few southern departments. There were 400 monarchists, 214 of them Orleanist, 182 legitimists mostly from the west and south-west; 78 moderates who were to become conservative republicans; 150 republicans, about 40 of a radical tinge; Bonapartism was reduced to a mere 20, only 4, and these in Corsica, daring to proclaim themselves as such. Some third of the new Assembly was *noblesse*; only 175 had ever sat in an Assembly before; their average age was fifty-three.

It was an exceptional body, elected under exceptional conditions, for a single purpose – to make peace. The shadow of things to come might have been seen in the election as President of the Assembly of Jules Grévy, the republican who had warned in 1848 against the constitutional arrangements which opened the door to Louis Napoleon. Thiers, for whom the election had practically been a plebiscite, with 2,000,000 votes accumulated in multiple candidatures and election in 26 departments, was

The Second Republic and the Second Empire

the almost inevitable choice as head of the Executive. France invariably looks to those it has known for many years when a national crisis emerges. Nevertheless, an overwhelmingly monarchist assembly had begun by placing in the key positions two republicans; and Thiers' three leading ministers, Favre, Picard, and Simon, were also republicans.

But there was more than one kind of republican in the minority of the Assembly. Paris had sent a group of deputies, including Louis Blanc, Victor Hugo, Delescluze, Ledru-Rollin, Rochefort, Quinet, whose names were like a roll-call of '48. To the monarchist majority they were intolerable and in fact were so little tolerated that some eight of them resigned. The National Assembly, under the leadership of Thiers, was determined to eliminate the danger from the left, and now this meant almost exclusively Paris. A court martial sentenced Blanqui and Flourens, as leaders of the 31 October rising, to death in their absence. The former Bonapartist, d'Aurelle de Paladines, dismissed by Gambetta, was put in command of the Paris National Guard. The Assembly was brought back from Bordeaux to Versailles instead of to Paris. Finally, Thiers gave orders for the 400 guns in the hands of the National Guard of Paris to be removed on 18 March. It has been described as a deliberate provocation, which Thiers never expected to succeed in any other respect; but he did not expect his troops from Versailles to fraternize with the Parisians, and he expected the National Guard from the middle-class quarters of Paris to give his policy support. This was to underestimate the effect of two fatal measures passed by the Assembly. The first had ended the moratorium on the promissory notes through which much of the business of Paris was conducted; the second was to make rents which had remained unpaid during the war immediately payable. These decisions seemed very reasonable to the landed gentry of the Assembly, to the financiers who had speculated in paper and rents, and to Thiers. They spelt ruin to the lower middle classes of Paris.

Thiers's attempted seizure of the guns was the spark

which set off revolution in Paris. After a riot and a few murders, he ordered the abandonment of Paris by all the legal authorities. The only organized body left in the city was the moderate Central Committee of the National Guard, which found itself obliged to take over the essential services, abandoned by Thiers's orders. Naturally those who came to the front in this emergency were the stronger and extremer leaders, bred in the red clubs which had flourished during the siege of Paris. The eternal conspirator, Blanqui, temporarily not the eternal prisoner, had been the inspiring genius of the most famous of the clubs, meeting in the Halles. His *club rouge* has been described as 'a chapel consecrated to an orthodox classical cult of conspiracy, in which the doors were wide open to everyone, but to which one only returned if one was a convert'. Blanqui himself presided over the cult, with 'his delicate, superior, calm countenance, his narrow, piercing eyes shot across now and again with a dangerous, sinister light' – an unusually favourable picture of the conspirator described by Victor Hugo as 'a sort of baleful apparition in whom seemed to be incarnated all the hatred born of every misery'.

The Blanquists were only a tiny fraction, the rest of the Parisian rebels felt the need to legitimize their position by holding elections. A municipal government, to be known by the historic but alarming name of Commune, was elected on 26 March. The name of the Commune was a memory of the year 11, of the Jacobins of Robespierre and the sansculottes of Hébert. It was a symbol beneath which the most opposed schools of revolutionary thought could rally. Four separate groups can be distinguished among its members – the pure revolutionaries, divided between Blanquists and Jacobins, the federalists following Proudhon, and the adherents of the First International. The conservatives or moderates returned in the first election of the Commune resigned, and after complementary elections there was a revolutionary majority of some 57 Blanquists and Jacobins, and a socialist and Proudhonist minority of about 22.

It is a mistake to regard the Commune as Marxist in

The Second Republic and the Second Empire

inspiration; only one of its members can be described as a Marxist. Equally it was not a government of the working-class. Though there were 25 *ouvriers*, there were more than twice as many lesser bourgeois or professional men. The 'Declaration to the French People' issued by the Commune on 19 April represents the federalist tendencies of the minority. As soon as the active struggle began, the Blanquists, weakened by the absence of their prophet, who had been arrested and returned to jail as soon as danger began to threaten Paris, and the Jacobins, headed by Delescluze, took control in a temporary alliance, to be followed, as in 1793, by bitter quarrels. On 1 May they set up a Committee of Public Safety by 45 votes to 23.

The second siege of Paris began on Palm Sunday, 2 April, by a Versailles army in a wretched state of disorganization and lack of material and morale. Its first military achievement was to shoot five prisoners. The forces of the Commune retaliated with a wild sortie in the direction of Versailles, which was easily dispersed with the loss of some 1,000 prisoners captured by the Versaillais, who picked out those they thought were the leaders and shot them. Given a small measure of capacity and unity, at the outset the Commune should have been able to take the offensive with success. It had many more men and guns than Versailles, and a base in the fortified camp of Paris which could be provisioned through the neutral Prussian lines. These advantages were gradually lost. While the leaders of the Commune talked and small bodies of men defended the forts, the life of Paris, theatres, concerts, the busy traffic of the streets, went on much as usual and far more normally than during the Prussian siege. Such changes as were deliberately debated and brought about by the Commune were hardly of major importance. The old revolutionary calendar was revived and May 1871 became *floréal* year LXXIX. The Vendôme column was pulled down in a great public ceremony.

Meanwhile the military strength of Versailles was growing. On 8 May a general bombardment of the fortifications began. The forts round the south of Paris, gallantly defended by isolated groups of men, fell one by one. On 21 May a section of the walls near the porte de Saint-Cloud was discovered to be undefended, and by nightfall the Versaillais had a large body of men within Paris. On the same day the Commune held its last official meeting, devoted typically to a trial of its own military commander. Both he and his successor had failed to secure a reasonable measure of military behaviour from the forces of the Commune. Now that Paris was at bay, the old Jacobin Delescluze proclaimed a war of the people, not conducted by staff officers and military discipline, but by the people, the *bras nus*. And now that all was really lost the Communards at last began to fight in earnest, in the traditional way, the only way that the people of Paris knew. It was a street battle of barricades, which was to rage for seven days across the breadth of Paris from west to east.

The Versaillais, strong in the knowledge that they were defending order and public morality, throughout the fighting showed more barbarity than the Communards. Apart from the initial episode and the actual fighting, there were practically no shootings of opponents or suspected opponents in Paris until the last stages were reached, though hostages were seized. The Versaillais systematically shot their prisoners. This was one motive of the subsequent murders of hostages that accompanied the final battle in the streets of Paris; but also, it is true, there was a group of ruthless men among the leaders of the Commune, who had not distinguished themselves in the fighting but had had their eye on the hostages all the time. Now they had their chance, and particularly chose priests, including the Archbishop of Paris, for their victims. To the horror of the street fighting and massacres on both sides was added fire. Incendiary shells from the Versaillais, the burning of buildings by the Communards to clear lines of fire or form a barrier, destroyed much. The Tuileries and other public buildings were fired in a last act of defiance by desperate men, though the story of the *pétroleuses* is a mere piece of propaganda.

In its final phase the defence of the Commune degenerated

The Second Republic and the Second Empire

into uncoordinated episodes of heroism or cruelty. Delescluze, in the dress of a deputy of '48, top hat, frock coat, and red sash, cane in hand, all being now lost, mounted a barricade to be shot. The last combat of any size was among the graves of the cemetery of Père-Lachaise; and there, on the next day, against the wall that was to become a place of pilgrimage, 147 Communards were shot. Military justice continued to take its toll. The Versaillais lost about 1,000 dead in the fighting; the death roll of the Communards was probably not less than 20,000. Thiers had won a notable victory in the class war; the illusions of 1789 and 1792 had drawn the people of Paris into the bloodiest and most merciless of all its defeats; the Second Empire had ended in disgraceful surrender, revolution and repression, blood and tears; but it was an assembly of monarchists, under a conservative republican head of state, that first provoked and then put to fire and sword the people of Paris.

7. PLUS ÇA CHANGE

The collapse of the Second Empire ends the monarchical and Bonapartist phase in French history. Yet, just as the ghost of the legitimate monarchy haunted the century after its fall, so a disembodied Bonapartism without a Bonaparte was to be a sort of Pepper's ghost, periodically appearing and disappearing on the political stage during the hundred years after the collapse of the Second Empire. Politically, it was far from clear in 1871 whether France was going on to something new or merely back to stale revivals of the past. In art and literature, also, 1871 was not a dividing line. The rebel movements of the third quarter of the century had already inaugurated what was to be one of the great ages of French painting and letters. Above all, in its basic pattern French society seemed to be, and indeed was, unaffected by the passing of an Empire.

If, having said all this, and admitting the artificiality of such divisions in history, we nevertheless have to end one volume and begin another in 1871, this is because there is, after all, something significant in the political calendar. The major changes in political institutions that resulted from the fall of the Second Empire were a determining factor in a fundamental though gradual transformation of French society, and without its opening years the history of the Third Republic would be robbed of the political developments that are essential for its understanding. There is another reason why we must make the break here. The disaster that befell the army, the unresisted collapse of the political system, the social *stasis* that burst out in the bloody class war of the Commune, all inflicted a psychological shock that, if the first result was to numb the national spirit, in the end stimulated it to new endeavour. Although, therefore, the disappearance of Napoleon III from the scene was not like that of a Louis XIV or a Napoleon I – it did not mark an epoch and hardly left a void – there are reasons for accepting the division of French history at this point and pausing to reflect on the significance of the generations that had elapsed between eighteenth *brumaire* and Sedan.

It is revealing to look back even earlier to 1770, when Louis XV had been making a new political experiment, as Louis Napoleon was in 1870, and consider the passage of an eventful hundred years, in the course of which France had experienced three major revolutions and moved backwards and forwards between monarchy, republic, and empire. How much during this century had French society really changed? If we imagine a Rip van Winkle who fell asleep in France, and alternatively in England, in 1770, and woke again in 1870, and ask him in which country there had been a series of revolutions, there can be little doubt what his answer would be. He would remember eighteenth-century England as a small, rural community of country towns, villages, and hamlets, with sea-ports, but with no great centre of population outside London, its communications by coach on the new turnpike roads where they existed or by pack-horse along tracks, its industry mainly carried on, in town or country, in the homes of domestic workers. Much of

The Second Republic and the Second Empire

this could also apply to the France of 1770, except that in England an agrarian revolution was already under way, while in France the ports were finer and urbanization had produced a crop of elegant provincial towns; also that France was a country with a population of over twenty millions, about three times that of Great Britain. Politically and socially there were more significant differences, but in both countries the powers of monarchy were in practice strictly limited by the influence of the aristocracy, which in turn had to respect the interests of a rising middle class.

Waking in 1870, the sleeper for a hundred years would find changes in England such as he would hardly credit. An industrial revolution that had transformed the appearance of large tracts of country, a population multiplied by five, an urgent political life, with two great parties which had brought political consciousness and activity to large sections of the community, an empire spreading to the four corners of the world: this was the England of Queen Victoria and Mr Gladstone. What was the France of Napoleon III and Ollivier?

It was a country which seemed in many ways never to have left the eighteenth century. There was an Emperor who was the effective head of the government, instead of a king who was only its nominal head; a court at Saint-Cloud instead of Versailles, with fewer old names and more *ennoblis*; a parliament, it is true, but one which lacked the independence, for good or ill, of the juridical *parlements* of the *ancien régime*; there were still great financiers, and they still exercised some political, and even more social, power; the Church was again in alliance with the state, and again used its influence to frustrate national policies and obstruct reforms; Paris was swollen and rebuilt, its poorer population expelled to the periphery, and the city itself even more than formerly the centre of administration and government, art and letters, finance and banking. Provincial France, apart from isolated patches of industrialization, and the railways that had been driven across it under the Second Empire, remained very much as it had been a century

A History of Modern France

earlier, administered in *départements* by prefects instead of in *généralités* by intendants. For the ordinary man the pattern of daily life, the food he ate and the way in which he ate it, his social relations, his interests, his upbringing and his formal education, had changed little; for the peasantry life had changed hardly at all.

If we ask the reason for the intense conservation of such a politically revolutionary country as France, we must first look at its economy, its ways of earning and spending. The Second Empire, under the inspiration of the Saint-Simonians, had inaugurated a minor industrial revolution, and in particular endowed France with a railway system. This was a sign of new things stirring, like the rebuilding of Paris by Haussmann, and of Lyon by Vaïsse. But it was attributable to the inspiration of Louis Napoleon himself, with a small group of advisers, and forced through against the opposition of the established powers of French society, just as had been the lesser efforts at economic progress of the Orleanist régime; the main financial and business interests of France seemed to have a vested interest in social conservatism and economic backwardness. The powerful Bank of France, whose two hundred regents formed the central citadel of wealth, had been given the task, from its Napoleonic beginnings, of guarding against social or economic change. A stable currency, unaffected by wars or revolutions, was one proof of its success. Industry was similarly guarded against experiment or change. In the nineteenth century it was impossible to keep technical improvements out entirely, or to prevent the appearance of some large-scale enterprises. But these were exceptional, and until Napoleon III forced through, against bitter opposition, his new commercial policy, a rigid protectionism shielded French industry from competition and the compulsion of progress.

However, industrialists and financiers and commercial men were not a dominant factor in French society. Men of property and rentiers were the main constituents in the structure of the French upper classes. Their ideas were supplied to them by professional men and writers who were

The Second Republic and the Second Empire

equally conservative in their intellectual formation. They were men of property on the Forsyte model, interested in the accumulation of land and houses, or the collection of government bonds, in which they had a pathetic faith, playing for safety as they thought, and content with modest gains so long as no risks were taken. Ordinary business they rather despised. England in these days was still damned, in Napoleonic phrase, as a nation of shopkeepers. *'La France'*, Michelet truly said and he meant it as praise, *'n'a pas d'âme marchande.'* The French élite in the nineteenth century was an élite of bourgeois, but their aim was to be, as in the eighteenth century, *bourgeois vivant noblement.*

The ideal of a stable, unchanging society seemed one that was capable of achievement at the time. The pressure which, in the eighteenth century and the earlier part of the nineteenth, produced social unrest and forced speculation about ways to remedy it, the pressure of population on a country already over-populated in relation to its productivity, had lackened. Above all, France remained rural, the masses of the nation scattered in small country towns, villages, or hamlets, where a class of peasant proprietors, however lacking in worldly goods or the amenities of life they may have been themselves, were acutely conscious of their interests as property owners, intensely suspicious of anything which seemed to offer the threat of change in the pattern of French agrarian society.

Thus a revolution had laid the foundations of an intensely conservative society, nor is this difficult to understand. The classes which consolidated their victory in the Revolution were the peasant proprietors in the country and the men of property in the towns, neither with any vision beyond the preservation of their own economic interests, conceived in the narrowest and most restrictive sense. A Church devoted – apart from an occasional easily crushed rebel – to the interests of the wealthy propertied classes provided the moral justification for their wealth, and spiritual sanctions against those who would attack it. The small Huguenot minority was, if possible, even more devoted to the protection of the interests of property than the great Catholic majority. A powerful, centralized administrative structure and judicial system, recruited almost exclusively from the upper sectors of society, strengthened the defences of the existing order. If this was bourgeois society, it was an economically reactionary and backward bourgeoisie that it represented, having nothing in common with the inventors and entrepreneurs, the ruthless financiers, the cut-throat competition of the builders and makers of industrial capitalism. The society which emerged in France from the revolutionary decade and was stabilized by Napoleon, under whom the pattern was fixed which it was to keep with little change for the next three-quarters of a century, was a far more static society than the one which had entered the Revolution with such high hopes.

It was also a society torn by periodic gusts of violent and bloody political disturbance. The paradox is not in the political instability, but in the fact that this also is evidence of the conservatism of a society stuck with an unfinished revolution on its hands, one which it seemed under the compulsion to try to re-enact periodically, not because of any social necessity, but because it was now part of the national tradition, a set pattern of behaviour that had to be repeated whenever the coincidence of political and economic crises provided the appropriate stimulus. Then, while some took up the traditional revolutionary stances, others dreamed of reviving the counter-revolution. But since the balance of society remained essentially unchanged, when the smoke had cleared away and the turmoil died down, it was seen that nothing fundamental had changed. Different actors might now be in the front of the stage, but they were still performing the same play.

For this reason the revolutions of 1830, 1848, 1870, though not the frustrated revolution 1871, each in turn give the impression of being the result of a chapter of accidents. This is in fact what they were, but it does not mean that they were of no importance and had no effect on national history. What they did was successively to remove most of the

The Second Republic and the Second Empire

political, and in some cases even the administrative personnel of the previous régime, sometimes only temporarily, but sometimes permanently. In addition, they destroyed the reputations and prospects of many of the leaders of revolution themselves. Seldom has a great nation been so wasteful of its élites. Regularly, generation after generation, those who had acquired political or administrative experience were thrown on the scrap-heap of a usually remunerative retirement.

What kept France going, apart from the stability of its social structure, was the rigid framework of a centralized administration, staffed in all its higher levels by the sons of the same propertied class that controlled the nation's economy. So long as their property and their jobs were safe, they were prepared to serve any régime. France has often been taken as the awful example of a country whose politics have been blighted by the curse of ideology. The strong, but unfortunately not silent, men in our universities who advocate a highly principled lack of political principle, and have tried to deny the legitimacy of rational thought about ends and means in politics, have looked to France to illustrate the danger of having ideas in politics, whereas Great Britain shows the virtue of a happy empiricism, not sicklied over by the pale cast of thought. Historically, this is the most arrant nonsense. The interplay between rational political thinking and empirical politics, which was a dominant feature of British political life for four centuries, was lacking in France. The influence of Rousseau on the French Revolution is a legend. The theocrats may have been too lunatic, and the doctrinaires too rational, but the failure of the Restoration was nothing to do with either, any more than the July Monarchy or the Second Republic were influenced by the Utopian Socialists. Benjamin Constant and de Tocqueville were both distinguished political thinkers, but if they were recognized as such, and had any practical influence, it was in England not in France.

In nineteenth-century France political life was the expression of the most blatant materialism. France between 1799 and 1871 was a working model of the instability of a political system without moral and ideological bases. The Napoleonic Empire naturally had none; it was a war dictatorship, with no more principle behind it than the Golden Horde, probably a good deal less. The Restoration came to a nation which had already made many compromises with the revolutionary and Napoleonic state, and could not return to the *ancien régime*, which anyhow had already lost its intellectual justification before it met its violent end. The revolution of 1830 merely demonstrated that France could not recover an age that was lost, and that 1789 was irreversible. The raison d'être of the July Monarchy was to protect the interests of property, and when Louis-Philippe was no longer able to do so, after a brief interval Louis Napoleon took up the task. With Saint-Simonian inspiration, the Second Empire came a little closer to grips with the problems of French society. If it had not been for the disaster of the Franco-Prussian War, the Liberal Empire might have survived and merged into a parliamentary régime not so very different from that of the Third Republic. But it could only have done this by giving some real content to the principle of the sovereignty of the people to which it paid lip service, and this meant in effect the Republic.

If the Revolution had any ideological basis it was the sovereignty of the people; and if this idea had any honest meaning (which is doubtful) it was universal suffrage. Again it will be enlightening to draw a comparison with England. Once the theoretical democrats of the revolutionary period – never very influential in practice – had been defeated, the extension of the franchise in Great Britain had been argued mainly on practical, utilitarian grounds, as a means of winning improved conditions of life for successive layers of the population. In France politics and economics were curiously separated. The case for universal suffrage was argued as a political right of the individual, a sort of magical gesture. Sovereignty of the people became an incantation, a secular religion. It had its prophets, chiefly concerned with their own spiritual sanctity, its dervishes, prepared to suffer

The Second Republic and the Second Empire

or inflict any pain in the service of the cult, and a political priesthood, anxious above all that no doctrines should be taken so seriously as to endanger vested interests.

Electoral management for a time succeeded in controlling the popular vote, but even in a restricted franchise the electorate sometimes refused to be managed, as the history of the Restoration and the July Monarchy showed. The only alternative, since the one-party state had not yet been invented, was the Bonapartist plebiscitary dictatorship. Beyond this we need not ask what Bonapartism was: it was the party of the men with property and jobs, as Orleanism had been before it, and as Legitimism had tried with less success to be during the Restoration. There was no Bonapartist, just as there was no Orleanist ideology. French politics between 1815 and 1870 was a Namierite paradise, with no Burke to distort the play of self-interested political intrigue, a model machine for the demonstration of politics as a self-sufficient activity.

The trouble is that real life will keep breaking in, disturbing the happy meaninglessness of the Namierite or Oakeshottian political game, in which every ladder has its corresponding snake and the game is never-ending, for it has no goal just as it had no beginning. Unfortunately, as we discover in the last resort, and sometimes even earlier, it cannot always be kept on the level of a game. So the history of nineteenth-century France showed. There were vital issues, which politicians and *fonctionnaires* might try to ignore, but which periodically took charge of the players; and then the ladders soared to the skies and the snakes devoured their victims.

The instability of French politics did not just arise out of the throw of the dice. There were real issues at stake. One of these was religion. To what extent religion in the West has ever been a cement of society is a matter of doubt. In France it certainly was not so in the century of the religious wars, or in that of the persecution and destruction of the Huguenots, or when the Jansenist controversy was bedevilling Church and state. The Revolution created a new

A History of Modern France

religious schism which was dangerous because the anti-clerical minority was large and influential. The constant attempts of the Church to use the machinery of the state to recover its influence over society, to interfere in secular matters and especially to control education, built up an anti-clerical opposition, which was not conciliated by the rise of a proselytizing spirit and a militant ultramontanism which aroused national and Gallican hostility as well. Although many unbelievers in the propertied classes were prepared to accept the power of the Church as a means of keeping the lower orders in the station to which God had called them, they could not enthusiastically support clerical influence over government. They were glad enough to have their daughters brought up in purdah and general ignorance by nuns, but they wanted a better education for their sons. As for the lower orders, whom religion was supposed to be keeping in a state of proper respect, they were steadily being alienated by a Church which seemed to be devoted exclusively to the protection of the interests of the rich. After 1794, however, anti-clericalism never offered a serious threat to the Church in this period, while clericalism was never strong enough to put the clock back to the seventeenth century as it might have liked. This conflict, therefore, produced tension in society, but no dangerous cleavage as yet.

The class conflict, which was not unconnected with this one, was more immediately alarming. Its nature must not be misunderstood. It was not the class conflict of a modern industrial society, with organized labour waging war for improved conditions and higher wages. Only in Lyon was there, on a small scale, something like this pattern. In the country – and France remained overwhelmingly rural – the peasant proprietors, with no vision beyond their commune, were more concerned to guard their own petty privileges against the rural proletariat than to envisage anything better for themselves. As men of property they could always be called on to rally to the defence of property against the 'anarchists' of Paris. Only in the capital was there a suffi-

The Second Republic and the Second Empire

ciently large proletariat to offer a real threat to the established order and here it was in the form of an unorganized horde, living in depression and degradation, capable – as in 1789 – of being called out by political leaders in the interests of a change of régime, but not capable of conceiving or fighting for a programme of economic reform to better its own conditions. The Parisian populace was a threat, in fact, not to the social system, which seemed irrefrangible, but to political stability.

It is true that in this intensely conservative society ideologies proliferated. Their numbers and their wildness bore witness to their remoteness from practicality. An ineffective left-wing now acquired the tradition of irresponsibility which comes from the divorce from political power, and which the right had inherited from the frondeur aristocracy of the *ancien régime*; while the various parties of the centre, sunk in a squalid defence of their vested interests, squabbled, and sometimes fought, for power and places and the rewards that went with them.

The picture is a depressing one, of a society which had forgotten most of the ideals inherited from the age of the Enlightenment and the earlier days of the Revolution and from which all who held to these, or to newer ideals, felt themselves alienated. Despairing of political and economic life, finding little solace in religion, they turned to art and literature and inaugurated the tradition of a divorce between these and society, the mutual contempt of the artist and the bourgeois. Instead of a mirror in which were reflected the highest values of contemporary civilization, the arts in France became a protest against a society which rejected them and which they rejected. Victor Hugo with the victims of justice and property in *Les Misérables*, Daumier in his drawings of the Orleanist bourgeoisie – lawyers and men of affairs, with greed, envy, malice, and all uncharitableness written in their countenances, Flaubert and the empty life of the Paris rentier or the provincial lady of fashion, Courbet painting the cold, pinched faces of poverty or the leer of success in Church and state – in these there was conscious social comment; in Gautier and others a turning away from contemporary society to art for art's sake, a rejection of bourgeois values, of the moral and religious phrases that provided the alibi for unfeeling hearts, and of the repetition of stereotypes that was a substitute for thought in obtuse heads. To those who could not accept gross and philistine standards the life of the rich was a spiritual void and that of the poor a material hell. In a sordid cult of dirt, drugs, and debauchery, the artist sought an artificial paradise, which yet in a Baudelaire could reach to the heights of poetry.

The *vie de Bohème* was a conscious protest against bourgeois values, but it was a pathetically unavailing protest. The aristocracy and bourgeoisie of the eighteenth century had kissed the rods that chastised them: Montesquieu, Voltaire, Rousseau, the Encyclopedists were their idols. Orleanists and Bonapartists just ignored their critics. The age enclosed by the two Napoleons, looked at from the point of view of the high hopes of the Enlightenment and 1789, is bound to seem disappointing and disillusioning. The achievements of the Frenchmen of that age were unimpressive even to themselves, and they remain unimpressive in retrospect. The exciting new developments of the nineteenth century passed France by. In an age of change the French nation appeared to have chosen stagnation without stability. The more the kaleidoscope of its politics changed, the more France remained the same.

Yet, looking forward, it will be seen that this could not have been the whole story. The First Republic succeeded to a great age of reform, and sadly misused its heritage. The Third Republic was to come into a much less promising inheritance and great things were to be made of it. But if this can be said, then there must be a different way from that which I have adopted of summing up the France of the monarchies and the empires. Under the frozen surface of sterile egoism we should detect the early shoots of the creative achievements of the Third Republic. These beginnings have been passed over slightly or not mentioned in this volume. They can be brought in more appropriately later, when they were coming to fruition. For the moment, in 1871, there was little enough evidence of a more hopeful future. It was the end of an unattractive chapter in the history of France. It was not the end of the whole story.

CHRONOLOGICAL TABLE

1799 November. Coup d'état of 18 *brumaire*
  December. Constitution of year VIII. Bonaparte First Consul
1800 February. Foundation of Bank of France
  Law of 28 *pluviôse* year VIII establishes prefectoral system
  Pacification of the West
  June. Marengo
  December. Hohenlinden
  Royalist bomb plot
1801 Armed Neutrality
  February. Treaty of Lunéville
  April. Copenhagen
  August. French army in Egypt capitulates
1802 Chateaubriand's *Le Génie du Christianisme*
  March. Peace of Amiens
  April. Concordat promulgated
  May. Bonaparte Consul for life
1803 April. British ultimatum
  May. Renewal of war with Great Britain
  Sale of Louisiana to United States
1804 March. Civil Code promulgated
  Cadoudal plot
  Execution of duc d'Enghien
  May. Proclamation of Empire
  Camp at Boulogne
  2 December. Coronation of Napoleon
1805 August. Third Coalition
  15 October. Ulm
  21 October. Trafalgar
  2 December. Austerlitz
1806 January. Peace of Pressbourg
  June. Confederation of the Rhine formed
  July. Maida
  October. Jena
  Auerstädt
  November. Berlin decrees
1807 February. Eylau
  June. Friedland
  July. Treaty of Tilsit

Chronological Table

- 1807 October. Invasion of Portugal
  November, December. Milan decrees
- 1808 Establishment of the University
  May. Joseph Bonaparte King of Spain
  July. Capitulation of Baylen
  August. Vimiero
  Convention of Cintra
  December. Napoleon invades Spain
- 1809 January. Corunna
  March. Invasion of Portugal
  April. Austrian offensive
  Disgrace of Talleyrand
  May. Annexation of Papal States
  Imprisonment of Pius VII
  July. Wagram
  October. Peace of Schönbrunn
- 1810 Divorce of Josephine
  April. Marriage of Napoleon to Marie-Louise
  Disgrace of Fouché
  Mme de Staël's *De l'Allemagne*
  September. Lines of Torres Vedras
- 1811 Economic crisis
- 1812 24 June. Grand Army crosses the Niemen
  September. Borodino
  14 September–14 October. Occupation of Moscow
  October. Malet plot in Paris
  27 November. Crossing of Beresina
  14 December. Ney recrosses Niemen
- 1813 May. Lützen
  Bautzen
  June. Vittoria
  August. Dresden
  October. Leipzig
  Wellington crosses the Pyrenees
- 1814 January. Allied invasion of France
  February. March. Negotiations at Châtillon
  31 March. Capitulation of Paris
  6 April. Abdication of Napoleon
  10 April. Toulouse. Defeat of Soult by Wellington
  11 April. Treaty of Fontainebleau
  1 May. First Treaty of Paris
  2 May. Declaration of Saint-Ouen

A History of Modern France

- 1814 4 June. Constitutional Charter of Louis XVIII
  September. Congress of Vienna meets
- 1815 1 March. Napoleon lands at Fréjus
  20 March. Napoleon enters Paris
  16 June. Ligny and Quatre-Bras
  18 June. Waterloo
  22 June. Second abdication of Napoleon
  8 July. Second Restoration
  Government of Talleyrand-Fouché
  White Terror in Midi
  August. Election of *Chambre introuvable*
  September. Talleyrand and Fouché resign
  Richelieu ministry
  November. Second Treaty of Paris
  December. Execution of Marshal Ney
- 1816 September. Dissolution of *Chambre introuvable*
  Election of new Chamber
- 1818 November. Occupation of France ended
  December. Richelieu replaced by Decazes
- 1819 de Maistre's *Du Pape*
  Géricault's *The Raft of the Medusa*
- 1820 February. Assassination of duc de Berry
  Recall of Richelieu
  September. Birth of comte de Chambord
- 1821 Death of Napoleon
  Revolutionary movement of the Charbonnerie
  December. Fall of second Richelieu ministry. Ultras take over government
- 1822 March. Plot of four sergeants of La Rochelle
  September. Villèle President of the Council
- 1823 April. Expedition into Spain
- 1824 March. Elections return an Ultra Chamber
  June. Dismissal of Chateaubriand
  Delacroix's *The Massacres of Scio*
  September. Death of Louis XVIII
  Succession of Charles X
- 1825 Law against sacrilege
  Indemnity to *émigrés* voted
  May. Coronation of Charles X at Reims
- 1827 Victor Hugo's *Cromwell*
  October. Battle of Navarino
  November. Elections

Chronological Table

- 1827 December. Fall of Villèle
- 1828 January. Government of Martignac
- 1829 August. Polignac government
- 1830 Victor Hugo's *Hernani*
  Berlioz's *Symphonie Fantastique*
  June. Elections
  July. Capture of Algiers
  25 July. Four Ordinances
  28-30 July. Revolution in Paris
  31 July. Duke of Orleans accepts lieutenant-generalcy of France
  2 August. Abdication of Charles X
- 1831 Victor Hugo's *Notre-Dame de Paris*
  Stendhal's *Le Rouge et le Noir*
  February. Anti-clerical riots
  March. Casimir-Périer ministry
  August. French expel Dutch from Belgium
  October-November. Revolt in Lyon
- 1831-32. Cholera epidemic
- 1832 Death of duc de Reichstadt
  May. Attempt of duchesse de Berry to rouse Vendée
  Death of Casimir-Périer
- 1833 Guizot's education law
- 1834 Revolt in Lyon
  Massacre in rue Transnonain
  Lamennais' *Paroles d'un croyant*
  Balzac's *Le Père Goriot*
  Louis Blanc's *L'Organisation du travail*
- 1835 July. Fieschi bomb plot
  Gautier's *Mademoiselle de Maupin*
  Vigny's *Chatterton*
- 1836 Attempt of Louis Bonaparte at Strasbourg
  September. Government of Molé
- 1838 Rachel plays in Racine
- 1839 Revolt of Abd-el-Kader
  March. Fall of Molé
  Louis Bonaparte's *Les Idées napoléoniennes*
- 1840 Re-burial of Napoleon in the Invalides
  Attempt of Louis Bonaparte at Boulogne
  March. Government of Thiers
  Mehemet Ali crisis
  October. Fall of Thiers

A History of Modern France

- 1840 Ministry of Guizot
  Proudhon's *Qu'est-ce que la propriété?*
- 1841 Entente cordiale of Aberdeen and Guizot
- 1842 Comte's *Cours de philosophie positive* completed
  Sue's *Les Mystères de Paris*
  Death of duc d'Orléans
  Guizot's railway law
- 1842-6 Railway mania
- 1844 Pritchard affair in Tahiti
  Dumas' *Le Comte de Monte-Cristo*
- 1846 Escape of Louis Napoleon Bonaparte from Ham
  October. Spanish marriages
- 1847 Economic crisis
  Capture of Abd-el-Kader
  May. Teste trial
  August. Murder by duc de Praslin
  July-December. Campaign of banquets
- 1848 23 February. Revolution in Paris. Resignation of Guizot
  24 February. Abdication of Louis-Philippe
  Provisional Government set up
  Proclamation of Universal Suffrage
  Abolition of slavery
  16 March. Demonstration of *bonnets à poil*
  17 March. Left-wing demonstration
  23 April. Election of Constituent Assembly
  15 May. Demonstration of the clubs
  22-26 June. June Days
  Government of Cavaignac
  4 November. Constitution of Second Republic
  10 December. Election of Louis Napoleon Bonaparte as President
  Government of Odilon Barrot
- 1849 April. Expeditionary corps sent to Rome
  May. Election of Legislative Assembly
  13 June. Attempted rising in Paris
  July. Fall of Roman Republic
  October. Dismissal of Barrot Ministry
- 1850 March. *Loi Falloux* on education
  Left-wing victories in by-elections
  May. Law restricting franchise
- 1851 July. Legislative Assembly fails to accept constitutional reform

Chronological Table

- 1851 2 December. *Coup d'état*
  - 14 December. Plebiscite
- 1852 January. Constitution
  - 20-21 November. Plebiscite on Empire
  - 1 December. Proclamation of Empire
  - Foundation of Crédit Foncier and Crédit Mobilier
- 1853 January. Marriage of Napoleon III and Eugénie
- 1854 March. War with Russia
  - September. Siege of Sebastopol
- 1854–65 Faidherbe in Senegal
- 1855 Paris Exhibition
  - September. Fall of Sebastopol
- 1856 Peace Congress in Paris
- 1857 Prosecution of *Madame Bovary* and *Les Fleurs du Mal*
  - Port of Dakar founded
- 1858 January. Orsini bomb plot
  - July. Conference of Napoleon III and Cavour at Plombières
  - Vision at Lourdes
- 1859 Construction of Suez Canal begun
  - Amnesty
  - April. War of Italian Unification
  - June. Magenta
  - Solferino
  - July. Armistice of Villafranca
- 1860 Annexation of Savoy and Nice
  - Free-trade treaty with Great Britain
  - Anglo-French occupation of Pekin
  - Expedition to Syria
  - First Constitutional changes
- 1861 October. Expedition to Mexico
- 1862 Annexation of Cochin-China
  - French troops remain in Mexico
- 1863 Revolt of Poland
  - Renan's *Vie de Jésus*
  - Salon des Refusés
  - Manet's *Le Déjeuner sur l'herbe*
  - May. Legislative elections
  - Fall of Persigny
  - Rouher Minister of State
- 1864 Schleswig-Holstein War
  - Maximilian proclaimed Emperor in Mexico
  - Papal Syllabus of Errors

A History of Modern France

1865 Death of Morny
Educational reforms of Duruy
1866 Austro-Prussian War
French troops evacuate Mexico
1867 January. Letter of Napoleon III announcing constitutional changes
February. Proposals for rearmament
Crisis of Crédit Mobilier
June. Execution of Maximilian
November. Garibaldi repelled at Mentana
1868 May. Press laws relaxed
1869 Flaubert's *L'Éducation sentimentale*
Suez Canal opened
May. Elections
Election of Gambetta on Belleville programme
Government of Ollivier
1870 May. Plebiscite on constitutional changes
June. Hohenzollern acceptance of throne of Spain, subsequently withdrawn
14 July. Ems telegram
19 July. French declaration of war on Prussia
August. French defeats
Fall of Ollivier
1 September. Surrender of Napoleon III and MacMahon at Sedan
4 September. Government of National Defence set up
19 September. Paris besieged
10 October. Gambetta arrives at Tours
27 October. Capitulation of Bazaine at Metz
November. Victory at Coulmiers
Reoccupation of Orleans by French
1871 19 January. Failure of *sortie en masse* from Paris
28 January. Armistice
8 February. Election of Assembly
Government of Thiers
1 March. Terms of peace ratified by National Assembly
18 March. Troops fail to remove guns from Montmartre
28 March. Election of Commune
10 May. Treaty of Frankfurt
21 May. Versaillais enter Paris
28 May. End of the Commune

FURTHER READING

THE fullest general history of France in the nineteenth century is still Lavisse, *Histoire de France contemporaine* (1920–22); reference to specific volumes will be made later. There are useful bibliographies in these, in the volumes of the *Peuples et civilisations* series, in Gordon Wright: *France in Modern Times, 1760 to the Present* (1962), and in *Clio*: L. Villat: *La Révolution et l'Empire, ii. Napoléon* (1936); *L'Époque contemporaine*, i. Droz, Genet et Vidalenc: *Restaurations et révolutions 1815–1871* (1933). Excellent general histories, in less detail than Lavisse, are J. P. T.Bury: *France 1814–1940* (2nd ed. 1951); *Histoire de la France pour tous les Français*, G. Lefebvre: *de 1774 à 1815*, C. H. Pouthas: *de 1815 à 1878;* and M. Reinhard's finely illustrated *Histoire de France ii. de 1715 à 1946;* J. Vidalenc: *Le Premier Empire, la Restauration;* L. Girard: *Le Règne de Louis-Philippe, La Révolution de 1848, Le Second Empire.* A selection of works on special aspects of French history since 1799 follows.

The best short account of French constitutional developments is given in the Introduction to the earlier editions of Duguit, Monnier et Bonnard: *Les Constitutions et les principales lois politiques de la France depuis 1789.* M. Deslandres: *Histoire constitutionelle de la France depuis 1789 jusqu'à 1870,* ii (1932) is long and rather arid but it contains useful material that cannot easily be obtained elsewhere. An interesting sketch of right-wing movements, perhaps unduly schematized, is R. Rémond, *La Droite en France de 1815 à nos jours* (1954). An essential book for understanding the operation of parliamentary institutions in France is D. W. S. Lidderdale's *The Parliament of France* (1951).

French historians are only now beginning to work on the economic history of nineteenth-century France. J. H. Clapham's *Economic Development of France and Germany 1815–1914* (4th ed. 1936) is an able survey on the basis of the material available when it was written. The trade policies of France are traced by S. B. Clough in *France, a History of National Economics, 1789–1939* (1939), a useful book though written to a theme which does not necessarily command acceptance. An account of religious developments is given by C. S. Philips in *The Church in France, 1789–1907* (2 vols. 1929, 1936), and more recently in the series edited by Fliche and Martin, especially *La Crise révolutionnaire 1789–1846* (1949) by J. Leflon. The study of the interaction of Church and State in France by P. H. Spencer in *The Politics of Belief in Nineteenth-Century France*

A History of Modern France

(1954) is thoughtful and illuminating. Concise and impartial summaries of foreign problems and policies, with bibliographies, are given in the *Histoire des relations internationales*, edited and in these volumes written by P. Renouvin – *Le XIXe siècle: i. 1815–71 L'Europe des nationalités et l'éveil de nouveaux mondes, ii. 1815–71 L'Apopée de l'Europe* (1954–5). On French colonies a competent survey with sufficient detail for the non-specialist is the *Histoire de la colonisation française* (1946) by H. Blet, while the ideas behind French colonization are described in H. Deschamps' *Méthodes et doctrines coloniales de la France du XVI siècle à nos jours* (2 vols., 1953). R. Girardet's *La Société militaire dans la France contemporaine 1815–1939* (1953) has interesting *aperçus* on the history of the army but is rather slight. A more scholarly work, containing much new material, is P. Chalmin, *L'Officier français de 1815 à 1870* (1957). In place of various rather dull histories of education may be mentioned G. Duveau's *Les Instituteurs* (1957), slight and opinionated but also lively and realistic. A well-documented study of the press laws is *The Government and the Newspaper Press in France 1814–1881* (1959) by Irene Collins. It is difficult to pick out a single book on French art for mention, but a stimulating general history of architecture is P. Lavedan's *French Architecture* (1944, trans. 1956). The *Oxford Companion to French Literature* (1959) is a useful work of reference. R. Soltau's *French Political Ideas in the Nineteenth Century* (1931) is a helpful if uninspired survey. Selections from a number of leading French social and political thinkers, with introductory notes on their authors, are edited by A. Bayet and F. Albert under the title, *Les Écrivains politiques du XIXe siècle* (1907).

Turning to special periods, we find the nineteenth century very unevenly served by secondary works. The literature on Napoleon I is immense. The best life in English is J. M. Thompson's *Napoleon Bonaparte: his Rise and Fall* (1952), though the arrangement is a little confusing. F. M. H. Markham's *Napoleon and the Awakening of Europe* (1954) is a well-written and judicious short account. In French may be mentioned G. Lefebvre's *Napoléon* (1935) in the *Peuples et civilisations* series, and the brief survey by F. Ponteil, *Napoléon Ier et l'organisation autoritaire de la France* (1956). The changing views on Napoleon during the subsequent century are summarized by P. Geyl in *Napoleon For and Against* (trans. 1949). A well-presented collection of contemporary verdicts which takes some of the gilt off the Napoleonic gingerbread is J. Savant's *Napoleon in his Time* (1954, trans. 1958). Works on special aspects of the meteoric career of the Emperor from one little island to

Further Reading

another, and on all those who impinged on it from his marshals to his mistresses, are so many and so detailed that the effort to pick out particular volumes for mention here has had to be abandoned. The histories already referred to will provide an introduction to the voluminous Napoleonic bibliography.

The counter-revolution and the opposition to Napoleon has been served much less well, but its importance for the future intellectual development of France is indicated in F. Baldensperger's *Le Mouvement des idées dans l'émigration française, 1789–1815* (1924). There is now an excellent history of the evanescent but unduly depreciated régime that followed the catastrophe of Napoleon, in G. de Bertier de Sauvigny's *La Restauration* (1955). Sympathetic to the Catholic and royalist ideals of the Restoration, it is therefore perhaps a little hard on parliamentarians like Decazes and Villèle.

The July Monarchy lacks any good recent general history and even specialized studies are comparatively rare. Competent accounts of the reign of Louis-Philippe are the volume in Lavisse by S. Charléty, *La Monarchie de juillet* (1921) and P. de la Gorce, *Louis-Philippe 1830–1848* (1931). A useful light on the politics of the reign is thrown by S. Kent in *Electoral Procedure under Louis-Philippe* (1937). The economic and social problems of a still mainly pre-industrial society have not been adequately studied, but indications are to be found in C. H. Pouthas, *La Population française pendant la première moitié du XIXe siècle* (1956), L. Chevalier's authoritative *La Formation de la population parisienne au XIXe siècle* (1950), the same author's stimulating *Classes laborieuses et classes dangereuses à Paris pendant la première moitié du XIXe siècle* (1958), and J. B. Duroselle's *Les Débuts du catholicisme social en France 1822–70* (1951).

With the Second Republic and the Second Empire we come to a period in which our problem is not to find titles to include, but rather to know what to omit. The best history of the Second Republic is the volume in Lavisse by C. Seignobos, *La Révolution de 1848 et l'Empire* (1921), which reflects a great deal of archival research, unfortunately – for lack of references – all to be done again. One traditional misinterpretation was eliminated by D. C. MacKay in *The National Workshops, a Study in the French Revolution of 1848* (1933); and something to rescue the reputation of Ledru-Rollin from excessive contempt was achieved by A. R. Calman's *Ledru-Rollin and the Second French Republic* (1922). Karl Marx's *Class Struggle in France 1848–50* was a brilliant analysis for its time but is naturally inadequate by the standards of modern economic history. F. A. Simpson's *Louis Napoleon and the Recovery of France 1848–56* (1930. 3rd edition 1956) is well written but lacks the research that might have given it more lasting value. The same author's *Rise of Louis Napoleon* (1909) is brilliantly written and amusing but very slight, and H. A. L. Fisher's *Bonapartism* (1914) is somewhat misleading. Louis Napoleon's own *Des idées napoléoniennes* (1839) is essential for the understanding of the Second Empire. Karl Marx's *The Eighteenth Brumaire of Louis Bonaparte* is a brilliant piece of contemporary history.

Among general histories of the Second Empire the volumes by Seignobos in Lavisse are probably still the best. A. L. Guérard's *Napoleon III* (1943) is a bright account and J. M. Thompson's *Louis Napoleon and the Second Empire* (1954) is of value as a study of the personality of Napoleon III. A thoughtful introduction to the economic policy of the Second Empire is H. N. Boon's *Rêve et réalité dans l'œuvre économique et sociale de Napoléon III* (1936). There is a thorough and well-documented study of the Chevalier-Cobden commercial negotiations in *The Anglo-French Treaty of 1860* (1930) by A. L. Dunham. D. H. Pinkney's *Napoleon III and the Rebuilding of Paris* (1958) is a well-balanced account based on original sources. A competent life of the rebuilder of Paris, derived from printed materials, is *The Life and Times of Baron Haussmann* (1957) by K. M. and Brian Chapman. L. Girard's *La Politique des travaux publics du second empire* (1952) is authoritative. On the other side of the medal is the detailed but impressionistic *La Vie ouvrière en France sous le Second Empire* (1946) by G. Duveau. The membership of the legislative assemblies is sketched by T. Zeldin in *The Political System of Napoleon III* (1958), which combines the brilliance and the narrowness of the Namier approach. A revealing picture of political life under the Second Empire can be obtained from biographies, such as R. Schnerb's thorough and penetrating *Rouher et le Second Empire* (1949). There are many studies of the foreign policy of Napoleon III. One of the most illuminating, which uses the reports of the procureurs, is L. M. Case, *French Opinion on War and Diplomacy during the Second Empire* (1954). The Franco-Prussian War belongs as much to European as to French history and has an extensive literature of which *The Franco-Prussian War* (1961) by Michael Howard is now authoritative. A detailed though rather anti-French account of *The Siege of Paris 1870–1871* (1950) is by M. Kranzberg. The attempt of France to fight back after the collapse of the Empire is well described by J. P. T. Bury

Further Reading

in *Gambetta and the National Defence* (1936). F. Jellinek's *The Paris Commune of 1871* (1937) is lively but to be used with caution. A scholarly account of the ideological conflicts among the Communards is given by C. Rihs in *La Commune de Paris* (1955).

Contemporary writers are, of course, very enlightening to the historian, perhaps particularly so in France where literature has so often been 'engaged'. The list that follows represents merely a sample of the riches that French literature holds for the historian. Chateaubriand's *Mémoires d'outre-tombe* is better for conveying atmosphere than facts. In *Choses vues* Victor Hugo gives a series of political and social vignettes, largely of the period of the July Monarchy. De Tocqueville's *Souvenirs* contain a penetrating study of the social and political errors, in which the author shared, of the Second Republic. The comte de Falloux's *Mémoires d'un royaliste* reveal the limitations of the clerical and conservative mind. In *L'Éducation sentimentale* Flaubert sets the gradual disillusionment of a young bourgeois, haunting the Paris boulevards with no end in life, against the tragic events of revolution and class war. Zola wrote, under the Third Republic, the *Rougon Macquart* cycle of twenty novels, portraying in lurid detail a Second Empire society made up almost wholly of an amalgam of luxury, crime, misery, and vice. The *Journal* of the Goncourts describes literary and artistic society in the second half of the nineteenth century. Nor should the kind of literature with no apparent political reference be forgotten. Balzac's novels were deliberately conceived as a many-faceted reflection of the *Comédie humaine* in the first thirty years of the nineteenth century.

INDEX

Abadie, 116
Abd-el-Kader, 110-12
Aberdeen, Lord, 113
Académie Française, 118
Academy of Moral and Political Sciences, 37
Acte additionelle, 68
Affre, mgr, 126
d'Aguesseau, 27
Aide-toi, le ciel t'aidera, 89
Albert, Alexandre Martin, 137-8
Alexander I, 44, 59-60, 64
Alexander II, 181
Algeria, Algiers, 41, 90, 110-12, 145, 158, 175-6
Alsace-Lorraine, 202
Amiens, Treaty of, 16, 19, 30, 38, 41-2, 48
Ampère, 37, 84
Anglo-French entente, 112-13
Angoulême, cathedral of, 116
Angoulême, duc d', 64
anti-clericalism, 83, 87, 100-1, 126, 133, 154, 190, 224
Arago, François, 37, 123, 137
architecture, French, 36-7, 116
Armed Neutrality, 16
army, French, 45-7, 66, 146, 195
Army Law of 1868, 195
Artois, comte d', 65, 68, 73, 77, 81
   See also Charles X
Aumale, duc d', 107, 112, 131
d'Aurelle de Paladines, 206, 211
Austerlitz, battle of, 44, 58, 112, 157
Austro-Prussian War, 181-2
l'Avenir, 100

Balzac, Honoré, 98, 118, 121-2
Bank of France, 28, 218
banquets, reform, 128-9
Barante, baron de, 77, 84, 152

Barbès, Armand, 143
Barère de Vieuzac, 48
Baroche, Pierre-Jules, 194, 197
Barrot, Odilon, 127, 137, 150-2, 154
Batavian republic, 15, 44
Baudelaire, 226
Baudin, Dr, 157, 191
Bautzen, battle of, 61
Bayeux tapestry, 43
Baylen, Capitulation of, 57, 66
Bazaine, marshal, 183, 203, 205
Beauharnais, Eugène, 45, 54, 167
Beauharnais, Hortense, 160, 186
Beauregard, comtesse de, 151, 163
Belgian revolution of 1830, 96, 108
Belleville programme, 205
Benedetti, 201
Béranger, 121, 151
Beresina, crossing of, 60
Berlin Decrees, 51
Berlioz, 84
Bernadotte, marshal, Charles XIV of Sweden, 60, 62
Berry, duc de, 26, 79-80, 85, 100, 170
Berry, duchesse de, 101-2
Berryer, Antoine, 193
Berthier, marshal, 20
Berthollet, Claude-Louis, 48
Billault, Adolphe-Augustin, 193
Bismarck, 179, 181-2, 199, 201, 205, 207
Blanc, Louis, 121, 137-8, 211
Blanqui, Auguste, 143, 208, 211-12
Blanquists, 212-13
Blucher, marshal, 69
Bonald, Louis de, 78, 82
Bonaparte, Caroline, 45
Bonaparte, Jerome, 44-5
Bonaparte, Joseph, 45, 54, 57, 85
Bonaparte, Louis, 44, 53-4, 160

240

Index

Bonaparte, Louis Napoleon, *see* Napoleon III
Bonaparte, Lucien, 20, 24
Bonaparte, Napoleon, *see* Napoleon I
Bonapartism, 107, 148–50, 152, 163, 215, 223
Bordeaux, 53, 64, 206
Borodino, battle of, 19, 60
Bossuet, 92
Boulogne, attempt of Louis Bonaparte, 107, 114, 149
Boulogne camp, 43
Bourbaki, general, 206
Bourbon, île, 89
Bourmont, marshal, 88, 90
Broglie, Jacques-Victor-Albert, duc de, 188
Broglie, Victor, duc de, 77, 95, 106
brumaire, *coup d'état* of, 12
Buchez, Pierre-Joseph-Benjamin, 120
Buffon, 84
Bugeaud, marshal, 110, 130–1

Cabanis, Georges, 37
Cabet, Étienne, 120–1
Cadoudal, Georges, 16–17
Cambacérès, 54
Cambodia, 177
Campan, mme, 54
canals, 123
Carbonari, 80, 160, 172
Carnot, Hippolyte, 120, 141, 153
Carnot, Lazare, 15, 68
Carnot, Sadi, 84
Casimir-Périer, 95, 102–3, 105–6
Cavaignac, general, 112, 145–6, 148, 152–3
Cavour, 172–5, 179
Cayenne, 158
Cayla, comtesse de, 80–1
censorship of press, 35, 80, 97, 105
Chambord, comte de, 101,
Chambre introuvable, 76

Changarnier, general, 112, 136, 156
Chanzy, general, 206
Chaptal, 24, 56
Charivari, le, 118
Charles X, 79, 82–3, 85–92, 94, 103. *See also* Artois, comte d'
Charter of Louis XVIII, 68, 73–4
Charter of 1830, 97
Chateaubriand, 32, 35, 72, 77, 84, 86, 115, 151
Châtillon, negotiations, 63
Chevalier, Michel, 120, 164, 178
Chevaliers de la Foi, 64, 77, 87
cholera epidemic, 103
Cintra, Convention of, 57
Cisalpine republic, 15, 41
Cluny, abbey of, 116
Cobden Treaty, 177–8
Cochin-China, 177
Code Napoléon, 27–8
Colbert, 27
colonies, French, 38–41, 89–90, 110–12, 175–7
Comédie française, 35
Commune of Paris, 212–16
Comptoir d'Escompte, 165
Comte, Auguste, 120, 122, 163
Concordat, 30–3, 55–6, 82–3
Condorcet, 163
Confederation of the Rhine, 44
Congregation, Jesuit, 82, 87
Conseil d'état, 21–2, 95, 159
Constant, Benjamin, 68, 77, 221
Consulate, 12–38
Continental System, 44, 47–8, 51–4, 58, 60
Copenhagen, bombardment of, 16
Correspondant, le, 188
Corunna, battle of, 57
Coulmiers, battle of, 206
Courbet, Gustave, 171, 225
Courvoisier, Jean-Joseph-Antoine, 88
Crédit Agricole, 165
Crédit Foncier, 165
Crédit Lyonnais, 165

241

Index

Crédit Mobilier, 165, 192–3
Crémieux, Isaac, 137, 204
Crimean War, 172, 174
Cuvier, Georges, 37, 84

Dakar, 176
Darboy, mgr, 189
Daumier, Honoré, 104–5, 116, 118, 171, 225
David, Jacques-Louis, 35–6
Decazes, duc, 76–7, 79
Delacroix, Eugène, 84, 116
Delescluze, Louis-Charles, 153, 191, 208, 211, 213, 214, 215
Desai, general, 14–15
Destutt de Tracy, 37
doctrinaires, 77–8, 105, 221
Dresden, battle of, 62
Drouyn de Lhuys, 182
Dumas, Alexandre, 121
Dupanloup, mgr, 188–9
Dupont, general, 66
Dupont de l'Eure, 94, 153
Duruy, Victor, 190

École des Chartes, 84
education, 29, 33–5, 83, 88, 124–6, 154, 190
Egypt, 16, 41–2
Elba, 65–7
émigrés, 66, 73–4, 86–7, 94
empire, French overseas, *see* colonies
Ems telegram, 201
Enfantin, père, 120, 163
Enghien, duc d', murder of, 17
entente, Anglo-French, of Louis-Philippe, 112–13
Eugénie, Empress, 162, 182, 200–1, 203–4
l'Événement, 152
Exhibition of 1855, 171
Eylau, battle of, 44

Faidherbe, general, 176, 206
Falloux, comte de, 144, 151, 154, 188

Farmers General, Wall of, 9, 169
Favre, Jules, 185, 211
February days, 129–31, 136
Ferdinand of Spain, 57
Ferry, Jules, 196
Fesch, cardinal, 59
Fieschi plot, 105
finances, French, 28–9, 66, 76, 86, 139, 166, 192–3, 218
Flahaut, Charles de, general, 186
Flaubert, Gustave, 136, 145, 157, 225
Flocon, 137
Flourens, Gustave, 211
Fontanes, Louis de, 34
Forbach, battle of, 202
Fouché, 20, 31, 55–6, 58, 68–9, 71, 75–6
Fould, Achille, 151, 165, 178, 193–4, 196
Fourcroy, Antoine-François, 33, 48
Fourier, 120
Four Ordinances, 90
Fragonard, 35
Francis Joseph, emperor, 175
Franco-Prussian War, 199–209, 222
Frayssinous, mgr, 83
free trade treaties, 177–9
freemasons, freemasonry, 190
Fresnel, Augustin, 84
Freycinet, Charles de, 205, 210
Friedland, battle of, 44
Fröschwiller, battle of, 202

Gallicanism, 31, 82, 189
Gambetta, 192, 204–8, 210, 211
Garibaldi, 182
Garnier, Charles, 170
Garnier-Pagès, Louis Antoine, 137, 153
Gaudin, duc de Gaète, 20, 28
Gautier, Théophile, 115, 121, 226
Genlis, mme de, 106

242

Index

Gérard, marshal, 94
Géricault, 36, 84, 116
Girardin, Émile de, 152
Giselle, 115
Goncourt, Edmond de, 207
Gorée, 89
Goya, 36
Gramont, duc de, 199–201
Grandville, 105
Gravelotte, battle of, 203
Grégoire, bishop, 79
grève du milliard, 192
Grévy, Jules, 147–8, 210
Gros, baron, 36
Guadeloupe, 40, 89
Guiana, French, 89
Guibert, cardinal, 141
Guibert, general, 47
Guizot, François, 77, 84, 94, 103, 106, 109–13, 124–30, 136, 180

Ham, castle of, 149
Haussmann, baron, 167–70, 193, 196–7, 218
Helvetic republic, 15, 45
Hohenlinden, battle of, 15–16
Hohenzollern candidature, 199–201
Howard, Miss, 151, 163
Hugo, Victor, 84–5, 112, 115–18, 122, 130, 146, 151–2, 157, 168, 171, 211, 212, 225
Hundred Days, 67–70, 75–7

Industry in France, 48–9, 52–3, 118–19, 122–4, 166, 178, 192, 218
Ingres, Jean-Auguste-Dominique, 36
Intransigents, clerical, 189
Ionian islands, 44
Isabella, queen, of Spain, 113–14
Italian War, 174–5, 185, 190

Jacobins, 16, 24, 212–13
Jemappes, battle of, 97
Jena, battle of, 44, 181
Jessaint, prefect, 26
Jesuits, 31, 82, 87, 126, 188
Jeune France, 89
Joinville, prince de, 107
Josephine, empress, 18, 36, 40, 55, 58–9, 160
Journal des débats, le, 86
Juarez, president, 183
June Days, 136, 143–6, 154, 171

Labiche, Eugène, 171
La Bourdonnaye, 75, 88
Lacordaire, père, 100, 170, 187–8
Lafayette, 80, 88, 94–5
Lafitte, Jacques, 89, 91, 95, 102–3
Lafon, l'abbé, 61
Lagrange, Joseph-Louis, 37
Lamarck, Jean-Baptiste de, 37, 84
Lamarque, general, funeral of, 102
Lamartine, 84, 114–15, 137, 142, 148, 152–3
Lamennais, 78, 82, 100, 119, 170
Lamoricière, general, 112
Lampedusa, 42
Lanson, Gustave, 121
Lanterne, la, 191
Laplace, Pierre-Simon de, 37
La Rochelle, four sergeants of, 80, 146
La Valette, 194
Lavoisier, 37, 48
Laws, Napoleonic Code of, 27–8
Le Bas, Philippe, 160–1
Lebrun, consul, 54
Leclerc, general, 40
Le Creusot, 166
Ledru-Rollin, 127, 137, 139–42, 147–8, 152–4, 158, 185, 211
Legion of Honour, 54
legitimism, legitimists, 100–1, 107, 126, 223
Leipzig, battle of, 62
Lemaître, Frédéric, 118

243

Index

Leroux, Pierre, 120
Lesseps, Ferdinand de, 177
Liberal Empire, 198-9, 222
Ligurian republic, 15, 41
livret, 49
Loi Falloux, 154, 188
Louis XVIII, 65, 67-9, 71-3, 75-7, 80-2, 84-6
Louis, baron, 66, 94
Louis Napoleon Bonaparte, *see* Napoleon III
Louis-Philippe, 96-7, 102-3, 105-14, 117-18, 130-1, 133, 158-61, 180, 222
Louisiana, 38, 40, 182
Lourdes, 188
Lunéville, treaty of, 15, 30
Lützen, battle of, 61
lycées, 34
Lyon, 53, 67, 167, 218, 224; revolt in, 99-100, 103-4

Macaire, Robert, 118
Mack, general, 44
MacMahon, marshal, 203
Madagascar, 89
Magenta, battle of, 174, 195
Maida, battle of, 45
Maistre, Joseph de, 35, 78, 82
Malet conspiracy, 61
Malta, 41-2
Marengo, battle of, 14-15
Marie-Amélie, queen, 107
Marie-Antoinette, queen, 54
Marie-Louise, empress, 58, 64
Marie, Alexandre-Thomas, 137-8, 153
Marmont, marshal, 65, 90
Marrast, Armand, 126, 137, 153
Martignac, vicomte de, 88
Martinique, 89
Marx, Karl, 136
Massiac, club, 39
Maupas, Charlemagne Émile de, 156
Maximilian, emperor, 183-4

Mehemet Ali, 108-9, 112-13
Mentana, battle of, 182
Mérimée, Prosper, 84, 116, 121
Metternich, 58, 68
Metz, 203, 206
Mexican expedition, 183-4
Michelet, Jules, 126, 219
Mignet, François-Auguste, 84, 89, 91, 97
Milan Decrees, 51
Millet, Jean-François, 171
Miquelon, 89
Mirari vos, 100
Molé, count, 106, 108, 130-1
Monge, Gaspard, 37
Montalembert, Charles Forbes, comte de, 100, 116, 126, 141, 151, 188
Montmorency, Mathieu, duc de, 77, 86
Montpensier, duc de, 107, 113
Moore, general, 57
Moreau, general, 14-17, 61-2
Morny, duc de, 156, 168, 183, 185-7, 190, 194, 198
Mortier, marshal, 57
Moscow, 60
Mulhouse, 53
municipal law of 1831, 99
Murat, Joachim, marshal, 45, 54-5, 62
Musset, Alfred de, 115

Napoleon I, 12-70, 148, 167, 220; his personality, 12, 14-15, 17-19, 21, 27, 30, 33, 46-7, 56
Napoleon III, 107, 114, 120, 148-204, 216, 218, 222
Napoleon, Prince, 198
National, le, 89-90, 126, 129, 152-3
National Guard, 87, 94-5, 99, 101-2, 104-5, 129, 137, 139, 143-6, 156, 204, 206, 211
National Workshops, 138, 143-4
Navarino, battle of, 88
Nemours, duc de, 96, 107

244

Index

Nerval, Gérard de, 116, 122
Ney, marshal, 57, 61, 67, 69, 75
Nice, 175

Offenbach, 171
Oldenburg, annexation of, 59
Ollivier, Émile, 173, 185, 187, 190, 194, 198, 200–3
Opera, Paris, 170
Organic Articles, 30–1
Orléans, duc d', 91. *See also* Louis-Philippe
Orléans, Ferdinand-Philippe, duc d', 107, 117, 131
Orléans, Hélène, duchesse d', 118, 137
Orleanism, 94, 165, 223
Orsini plot, 170, 173
Ossian, 35
Otranto, duc d', *see* Fouché
Oudinot, marshal, 154
Ouvrard, Gabriel-Julien, 86

Painting, French, 35–6, 84, 116, 171
Palmerston, Lord, 113
Panthéon, 83, 188
Papal States, annexation of, 45, 56
Paris, 9–11, 37, 118–19, 134–5, 167–70, 196, 217, 224–5; Commune of, 212–15; comte de, 131; Congress of, 172, 177; siege of, 204–8
Paul I, assassination of, 16
Pekin, occupation of, 176
Peninsular War, 56–8
Péreire brothers, 120, 152, 165, 193, 196
Persigny, Victor Fialin, duc de, 156, 186, 198
phylloxera, 192
Picard, Ernest, 185, 211
Pichegru, general, 16–17
Pitt, William, 16, 48
Pius VII, 17, 30
Pius IX, 154, 189

plebiscite of 1799, 13; of 1804, 17; of 1852, 160
Plombières, meeting at, 173
Poitiers, committee of rue de, 153
Poland, 142, 181
Polignac, Jules, prince de, 77, 88–90, 94
population, 11, 93, 118, 135, 166, 217, 219
Positivism, 122
Praslin, duc de, 128
prefects, 23–6, 55, 79, 102, 110, 140, 156, 159–60
press laws, 35, 74, 80, 105, 159, 191
Pressburg, treaty of, 44
Presse, la, 152
Prince Imperial, 163, 204
Pritchard incident, 113
Protestants, French, 33
Proudhon, Pierre-Joseph, 121, 212
Prud'hon, Pierre, 36

Quatre-bras, battle of, 69
Quinet, Edgar, 126, 211

Rachel, 121
railways, 123–4, 165–6, 217–18
Raspail, François-Vincent, 148, 152
Réal, Pierre-François, comte, 18
Réforme, la, 127, 129, 152
Reichstadt, duc de, 59, 64, 107, 161
religion, 29–33, 74, 82–3, 97, 100, 114–15, 119, 126, 187–90, 223–4
Rémusat, Charles de, 78
Renan, Ernest, 122
Restoration, First, 64–7; Second, 71–5
Revocation of Edict of Nantes, 92
Richelieu, duc de, 76–7, 79–80
Robespierre, 12, 15

245

Index

Rochefort, Henri, 191, 211
Roederer, Pierre-Louis, 21, 33
Roman republic, 154
romanticism, 115–17, 121
Rome, French garrison in, 182; king of, *see* Reichstadt, duc de
Rossini, 84
Rothschilds, 193, 196
Rouher, Eugène, 159, 182, 193–8, 200
Rousseau, Jean-Jacques, 18, 30, 83, 115, 120, 221
Royer-Collard, Pierre-Paul, 77
Ruhr, 52
Russo-Turkish War, 172

Saar, 70
sacrilege, law of, 83
Sadowa, battle of, 195, 199
Saint-Antoine, faubourg of, 10, 15
Saint-Arnaud, general, 156
St Domingo, 38–40
Saint-Germain, faubourg of, 98
Saint-Germain d'Auxerrois, riot of, 100–1
Saint-Omer, declaration of, 65
Saint-Pierre, Bernardin de, 115
Saint-Pierre, île de, 89
Saint-Simon, comte de, 117, 119–20, 122, 163–4
Saint-Simonianism, Saint-Simonians, 120, 152, 163–4, 193, 218, 222
Salon des Réfusés, 171
Sand, George, 115, 117, 122
Savoy, 175
Schleswig-Holstein, 181
Schneider brothers, 166
Sébastiani, marshal, 41–2, 94
Sebastopol, 172
Sedan, 203–4, 206
Ségur, Philippe de, 66
Sénégal, 89, 176
Sibour, archbishop, 187
Sieyes, 13
Simon, Jules, 211

slavery, slave trade, 39–40, 137
Société des Amis des Noirs, 39
Society of the Rights of Man, 103, 105
Solferino, battle of, 174–5
Solidarité Républicaine, 153
Soult, marshal, 58, 64–5, 106, 108–9
Spain, French invasion of, 1823, 85–6; Napoleonic War in, 56–8
Spanish marriages, 113–14
Staël, mme de, 35, 84, 115
Stendhal, 84, 121
Strasbourg, attempt of Louis Bonaparte, 107, 114, 149
Stuart, general, 45
Sue, Eugène, 117, 121–2, 155
Suez canal, 177
Surcouf, 51
Syllabus of Errors, 189
Syria, expedition of 1860, 177

Tahiti, 113
Taine, Hippolyte, 25, 122
Talleyrand, 20, 55–6, 58, 64, 66, 68, 71, 75–6, 79, 89, 96, 186
Ternaux, Guillaume-Louis, baron, 49
Teste affair, 128
theocrats, 78, 221
Thierry, Augustin, 84, 119
Thiers, Adolphe, 84, 89–91, 95, 103, 106–9, 113, 123, 127–8, 131, 150–52, 154–5, 182, 186, 201, 204, 208, 210–12, 215
Third Coalition, 43
Thomas, Albert, 138
Tilsit, Congress of, 44, 47, 55, 59
Tocqueville, Alexis de, 23, 127, 136, 143–4, 147, 151, 221
Toulouse, battle of, 65
Toussaint-Louverture, 40
Trafalgar, battle of, 43, 47
Transnonain, massacre of the rue, 104
tricolore, 96

Index

Trochu, general, 204, 208
Tussaud, madame, 36

Ulm, battle, of, 44
ultramontanes, 82, 189, 224
ultra-royalists, 77-8, 87, 96
l'Univers, 126, 189
universal suffrage, 114, 127, 137, 139, 155
universities, 34

Vaisse, 167, 218
Vendée, pacification of, 30; revolts in, 68, 93, 101
Vendôme column, 37, 107
Vera Cruz, 183
Vernet, Horace, 36
Veuillot, Louis, 126, 188-9
Victor, marshal, 57
Victoria, queen, 113, 160-1
Vigny, Alfred de, 84, 115-17
Villafranca, armistice of, 175
Villèle, comte de, 77, 79, 81, 85-8

Villeneuve, admiral, 43
Vimiero, battle of, 57
Viollet-le-Duc, 116, 168
Voltaire, 10, 83

Wagram, battle of, 58
Walcheren expedition, 58
Walewski, comte, 175, 178, 190
Warsaw, Grand Duchy of, 45, 59-60
Waterloo, battle of, 69
Weber, 84
Wellington, Duke of, 19, 57, 62, 64-5, 69, 71, 76
West Indies, French, 38-40
Westphalia, kingdom of, 44
White Terror, 75, 88
Windham, William, 16
Winterhalter, 162
Wissembourg, battle of, 202

Young, Arthur, 11

*Some more Pelican books on
history are described on
the following pages*

Lionel Kochan

THE MAKING OF MODERN RUSSIA

'This is a history of Russia from the earliest times up to the outbreak of the second world war. However, in keeping with his choice of title, Mr Kochan has concentrated on the modern period, devoting about as many pages to the eighty years following the Emancipation of the Serfs in 1861 as to the preceding 800-odd years. ... The result is a straightforward account of a complicated story. A successful balance has been held between such conflicting themes as foreign policy ... foreign influences and native intellectual trends. His book could be a valuable introduction to the general reader in search of guidance ... a commendable book'
– *Sunday Times*

'He handles his material with skill and sympathy. I cannot think of a better short book for acquainting the general reader with the broad outlines of Russian history. I hope many will read it' – Edward Crankshaw in the *Observer*

'Gives proper weight to economic, geographical, and cultural, as well as political and military factors, and which, while giving long-term trends their place, manages very often to convey a sense of real events happening to real people' – Wright Miller in the *Guardian*

'It reads easily, it is the ideal book for the general reader' – *Economist*

G. R. Storry

A HISTORY OF MODERN JAPAN

The rise, fall, and renaissance of Japan, within the space of less than a hundred years, is one of the most curious and dramatic stories of our time. The first part of this book gives the historical background to Japan's emergence as a modern state in the sixties of the last century. It then discusses in detail the stages of Japan's advance as a world power up to the tragedy of the Pacific War. This struggle and its aftermath – the Occupation – are vividly described and analysed. The last chapter, bringing the account right up to the present day, is a fascinating study of the new Japan that has come into being since the San Francisco Peace Treaty of 1951.

William G. Atkinson

A HISTORY OF SPAIN AND PORTUGAL

This book attempts to show as a whole the Peninsula made up of Spain and Portugal. Through its varied history a characteristic pattern of social life has emerged. The successive occupations of Roman, Visigoth, and Muslim span between them more than a thousand years. The Peninsula's great contribution to the modern age was the opening up of the New World in the west by Spain, and of new routes to the east by Portugal. 'And were there more lands still to discover,' wrote Camoens, 'they would be there too.' Over the last century and a half the history of both peoples provides a case-study in the essential relativity of forms of government. The reader will find here, too, a commentary upon great Spanish and Portuguese literary and artistic figures: Camoens, Cervantes, Lope de Vega, Calderón, Velázquez, Goya, and many more.

George Pendle

A HISTORY OF LATIN AMERICA

About Latin America and its problems there prevails what the *Economist* recently called an 'awe-inspiring ignorance'. An authoritative and concise introduction to an area of such great economic potentiality is certainly needed.

This history has been written by a specialist who has been closely connected with Latin America for the last thirty years. In tracing the development of civilization from the earliest times down to Fidel Castro – with the principal countries taking their place in the continental story – the author helps to place current events in their context.

Many races and classes have contributed to the civilization of this great land-mass, with its vast mountain ranges, rivers, prairies, forests, and deserts: Indians, European *conquistadores*, priests, planters, African slaves, *caudillos*, liberal intellectuals, commercial pioneers.

Simón Bolívar once classed the Latin Americans as a distinct variety of the human species, and in discussing their characteristics George Pendle identifies two notable qualities: the 'El Dorado spirit' and an inclination to prefer people to 'things and rules'.

Alfred Cobban

A HISTORY OF MODERN FRANCE
VOLUME I: 1715–1799

Professor Cobban writes, in his concluding chapter, 'The French eighteenth century is not a period of great, dominating political figures. Yet if no one man counted overmuch, more men – and women – counted for something than possibly at any other time. ... If it was not a century of greatness, for the student of *l'homme moyen sensuel* there is no more fruitful field. The eighteenth century was also something more: it was, and above all in France, the nursery of the modern world. Ideas and social forces, the seeds of which were sown much earlier, can be seen now pushing above the surface, not in the neatly arranged rows of the careful gardener but in the haphazard tangle of nature. Yet they *can* be seen and distinguished: the field is no longer a seed-bed but it is not yet a jungle, and a pattern is discernible. The simple interpretations imposed on eighteenth-century France by historians writing under the influence of later social and political ideologies may have to be abandoned, but the history that is beginning to emerge from more detailed studies, if it is more complex, is still coherent.'

Alfred Cobban

A HISTORY OF MODERN FRANCE
VOLUME III: 1871–1962

Alfred Cobban has now expanded *A History of Modern France* into three volumes and has added some completely new material. This volume covers the period from the Franco-Prussian war to de Gaulle.

Professor Cobban writes: 'For a thousand years France was a monarchy; it has been a republic for less than a hundred.' In spite of French traditionalism, in spite of a succession of weak governments and two disastrous world wars, this republic managed to survive and even to achieve greatness. The third Republic saw a splendid flowering of the arts; the fifth has finally achieved many of the long overdue social and international aims of France.

In this book, Professor Cobban steers the reader skilfully through the political and social problems besetting modern France. His balanced and stimulating account of the three republics is invaluable to anyone interested in the development and present position of a great European nation.

For a complete list of books available please write to Penguin Books whose address can be found on the back of the title page